Receipt

01/08/17
Order No:BP3145

Shipping Address	Billing Address
Christopher Boyd Morton Fraser LLP 145 St Vincent Street Glasgow G2 5JF United Kingdom	Christopher Boyd 3/1, 126 Kelvinhaugh Street Glasgow G3 8PP United Kingdom

Receipt

Quantity	Item	Taxes	Price
1 x	**Employment Tribunal Remedies Handbook 2017-18**	£0.00 VAT	£40.00

Paid with thanks as below

Subtotal price:	£40.00
Total tax:	£0.00
Shipping:	£3.50
Total price:	**£43.50**

If you have any questions, please send an email to info@bathpublishing.co.uk
Bath Publishing Limited, 27 Charmouth Road, Bath, BA1 3LJ
Company registered in England and Wales: 5209173. VAT Registration No: 826941114

EMPLOYMENT TRIBUNAL REMEDIES HANDBOOK

2017-18 Edition

General Editor:

Benjamin Gray

Littleton Chambers

Foreword

Judge Brian Doyle

President

Employment Tribunals (England & Wales)

First edition: Published April 2014

Second edition: Published April 2015

Third edition: Published August 2016

Fourth edition: Published June 2017

ISBN 978-0-9935836-3-6

Text © Bath Publishing Limited

Typography © Bath Publishing Limited

Bath Publishing Limited
27 Charmouth Road
Bath
BA1 3LJ
Tel: 01225 577810

email: info@bathpublishing.co.uk
www.bathpublishing.co.uk

Bath Publishing Limited is a company registered in England: 5209173
Registered Office: As above

FOREWORD

This is the fourth edition of the Employment Tribunal Remedies Handbook for which I have been pleased to write a Foreword. Benjamin Gray, the General Editor, has done a fine job in ensuring that this essential work is up-to-date and user-friendly, while Bath Publishing Ltd continues to ensure that it enjoys high publishing values.

Many Employment Judges will tell you that parties in Employment Tribunal litigation – whether professionally represented or not – often treat the question of remedy as an afterthought or as something that will be dealt with by the Tribunal in due course. My training as a judge has taught me over the last 23 years that one of the first questions to ask a claimant, whether at a case management hearing or at the outset of the final hearing, is what do you seek to achieve if you were to win your case? It is surprising how often a litigant in person or a legally represented party has given relatively little thought and analysis to what their claim is worth or what reductions to their expectations might have to be anticipated. The introduction of early conciliation, of tribunal fees and more recently of judicial assessment (a form of early neutral evaluation) means that such an approach to the valuation of a prospective claim is a luxury that neither prospective party can afford to indulge.

In recent years both standard and bespoke case management orders almost invariably require a claimant to prepare and to serve a statement or schedule of loss and remedy, addressing mitigation of loss as well as the calculation of remedy. In some cases, a counter-schedule might be appropriate or required of the respondent. Employment Judges hope that by this process both parties will give careful consideration to what a claim might be worth, taking account of the various permutations that might arise. The claimant might win on all counts, but what if they only succeed in part of the claim? What heads of loss might arise for consideration by the Tribunal? What are the chances that those heads of loss will be awarded or capped or time limited or excluded altogether? How do you value non-monetary loss, such as loss of a chance or injury to feelings or personal injury? What effect does interest or taxation or recoupment have upon the award? Does consideration need to be given to a *Simmons v Castle* uplift and, if so, how is that to be assessed? How is pensions loss compensation to be measured? How will any tribunal fees be recovered? These and many other questions need to be at the forefront of the thinking of the parties and their representatives at the very earliest stages of Employment Tribunal litigation.

In recent years, I have been very pleased to be associated as judicial representative with the advisory board behind Bath Publishing's Employment Claims Toolkit. This sophisticated online calculator not only takes the stress out of what are often quite complex calculations, but should give parties, practitioners and judges considerable confidence that they have accounted for all possible heads of loss and remedy and the variables that might inflate or deflate them. However, just as a school student using a calculator also has to understand the basic rules of arithmetic that underpin their calculations, so too does a party using the Toolkit need to understand the basic principles of remedies. The Handbook and the online Employment Claims Toolkit work well together in that regard, ensuring that parties, representatives and tribunals always have the best possible information to enable them to calculate compensation as fairly and as accurately as possible.

In that context, the publication of the Employment Tribunal Remedies Handbook 2017-18 is again very welcome. In this new edition, there are new entries on agency workers, early conciliation, judicial assessment/mediation and re-engagement/reinstatement. The entries on accelerated/decelerated receipt and physical/psychiatric injury have been substantially updated. Account has also been taken of the reduced discount rate. Later this summer new Presidential Guidance on pensions loss compensation will be issued. The General Editor's work is never done in this fast-moving area of litigation.

Judge Brian Doyle

President, Employment Tribunals (England & Wales)

27 June 2017

ALSO AVAILABLE FROM BATH PUBLISHING

Employment Claims Toolkit

The perfect companion to this book, the Employment Claims Toolkit takes all the rules and calculations presented here and puts them into practice by allowing you to create flexible, adjustable, accurate statements of remedy.

Find out more at www.employmentclaimstoolkit.co.uk

Employment Cases Update

The full text of every employment case from the EAT, High Court, Court of Appeal and Supreme Court in a single source and free to view. We have been publishing since 2010 and the site now contains over 2,600 cases with short summaries, keywords and links to other cases cited.

The website will also be updated once any changes to the calculation of pension loss have been announced.

You can also subscribe to our CPD service which transforms your reading into fully accredited CPD for only £75 a year.

Visit www.employmentcasesupdate.co.uk to sign up for our free weekly email or to browse the cases.

INTRODUCTION

Welcome to the new edition of the Employment Tribunal Remedies Handbook which once again is packed with information about the calculation of remedy in employment claims. Now into its 4th year, the Handbook is rapidly gaining a reputation as the 'go-to' resource when calculating remedy and has even been relied on by the EAT.

The handbook is an invaluable tool for potential claimants and respondents from before proceedings have been brought through to all stages of later litigation. It is as important as ever that potential claimants understand what their claims might be worth before embarking on employment tribunal litigation. It is also useful for respondents to a potential claim to know, for example, what their liabilities could be before undertaking disciplinary proceedings or a redundancy exercise. And with Early Conciliation now compulsory, both parties benefit from having the key remedy information available to enable them to reach a compromise.

All of this means that the information contained in the Employment Tribunal Remedies Handbook is essential at any stage of a dispute where the assessment and valuation of remedies is a possibility.

Each employment right that can be enforced in an employment tribunal is summarised, followed by the principles that will be applied to any remedies. For example, the common claims of unfair dismissal, discrimination and detriment are covered, and also all the numerous less litigated rights such as time off for study and training and the right of a TUPE transferee to be notified of employee liability information. For each such entry, the nature of any award is set out, such as the route to calculate a basic award or the principles that will be applied to calculate a compensatory award.

There are also separate entries for each element of a remedy and the principles used in its calculation, such as mitigation, loss of chance, tax and termination payments, grossing up, order of adjustments, recoupment, the definition of a week's pay, and many other elements of a remedy calculation. Each entry is cross-referenced to others, so it is possible to start anywhere in the book when a specific issue arises, not just at the particular right that is being enforced.

The text is supported by worked examples, to show clearly how the law is applied. 46 essential tables are included with up to date information on caps, limitation periods, fees, National Minimum Wage rates and much more, so that the information needed is always to hand.

What's new in the 2017-18 edition?

The book has been updated to include the latest limits and caps, changes in legislation and recent case law. Apart from the new figures, the main changes are set out below:

- Tax treatment of injury to feelings: The case of *Moorthy v Revenue & Customs* [2016] UKUT 13 (TCC) is due to be heard in the Court of Appeal in May 2017. It remains to be seen whether the ET will follow the upper tribunal's ruling (that injury to feelings should be taxed because 'injury' in section 406 refers to a medical condition and does not include injury to feelings), although it is likely that they will for the time being, and there will be more indemnity clauses written into remedy decisions which involve awards for injury to feelings.

- Four new entries have been added: Agency workers; Early conciliation; Judicial assessment/mediation; and Re-engagement and reinstatement.

- Following the consultation by the Office of Tax Simplification, in which it asked for feedback on its proposals to simplify the tax treatment of termination payments, several changes have been proposed to come into force from April 2018. However, the calling of the snap election meant that the measures were removed from the Finance Act 2017 in the wash-up period. The view of the Chartered Institute of Taxation is that a significant amount of the Bill would be re-enacted irrespective of who wins the election. We are therefore keeping these in for the present moment, but remind practitioners that these are currently proposals, and that they need to check to see what the law becomes in due course. The most notable changes are as follows:

  - Compensation for injury to feelings in a termination payment will be taxable to the extent that the £30,000 tax free allowance has been exceeded, except where the compensation is for a psychiatric injury or a recognised medical condition;

  - Employer (but not employee) NI will be payable on any amount of compensation that exceeds the £30,000 tax free allowance, thus further increasing the burden on employers;

- o All payments in lieu of notice (PILONs) will be taxable as earnings, whether or not there is a right to make the payment in a contract of employment;

- o The foreign service relief exemption for termination payments will be removed.

- The Court of Appeal has now confirmed that the 10% *Simmons v Castle* uplift should be applied to both injury to feelings and psychiatric injury (see *De Souza v Vinci Construction (UK) Ltd* [2017] EWCA Civ 879).

- The application of the ACAS uplift/deduction has been considered in several judgments over the last few months. In particular;

- o The ACAS uplift does not apply to ill health dismissals (*Holmes v Qinetiq* UKEAT/0206/15/BA);

- o Nor does it apply to dismissals for some other substantial reason (SOSR), where the dismissal is due to an irretrievable breakdown of the working relationship (*Phoenix House Ltd v Stockman & Anor* UKEAT/0264/15/DM);

- o It only applies if the grievance has been made in writing (*The Cadogan Hotel Partners Ltd v Ozog* UKEAT/0001/14/DM); and

- o It only applies to employees not workers (*Local Government Yorkshire & Humber v Shah* UKEAT/0587/11/ZT).

- "Physical and psychiatric injury" has been revised to consider the differences between "divisible" and "indivisible" types of harm, and the different approaches courts and tribunals must take to compensation in this area. A careful analysis of the authorities in this area suggests that indivisible harm should, in my view, be further divided into cases of "monocausal" and "multicausal" indivisible harms, to explain the true dividing line between "divisible" and "indivisible" harm, which has not always been easy to work out. The examples given are from industrial injury cases rather than employment discrimination cases as these are the traditional examples given in this area and it is easier to extrapolate the principles from them.

- The discount rate for personal injury compensation payments has also been changed from +2.5% to -0.75% as a result of falling investment returns – Ogden Table 27 has been updated to include the appropriate multipliers for the new rate.

- "Accelerated payment: discount for early receipt" has been renamed as "Accelerated/decelerated receipt" and updated to reflect the principle in *Melia v Magna Kansei Ltd* [2005] EWCA Civ 1547 that an uplift can be applied for decelerated, or delayed, receipt to ensure that past and future losses are treated consistently.

- Pensions: The GAD tables have been removed from this edition and replaced with Ogden Tables 15 to 26 as the 'Compensation for Loss of Pension Rights: Employment Tribunals' guidance has been withdrawn. At the time of writing, the Working Party is about to release new guidance for calculating pension loss – the pensions entry has been updated to outline the main changes.

As always, any comments or suggestions for improvement or additions for subsequent editions are most welcome. Please forward any comments to the publishers at info@bathpublishing.co.uk.

Benjamin Gray

Littleton Chambers

June 2017

CONTENTS

Contents

Contents

Case	Entry	Case	Entry
Ministry of Defence v Fletcher [2010] IRLR 25; [2009] UKEAT 0044/09/0910	Aggravated damages; Exemplary damages	O'Neill v Governors of St Thomas More Roman Catholic Voluntary Aided Upper School [1997] ICR 33	Discrimination
Ministry of Defence v Mutton [1996] ICR 590	Pension loss	Olayemi v Athena Medical Centre & Anor UKEAT/0140/15	Housing benefit; Physical and psychiatric injury
Ministry of Defence v Wheeler [1998] IRLR 23	Discrimination; Loss of chance	Optikinetics Ltd v Whooley [1999] ICR 984	Basic award; Contributory conduct
Mole Mining Ltd v Jenkins [1972] ICR 282	Week's pay	Orthet Ltd v Vince-Cain (2) [2004] IRLR 857; [2004] UKEAT 0801/03	Injury to feelings; Mitigation; Pension loss; Tax and termination payments
Montracon Ltd v Hardcastle UKEAT/0307/12/JO	Contributory conduct	Oti-Obihara v Commissioners for HM Revenue & Customs [2011] IRLR 386	Injury to feelings; Tax and termination payments
Moorthy v The Commissioners for Her Majesty's Revenue & Customs [2014] UKFTT 834 (TC)	Injury to feelings; Tax and termination payments	Paggetti v Cobb [2002] IRLR 861	Week's pay
Moorthy v Revenue & Customs [2016] UKUT 13 (TCC)	Injury to feelings; Tax and termination payments	Palfrey v Transco Plc [2004] IRLR 916	Effective date of termination
Morgans v Alpha Plus Security Ltd [2005] ICR 525	Incapacity benefit	Palmanor Ltd v Cedron [1978] ICR 1008	Week's pay
Mr A v Revenue & Customs (Income tax/Corporation tax: Employment income) [2015] UKFTT 189	Tax and termination payments	Parker Foundary Ltd v Slack [1992] IRLR 11	Basic award; Contributory conduct
Murray v Powertech (Scotland) Ltd [1992] IRLR 257	Injury to feelings	Parker Rhodes Hickmott Solicitors v Harvey UKEAT/0455/11/SM	Effective date of termination
National Westminster Bank Plc v Parry [2004] EWCA Civ 1563	Additional award; Arrears of pay (reinstatement/re-engagement)	Parsons v BNM Laboratories Ltd [1963] 2 All ER 658	Gourley principle
Norton Tool Co Ltd v Tewson [1973] All ER 183	Compensatory award; Mitigation	Phoenix House Ltd v Stockman & Anor UKEAT/0264/15/DM	ACAS
O'Donoghue v Redcar and Cleveland Borough Council [2001] IRLR 615	Injury to feelings; Loss of chance		

ACAS (The Advisory, Conciliation and Arbitration Service)

(see also Adjustments)

An award for compensation can be increased or reduced, by up to 25%, if the employer/employee (but not worker – see *Local Government Yorkshire & Humber v Shah* UKEAT/0587/11/ZT) has unreasonably failed to comply with a relevant code of practice relating to the resolution of disputes (see s207(A) TULRC(A) 1992). A relevant code of practice will have been issued either by ACAS or the Secretary of State under ss199 to 206 TULR(C)A. At present ACAS *Code of Practice 1: Disciplinary and Grievance Procedures* (2015) is the only relevant code of practice.

The ACAS Code is not engaged unless a grievance is raised in writing and therefore the ACAS uplift is not available if a grievance is raised orally (see *The Cadogan Hotel Partners Ltd v Ozog* UKEAT/0001/14/DM, paragraph 52).

The full list of tribunal jurisdictions to which s207A applies is detailed in Schedule A2 of TULR(C)A:

- s120 and s127 of the Equality Act 2010 (discrimination etc in work cases);

- s145A TULR(C)A (inducements relating to union membership or activities);

- s145B TULR(C)A (inducements relating to collective bargaining);

- s146 TULR(C)A (detriment in relation to union membership and activities);

- Paragraph 156 of Schedule A1 TULR(C)A (detriment in relation to union recognition rights);

- s23 of the Employment Rights Act 1996 (unauthorised deductions and payments);

- s48 of ERA 1996 (detriment in employment);

- s111 of ERA 1996 (unfair dismissal, but see below);

- s163 of ERA 1996 (redundancy payments);

- s24 of the National Minimum Wage Act 1998 (detriment in relation to national minimum wage);

- The Employment Tribunals Extension of Jurisdiction (England and Wales) Order 1994 (SI 1994/1623) (breach of employment contract and termination);

- The Employment Tribunals Extension of Jurisdiction (Scotland) Order 1994 (SI 1994/1624) (corresponding provision for Scotland);

- Regulation 30 of the Working Time Regulations 1998 (SI 1998/1833) (breach of regulations);

- Regulation 32 of the Transnational Information and Consultation of Employees Regulations 1999 (SI 1999/3323) (detriment relating to European Works Councils);

- Regulation 45 of the European Public Limited-Liability Company Regulations 2004 (SI 2004/2326) (detriment in employment);

- Regulation 33 of the Information and Consultation of Employees Regulations 2004 (SI 2004/3426) (detriment in employment);

- Paragraph 8 of the Schedule to the Occupational and Personal Pension Schemes (Consultation by Employers and Miscellaneous Amendment) Regulations 2006 (SI 2006/349) (detriment in employment);

- Regulation 34 of the European Cooperative Society (Involvement of Employees) Regulations 2006 (SI 2006/2059) (detriment in relation to involvement in a European Cooperative Society);

- Regulation 17 of the Cross-border Railway Services (Working Time) Regulations 2008 (SI 2008/1660) (breach of regulations);

- Regulation 9 of the Employment Relations Act 1999 (Blacklists) Regulations 2010 (SI 2010/493) (detriment connected with prohibited list).

Ill health capability dismissals

The ACAS Code only applies in cases where there is *'culpable conduct'* or performance correction or punishment (*Holmes v Qinetiq Ltd* UKEAT/0206/15). In *Holmes,* the claimant was dismissed because of ill-health. No disciplinary procedure was invoked because, apart from the effects of his illness, the claimant was able to perform the job of security guard and there was no suggestion that his conduct or performance gave rise to a disciplinary situation or involved culpable conduct. That meant the employer was not required to follow the ACAS Code of Practice on Disciplinary and Grievance Procedures and the uplift under section 207A(2) was not available.

Capability cases involving poor performance are capable of falling within the Code, but only where such performance involves *'culpable conduct'*. The

Code does not apply to a capability dismissal arising from ill-health or sickness absence *'and nothing more'*.

Dismissal for Some Other Substantial Reason (SOSR)

In *Phoenix House Ltd v Stockman & Anor* UKEAT/0264/15/DM the EAT held that the ACAS Code, and therefore the ACAS uplift/deduction, does not apply to dismissals for some other substantial reason where *'misconduct is not alleged and capacity is not in issue'*. Mitting J rejected the provisional view expressed by Laing J in *Hussain v Jury's Inn Group Ltd* UKEAT/0283/15/JOJ said that there were *'pointers in both directions'* on this issue, holding that *'clear words in the Code'* were needed for the ACAS adjustment to apply, and this was not the case in dismissals for Some Other Substantial Reason.

Order of Adjustments: Where a compensatory award for unfair dismissal falls to be adjusted for unreasonable failure to comply with a relevant code of practice, the adjustment is applied immediately before any reduction for contributory conduct (s123(6)) or reduction due to the receipt of an enhanced redundancy payment in excess of the basic award (s123(7)) (see s124A(a) and *Basic award, Compensatory award, Contributory conduct, Redundancy*).

Example 1

An ex-employee is awarded a basic award of £2,000, a compensatory award of £3,000 and damages for breach of contract of £500. The employer is found to have unreasonably failed to comply with a relevant code of practice and an uplift of 25% is applied to the applicable awards. The calculation would be as follows:

The basic award remains as £2,000 because the uplift does not apply to this award.

The compensatory award is now £3,000 x 1.25 = £3,750

The damages for wrongful dismissal are now £500 x 1.25 = £625

Example 2

An ex-employee would be awarded a basic award of £2,000, a compensatory award of £3,000 and damages for breach of contract of £500. However, he received an enhanced redundancy payment of £2,500. The employee is found to have unreasonably failed to comply with a relevant code of practice and a deduction of 25% is applied to the applicable awards. The calculation would be as follows:

The basic award is reduced to zero because of the

enhanced redundancy payment, but there remains £500 of enhanced redundancy payment to put into the calculation of the compensatory award: £2,500 - £2,000 = £500

The compensatory award is now (£3,000 x 0.75) - £500 = £1,750

The damages for wrongful dismissal are now £500 x 0.75 = £375

Statutory authorities: ERA 1996 s123(6), 123(7) and s124A(a); TULR(C)A Schedule A2

Relevant case law: *Holmes v Qinetiq Ltd* UKEAT/0206/15/BA; *Local Government Yorkshire & Humber v Shah* UKEAT/0587/11/ZT; *Phoenix House Ltd v Stockman & Anor* UKEAT/0264/15/DM

Accelerated/decelerated receipt

(see also Adjustments; Table 24; Ogden Table 27)

Accelerated receipt

If an award is made to a claimant to compensate for future losses, they are in fact receiving the money before they would have received it if they had not been dismissed. The idea behind the discount for accelerated receipt, therefore, is to take into account any interest that might in fact be earned on this money if it were invested as a lump sum, when it would not ordinarily have been available to the claimant to do so.

A discount for accelerated receipt can be made on awards for future loss, including the compensatory award and an award for financial losses in a discrimination claim. The reduction will only apply to future losses, such as future income and benefits.

No discount will need to be applied if the award for future loss is relatively small, as will often be the case (see *Les Ambassadeurs Club v Bainda* [1982] IRLR 5).

There is no established route to calculate the appropriate reduction. Tribunals sometimes merely apply a single percentage adjustment to recognise accelerated receipt. However, in *Bentwood Bros (Manchester) Ltd v Shepherd* [2003] IRLR 364 the Court of Appeal overturned a decision to make a single 5% reduction for an award that covered 10 years' loss. It will always be necessary for a tribunal to set out the method it has used and its reasons for using it.

Decelerated receipt

Melia v Magna Kansei Ltd [2005] EWCA Civ 1547 holds that in principle an uplift can be applied for decelerated, or delayed, receipt to ensure that past and future losses are treated consistently.

Such awards are rare in practice, and *Francois v Castle Rock Properties Ltd (t/a Electric Ballroom)* EAT/0260/10 observes that it is not the routine practice of tribunals to make such awards. The logic underlying decelerated receipt adjustments is unlikely to apply in discrimination cases, where there are already specific provisions for interest.

It is an open question whether such an adjustment should be applied in cases where there is no future loss: the principle of *Melia* is to treat the past and future losses consistently, an issue that does not arise where only one of the two awards is made.

A tribunal may choose to use a similar approach to that used for accelerated receipt (but in the opposite direction) to calculate the interest due on an award paid after the loss has been incurred.

In *Francois* the EAT observed that when considering an adjustment for decelerated receipt, the tribunal is considering '*the loss of the use of the money which the recipient should have had earlier. Interest may be a measure of that loss. Other measures may also be appropriate.*'

Example

If the future sum awarded is £10,000 and a discount percentage of 0.5% is to be applied over a period of 5 years the amount to be awarded will be calculated as follows:

Look down the left hand side of Ogden Table 27 and choose a term of 5. Look across to a percentage rate of 0.5. The discount factor is 0.9754. Multiply 10,000 by 0.9754 to get a figure of £9,754.

Adjustments: The discount/increase for accelerated/decelerated receipt should be made within the first stage of any calculation, namely calculating the loss suffered by the individual. Any adjustments will be made afterwards (see also *Adjustments*).

Statutory authorities: None

Relevant case law: Benchmark Dental Laboratories Group v Perfitt EAT/0304/04; Bentwood Bros (Manchester) Ltd v Shepherd [2003] EWCA Civ 380; Francois v Castle Rock Properties Ltd (t/a Electric Ballroom) EAT/0260/10; Les Ambassadeurs Club v Bainda [1982] IRLR 5; Melia v Magna Kansei Ltd [2005] EWCA Civ 1547; York Trailer Co Ltd v Sparkes [1973] IRLR 348

Accompaniment to a disciplinary, grievance or flexible working meeting

A worker has the right to be accompanied at a grievance or disciplinary meeting (s10 and s11 ERelA 1999), at a meeting to discuss their right to flexible working meeting (s14 and s15 FW(PR) Regs 2002) or at a meeting to discuss their right to make a request in relation to study or training (s63D to 63K ERA 1996) (Reg 16 and Reg 17 EST(PR) Regs 2010) and a worker is allowed to have time off to accompany the other worker to the meeting. The worker is allowed to postpone the meeting in certain circumstances.

Remedy: Where a tribunal finds a complaint of a failure to comply well founded, it may make an award of up to 2 weeks' pay.

Gross or net: Gross. A week's pay as defined in ss220 to 229 ERA 1996 applies (see *Week's pay*).

Limit on a week's pay: £489 (see Table 1 for historical rates).

Limit on number of weeks: 2

Any maximum or minimum: Maximum = £978; No minimum

Adjustments: None

Tax: The tax treatment relating to non-termination payments is not clear. If the claimant was claiming this head of loss alongside unfair or wrongful dismissal, it is arguable that any award under this head would be included in the compensatory award and therefore taxable under s401. If the claimant's employment has not been terminated however, it could be argued that no tax is payable - the award is not 'earnings', nor is it an award on termination of employment, or change of duties or earnings (see *Tax and termination payments*).

Recoupment: N/A

Statutory authorities: ERelA 1999 ss10 and 11; ERA 1996 s63D to 63K; EST(PR) Regs 2010 (SI 2010/155) Regs 16 and 17; FW(PR) Regs 2002 (SI 2002/3207) Regs 14 and 15

Additional award

(see also Arrears of pay; Re-engagement and reinstatement)

An additional award may be made where an employer has failed to comply with an order for reinstatement or re-engagement made under s113 ERA 1996, following a finding of unfair dismissal, and has failed to establish that it was not practicable for them to comply. See also s166 TULR(C)A 1992.

Remedy: The award differs according to whether there has been partial or total non-compliance. Only where there has been total non-compliance with the order will the additional award be made. In both cases, a separate award of compensation to cover financial losses will be made, subject to a statutory cap (see below).

Partial compliance: An employer will be ordered to pay compensation to an employee if an employee is reinstated or re-engaged pursuant to such an order, but the employer does not fully comply with the terms of that order (s117(1) ERA 1996).

The tribunal will award the amount it thinks fit having regard to the loss sustained by the employee in consequence of that failure to comply, but there is no power to order an additional award for partial compliance.

Total non-compliance: If an order for reinstatement or re-engagement is made, but the employee is not reinstated or re-engaged, a compensatory award will be made under s124 ERA 1996 and an additional award of compensation of between 26 and 52 weeks' pay will be made (s117(3)).

The additional award will not be made, however, if the employer satisfies the tribunal that it was not practicable to comply with the order. The hiring of a permanent replacement will not satisfy this condition unless it was not practicable to arrange for the employee's work to be done without hiring a permanent replacement (s117(4) and s117(7)).

Calculation: Additional award = number of weeks x gross weekly pay

Gross or net: Gross. A week's pay as defined in ss220 to 229 ERA 1996 applies (see *Week's pay*).

Limit on a week's pay: £489 (see Table 1 for historical rates).

Limit on number of weeks: Minimum is 26; Maximum is 52

Any maximum or minimum: Minimum depends on employee's gross weekly pay (but see *National Minimum Wage*); Maximum is £25,428

Adjustments: The following applies to compensation (but not the additional award itself): where the claimant has unreasonably prevented an order for reinstatement or re-engagement from being complied with, and where the tribunal makes an award of compensation for losses suffered (see above) the tribunal will take that conduct into account as a failure on the part of the claimant to mitigate his loss.

Cap: The statutory cap applies to an award under s117(1) and (2)and s123. ERA 1996. The statutory cap is currently the lower of £80,541 or 52 weeks' gross pay (as defined in ss220 to 229 ERA 1996) (see s124 ERA 1996). It should be noted that the cap will be lifted to the extent necessary to compensate for arrears of pay and any additional award:

- in the case of compensation awarded under s117(1) (where there has been partial compliance) the cap can be exceeded to the extent necessary to enable the award fully to reflect the amount specified as payable under s114(2)(a) or s115(2)(d) (see *Arrears of pay*). In other words, the employee is entitled to receive at least their arrears of pay, even if those arrears exceed the cap;

- in the case of an award under s117(3) (where the employer has not complied at all) the cap may be exceeded to the extent necessary to allow the aggregate of the compensatory and additional awards fully to reflect the amount specified as payable under s114(2)(a) or s115(2)(d) (see *National Westminster Bank Plc v Parry* [2004] EWCA Civ 1563).

This means that:

- if the arrears of pay exceed the cap on their own, the individual will receive the total amount of arrears;

- if the arrears of pay do not exceed the cap on their own they will be offset against the compensatory award.

Mitigation: The additional award is not expressly related to an employee's losses, or to mitigation, however a tribunal may well take into account an employee's losses and attempts to mitigate them in reaching the amount of the award, particularly perhaps if the statutory cap prevents full recovery of the employee's losses.

Tax: The additional award will be taxed under s401 ITEPA 2003 and can be taken into account within the £30,000 tax free amount at termination (see also *Grossing up*).

Recoupment: Recoupment does not apply to the

additional award but it does apply to any compensation awarded under s123 as a result of non-compliance with s113 and to arrears of pay which may have been ordered by ss114 or 115.

Statutory authorities: ERA 1996 ss113 to 118

Relevant case law: *National Westminster Bank Plc v Parry* [2004] EWCA Civ 1563; *Selfridges Ltd v Malek* [1998] ICR 268

Example 1

Basic award = £3,000

Financial losses = maximum available for this employee (52 weeks) = £25,000

Additional award = £15,000

Arrears of pay = £5,000 (The arrears of pay are included within the compensatory award with the remaining losses capped at £25,000 - £5,000 = £20,000)

Award = £3,000 + £25,000 + £15,000 = £43,000

Example 2

Basic award = £3,000

Financial losses = zero

Statutory cap for this employee is £25,000 (52 weeks' pay)

Additional award = zero (reinstatement or re-engagement order was partially complied with)

Arrears of pay = £28,000

Award = £3,000 + £28,000 = £31,000

Example 3

Basic award = £3,000

Financial losses = maximum available for this employee (52 weeks) = £30,000

Additional award = £25,000

Arrears of pay = £60,000

Aggregate of financial losses and additional award = £55,000, which is lower than the arrears of pay (£60,000) so replace the lower figure with £60,000.

Total Award = £3,000 + £60,000 = £63,000

Adjustments and order of adjustments

(see also ACAS; Accelerated/decelerated receipt; Contributory conduct; Interest; *Polkey*; Protected disclosure)

It is important that adjustments are applied to awards in the correct order since this can significantly affect the final figure.

This can be seen in *Digital Equipment Co Ltd v Clements* [1997] EWCA Civ 2899; [1998] ICR 258. Mr Clements argued that the redundancy payment of £20,685 should be deducted from the compensatory award of £43,136, leaving a balance of £22,451; which should then be reduced by 50% (*Polkey*) giving a compensatory award of £11,275. This would result in the then-maximum of £11,000 being payable. Digital argued that the tribunal should give full credit for the enhanced redundancy payment and first reduce the loss by 50%, leaving a compensatory award of £21,568 from which the tribunal should then deduct the £20,685, leaving a balance of £883. The tribunal ruled in favour of the claimant, but the decision was overturned by the EAT and the Court of Appeal, leaving the claimant with £883.

Different adjustments apply to the different types of award - these adjustments, and the correct order in which they should be applied, are listed below.

Adjustments to the compensatory award

1) Calculate the total losses suffered by the claimant;

2) Deduct any amounts received from the employer such as payment in lieu of notice or ex gratia payment which made to the employee as compensation for the dismissal (*Digital Equipment Co Ltd v Clements* [1997] EWCA Civ 289). This must exclude any enhanced redundancy payment above the basic award;

3) Deduct earnings which have mitigated the claimant's loss or a sum which reflects any failure by the claimant to mitigate his or her loss (ERA s123(4) 1996) (see also *Mitigation*);

4) A '*Polkey*' deduction to reflect the chance that the claimant would have been dismissed in any event had the employer acted fairly (*Polkey v AE Dayton Services Ltd* [1987] IRLR 50 (HL)) (see also *Polkey*);

5) Decrease/increase for accelerated/decelerated receipt of compensation in respect of future/past loss (*Bentwood Bros (Manchester) Ltd v Shepherd* [2003] EWCA Civ 380) (see also *Accelerated/decelerated receipt*);

6) Percentage increase or reduction up to a maximum of 25% to reflect an unreasonable failure by the employer or employee to comply with the ACAS disciplinary code

(s207A TULR(C)A) (see *ACAS*);

7) (From 25 June 2013) a percentage reduction, up to a maximum of 25%, if a protected disclosure was not made in good faith (see also *Protected disclosure*);

8) Any extra award for a failure by the employer to provide written particulars of employment (s38 EA 2002) (see also *Written particulars*);

9) Percentage reduction for any contributory conduct on the part of the employee (s123(6) ERA 1996). Note that this percentage does not have to be same as any such deduction to the basic award (see also *Contributory conduct*);

10) Deduction for any enhanced redundancy payment to the extent that it exceeds the basic award (s123(7) ERA 1996) (see also *Redundancy*);

11) Interest on past losses, if available (see also *Interest*);

12) Gross up (see *Grossing up*);

13) Apply the statutory cap if relevant (see *Statutory cap*).

Adjustments to the basic award

The basic award can be reduced in the following situations:

- By an amount that the tribunal considers to be just and equitable where the employee has unreasonably refused an offer of reinstatement (s122(1) ERA 1996);

- By an amount to reflect contributory conduct (s122(2) ERA 1996). Note though that s122(2) does not apply in redundancy cases except as provided for in s122(3) (see *Basic award* and *Basic award, minimum* below). This percentage reduction does not have to be the same as that for the compensatory award. Note the case of *Granchester Construction (Eastern) Ltd v Attrill* UKEAT/0327/12/LA, where a 50% *Polkey* deduction was made to the compensatory award, and both the basic and compensatory awards were also reduced by 10%. The EAT said *'Whereas it may be appropriate to moderate what would otherwise be the degree of contributory conduct that would reduce an award because there have been matters of conduct taken into account in assessing the chances of a fair dismissal, so that it might be in effect double counting to impose upon the claimant a further reduction by way of contributory conduct, that reasoning cannot*

apply to that part of the award to which the Polkey principle itself does not apply' (i.e. the basic award);

- By any redundancy payment paid on termination for a genuine redundancy or as ordered by the tribunal (but see also *Redundancy*) (s122(4) ERA 1996). This must be a redundancy in fact, rather than one incorrectly labelled as such by the employer, even if the employee accepted the label at the time (see *Bowyer v Siemens plc* UKEAT/0021/05/SM). Any excess goes towards reducing the compensatory award (see *Boorman v Allmakes* [1995] IRLR 553);

- By an amount that the tribunal considers to be just and equitable where the claimant has been awarded an amount under a designated dismissal procedures agreement (s122(3A));

- Where the dismissal is unfair by virtue of s104F (blacklists) the basic award will be reduced (or further reduced) by the amount of any basic award paid in respect of the same dismissal under s156 TULR(C)A (minimum basic award in case of dismissal on grounds related to trade union membership or activities).

The basic award cannot be:

- increased or decreased for the failure by the employer/employee to comply with the ACAS Code of Practice (see s124A and s118(1)(b) ERA 1996);

- increased following a failure to provide the employee with a written statement of terms and conditions of employment, as that increase is applied within the compensatory award (s38 EA 2002 and s124A and s118(1)(b) ERA 1996);

- reduced on account of the employee's failure to mitigate their loss;

- reduced under *Polkey* (unless it is an *'exceptionally rare case where such a (fair) dismissal might have taken place virtually contemporaneously with the unfair dismissal which actually occurred'* - see again *Granchester Construction (Eastern) Ltd v Attrill* UKEAT/0327/12/LA, paragraph 19).

Minimum basic award under s120 ERA 1996

If the minimum award of £5,970 has been made because the principal reason for a redundancy dismissal was one of the reasons set out in s120(1) the figure may still be reduced for contributory conduct, but the percentage reduction is applied to the difference between what the claimant would have received under the standard case and the minimum £5,970. For example, if the claimant would only have received £2,000 but does in fact qualify for the minimum £5,970, any contributory conduct will be applied to the difference, i.e. £ £3,970.

Adjustments to a discrimination award

1) Possibly contributory conduct (but see *Discrimination* for further information);

2) Failure to comply with the ACAS Code of Practice;

3) Interest can be added to the awards for injury to feelings, personal injury, aggravated damages and the award for financial loss (see *Interest*);

4) Where a dismissal is both discriminatory and unfair, the tribunal should make the award for compensation under the discrimination legislation, but may also make a basic award (see *D'Souza v London Borough of Lambeth* [1997] IRLR 677).

Adjustments to damages for wrongful dismissal

Damages for wrongful dismissal can be adjusted in 3 ways:

1) An increase/decrease for the failure by the employer/employee to comply with the ACAS Code of Practice (see s207A and Schedule A2 of TULR(C)A);

2) A deduction for any contingencies and any accelerated payment of damages, which is only likely to arise where the (unexpired) period of notice under the contract is substantial;

3) Interest may be awarded from the date of the cause of action to the date of the hearing but only in the County Court, High Court and Court of Appeal. The ET does not have jurisdiction to award interest on a breach of contract.

Grossing up and the statutory cap

Grossing up is applied after all the adjustments have been applied (see also *Grossing up*).

The statutory cap is applied after the grossing up calculation (see also *Statutory cap*).

Example 1
Awards
Basic award = £3,000

Financial loss = £10,000

Adjustments
Contributory conduct (basic and compensatory awards) = 10%

ACAS uplift = 25%

Calculation
Total award = (£3,000 x 0.9) + (£10,000 x 0.9 x 1.25 but see note below) = £2,700 (basic award) + £11,250 (compensatory award) = £13,950

Remember that adjustments are **multiplied** cumulatively. In other words, don't add/subtract the adjustment percentages to get the overall change (i.e. an increase of 25% and a decrease of 10% does **not** translate into an increase of 15%). The actual overall increase is 12.5% (because 1.25 x 0.9 = 1.125, where the .125 represents the 12.5%)

Example 2
Awards
Basic award = £3,000

Financial loss = £10,000

Award for lack of written particulars = 2 weeks' pay = £600

Credits
Ex gratia payment = £500

Earnings = £750

Adjustments
Contributory conduct (basic and compensatory awards) = 10%

Polkey deduction = 30%

Calculation
Basic award = £3,000 x 0.9 = £2,700 (*Polkey* does not apply to the basic award).

The order of adjustments for the compensatory award must be carefully considered because we have a mixture of multiplication (contributory conduct) and addition/subtraction (lack of written particulars, ex gratia payment and earnings). It is important that the order given on the previous page is followed.

The financial loss is first reduced by £500 and £750 and then the *Polkey* deduction is applied = (£10,000 - £500 - £750) x 0.7 = £6,125

Next, add the failure to provide written particulars = £6,125 + £600 = £6,725

Then apply the contributory conduct adjustment = £6,725 x 0.9 = £6,052.50

Total award = £2,700 (basic award) + £6,052.50 (compensatory award) = £8,752.50

Example 3
Awards
Basic award = £3,000

Financial loss = £10,000

Award for lack of written particulars = 2 weeks' pay = £600

Credits

Ex gratia payment = £500

Earnings = £750

Redundancy payment made on termination = £5,000

Adjustments

Contributory conduct (compensatory award only) = 10%

Polkey deduction = 30%

ACAS uplift = 15%

Calculation

First reduce the Basic Award by any redundancy pay received. The redundancy pay here exceeds the basic award, so this element is zero. The remainder (£5,000 - £3,000 = £2,000) goes towards reducing the compensatory award, but only at the end of the calculation.

The financial loss is first reduced by £500 and £750 and then the *Polkey* deduction and the ACAS uplift are applied = (£10,000 - £500 - £750) x 0.7 x 1.15 = £7,043.75

Next, the failure to provide written particulars is added = £7,043.75 + £600 = £7,643.75

Then contributory conduct has to be applied = £7,643.75 x 0.9 = £6,879.38

Finally, the remainder of the redundancy pay is deducted to the extent of the excess beyond the basic award = £6,879.38 - (£5,000 - £3,000) = £4,879.38

Total Award = £4,879.38

Example 4

This is identical to example 3 apart from the fact that the basic award also has contributory conduct applied to it.

Awards

Basic award = £3,000

Financial loss = £10,000

Award for lack of written particulars = 2 weeks' pay = £600

Credits

Ex gratia payment = £500

Earnings = £750

Redundancy pay paid on termination = £5,000

Adjustments

Contributory conduct (basic **and** compensatory awards) = 10%

Polkey deduction = 30%

ACAS uplift = 15%

Calculation

First the basic award needs to be reduced for contributory conduct = £3,000 x 0.9 = £2,700 Next it is reduced by any redundancy pay received. The redundancy pay exceeds the reduced basic award so the reduced basic award is zero. The remainder (£5,000 - £2,700 = £2,300) goes towards reducing the compensatory award, but only at the end of the calculation.

The financial loss is first reduced by £500 and £750 and the *Polkey* deduction and the ACAS uplift are applied = (£10,000 - £500 - £750) x 0.7 x 1.15 = £7,043.75

Next, the failure to provide written particulars is added = £7,043.75 + £600 = £7,643.75

Then contributory conduct is applied = £7,643.75 x 0.9 = £6,879.38

Finally, the remainder of the redundancy pay should be deducted to the extent of the excess of the **reduced** basic award = £6,879.38 - £2,300 = £4,579.38

Total Award = £4,579.38

Statutory authorities: EA 2002 s38; ERA 1996 ss118(1)(b), 120, 122(1) & (2), 123(4), (6) & (7) and 124A; The Industrial Tribunals (Interest on Awards in Discrimination Cases) Regulations 1996; TULR(C)A s207A & Schedule A2

Relevant case law: *Bentwood Bros (Manchester) Ltd v Shepherd* [2003] EWCA Civ 380; *Digital Equipment Co Ltd v Clements* [1997] EWCA Civ 2899; *Granchester Construction (Eastern) Ltd v Attrill* UKEAT/0327/12/LA; *Hardie Grant London Ltd v Aspden* [2012] I.C.R. D6 (EAT); *Polkey v AE Dayton Services Ltd* [1987] IRLR 50 (HL)

Adoption leave: see Detriment; Unfair dismissal; Table 28

Age discrimination: see Discrimination

Agency workers

Regulations 5, 12, 13 and 17(2) of the Agency Workers Regulations 2010/93 give agency workers a variety of rights, including the rights 'to the same basic working and employment conditions' as if they had been employed directly by those hiring them, where they have been working in the same role for the same hirer for 12 continuous calendar weeks (Regulation 5).

If a complaint to an Employment Tribunal in respect of a breach of the Regulations is held to be well-founded, regulation 18(8) directs the tribunal to take such of the following steps as it considers just and equitable:

1) Making a declaration as to the rights of the complainant in relation to the matters to which the complaint relates;

2) Ordering the respondent to pay compensation to the complainant;

3) Recommending that the respondent take, within a specified period, action appearing to the tribunal to be reasonable, in all the circumstances of the case, for the purpose of obviating or reducing the adverse effect on the complainant of any matter to which the complaint relates.

Any such compensation is to be 'such as the tribunal considers just and equitable in all the circumstances having regard to (a) the infringement or breach to which the complaint relates; and (b) any loss which is attributable to the infringement'. This loss is to be taken to include 'any expenses reasonably incurred by the complainant in consequence of the infringement or breach; and loss of any benefit which the complainant might reasonably be expected to have had but for the infringement or breach.'

This sum must not be less than 2 weeks' pay where the complaint is an infringement of Regulations 5 and 10, unless such a sum would not be a just and equitable amount 'taking into account the conduct of the claimant and the respondent', in which case a lower sum may be awarded.

An additional award may be granted where the agency or hirer is considered to have structured its assignments 'to prevent the agency worker from being entitled to, or from continuing to be entitled to, the rights conferred by Regulation 5', and but for that structure the agency worker would, or would continue to, be entitled to rights under Regulation 5. Such an award is not to be more than £5,000.

Alternatively, the tribunal may order the respondent to pay a penalty to the Secretary of State under s12A Employment Tribunals Act 1996.

If there is more than one respondent, the amount of compensation payable by either respondent is to be 'such as may be found by the tribunal to be just and equitable having regard to the extent of each respondent's responsibility for the infringement to which the complaint relates'. If an additional award is made, this is also to be apportioned on a 'just and equitable' basis 'having regard to the extent to which [the tribunal] considers each to have been responsible for the fact that' the assignments have been structured to avoid conferring Regulation 5 rights.

Failure to comply with any recommendation made by the tribunal, without reasonable justification, gives the tribunal the discretion (if it considers it just and equitable to do so) to increase the amount of any compensation ordered, or award compensation if it has not already done so.

The correct approach for a tribunal to take in assessing compensation has been set out by the EAT in *Amissah & Ors v Trainpeople.co.uk Ltd (Dissolved) & Anor* UKEAT/0187/16:

1) It must identify the infringement;

2) It must identify the responsibility of the hirer and the temporary work agency for the infringement;

3) It must decide whether to order either the temporary work agency or the hirer to pay compensation; and

4) When it does, it must determine what amount of compensation it would be just and equitable to award. It must have regard to (a) the infringement and (b) the loss attributable to the infringement. That loss should be taken to include the loss of any benefit that the claimant might reasonably be expected to have had but for the infringement.

In assessing the loss, the tribunal should ask itself what would have happened but for the infringement for which the relevant party was responsible.

Injury to feelings is excluded for claims under Regulations 5, 12, 13, 10(1)(a)-(d) (see Reg 18(15)) but it does appear to apply to unfair dismissal claims under the regulations.

Gross or net: The compensation is calculated according to a week's pay, which is a gross figure.

A week's pay is defined as the higher of:

• the average weekly pay received by the agency worker in the previous 4 weeks in relation to the assignment to which the claim relates; and

• the average weekly pay that the agency worker should have received in the previous 4 weeks in relation to the assignment to which the claim relates.

Only payments in respect of basic pay whether by way of annual salary, payments for actual time worked or by reference to output or otherwise should be taken into account.

Limit on a week's pay: None

Any maximum or minimum: Minimum is 2 week's pay, unless 2 week's pay is not a just and equitable amount of compensation, in which case the tribunal can reduce the amount as it considers appropriate; There is no maximum.

Additional award: No minimum; Maximum is £5,000

Adjustments: The award can be reduced for contributory conduct (Reg 18(17)).

Mitigation: The tribunal may reduce the amount if it considers that the claimant has failed to mitigate their loss (Reg 18(16)).

Tax: The tax treatment is not clear. To the extent that any sum awarded is compensation for lost earnings, it is likely to be taxed under s62 ITEPA 2003.

Statutory authorities: Agency Workers Regulations 2010/93; Employment Tribunals Act 1996 s12A

Relevant case law: *Amissah & Ors v Trainpeople.co.uk Ltd (Dissolved) & Anor* UKEAT/0187/16

Aggravated damages

Aggravated damages are available in discrimination claims in England and Wales, but not in Scotland. They are an aspect of injury to feelings, and are awarded only on the basis, and to the extent that the aggravating features have increased the impact of the discriminatory act on the claimant and thus the injury to his or her feelings. They are compensatory, not punitive. The appropriate acts include:

• Where the act is done in an exceptionally upsetting way: Underhill P in *Commissioner of Police of the Metropolis v Shaw* UKEAT/0125/11/ZT cites the phrase '*high-handed, malicious, insulting or oppressive*' behaviour;

• Motive: discriminatory conduct that is evidently based on prejudice or animosity or which is spiteful or vindictive or intended to wound is likely to cause more distress than if done without such a motive – for example as a result of ignorance or insensitivity. Naturally, the claimant has to be aware of the motive in question; and

• Subsequent conduct: for example, conducting the trial in an unnecessarily oppressive manner, failing to apologise, or failing to treat the complaint with the requisite seriousness. (*Bungay & Anor v Saini & Ors* UKEAT/0331/10 and *Zaiwalla & Co v Walia* [2002] UKEAT/451/00).

Tribunals must beware the risk of double recovery, and consider whether the overall award of injury to feelings and aggravated damages is proportionate to the totality of the suffering caused to the claimant.

It is good practice to formulate aggravated damages as a sub-heading of injury to feelings – i.e. '*injury to feelings in the sum of £x, incorporating aggravated damages in the sum of £y*'.

Remedy: There is no specific calculation but it would appear from the decided cases that £20,000 is the top end of the bracket for aggravated damages. The award is compensatory, not punitive. There is no minimum award.

Adjustments: Interest can be applied (see also *Interest*) but no other adjustments are applicable.

Mitigation: N/A

Tax: The award is likely to be treated in the same way as an award for injury to feelings (see also *Injury to feelings* and *Tax and termination payments*).

Recoupment: N/A

Relevant case law: *Bungay & Anor v Saini & Ors* UKEAT/0331/10; *Commissioner of Police of the Metropolis v Shaw* UKEAT/0125/11/ZT; *Ministry of Defence v Fletcher* [2009] UKEAT/0044/09; *Singh v University Hospital NHS Trust* EAT/1409/01; *Zaiwalla & Co v Walia* [2002] UKEAT/ 451/00

Ante-natal: see Time off for ante-natal care

Apprentices: see National Minimum Wage

Arrears of pay (reinstatement/re-engagement)

(see also Additional award)

Where a tribunal makes an order for reinstatement or re-engagement, the claimant is entitled to arrears of pay from the date of dismissal to the date of reinstatement/re-engagement in respect of any benefit that the employee might reasonably be expected to have had but for the dismissal. In the case of *National Westminster Bank Plc v Parry* [2004] EWCA Civ 1563 the court stated: *'Plainly that envisages a sum which will be payable whether or not the order for reinstatement is obeyed.'*

Reinstatement: if the claimant would have benefited from an improvement in his terms and conditions of employment had he not been dismissed, an order for reinstatement shall require him to be treated as if he had benefited from that improvement from the date on which he would have done so but for being dismissed. This could also include accrued holiday pay (s114 ERA 1996).

Re-engagement: again, the claimant is entitled to full back pay plus any accrued holiday pay. Arrears are normally calculated on the basis of the claimant's pay prior to dismissal, even if the new job on re-engagement is paid at a lower rate.

Remedy: The award will be the sum of any pay and benefits between the date of dismissal and reinstatement/re-engagement. Any payment in lieu, ex gratia payments paid by the employer, and any wages the employee has earned since dismissal should be deducted as well as any other benefits the tribunal thinks appropriate (see s114(4) and s115(3)).

Where an employer reinstates or re-engages an employee but fails fully to comply with the order, the loss suffered by the employee can be compensated for under s117(1), including any arrears of pay and benefits.

Where an employer fails to reinstate or re-engage a claimant, the losses suffered, including any unpaid arrears of pay and benefits, will fall to be compensated under the compensatory award (see s117(3)(a)).

Gross or net: Calculated on gross pay.

Adjustments: None

Cap: The statutory cap applies to an award under s117(1) and (2) ERA and s123. The statutory cap is currently the lower of £80,541 or 52 weeks' pay (as defined in ss220 to 229 ERA 1996) (see s124 ERA 1996). It should be noted that the cap will be lifted to the extent necessary to compensate for arrears of pay and any additional award:

- in the case of compensation awarded under s117(1) where the order for reinstatement or re-engagement has been partially complied with, the cap can be exceeded to the extent necessary to enable the award fully to reflect the amount specified as payable under section 114(2)(a) or section 115(2)(d). In other words, the employee is entitled to receive at least their arrears of pay, even if those arrears exceed the cap;

- in the case of an award under s117(3) (i.e. an award where the employer has not complied at all with an order for reinstatement or re-engagement) the statutory cap may be exceeded to the extent necessary to enable the aggregate of the compensatory and additional awards fully to reflect the amount specified as payable under section 114(2)(a) or section 115(2)(d) (see *National Westminster Bank Plc v Parry* [2004] EWCA Civ 1563).

This means that:

- if the arrears of pay exceed the cap on their own, the individual will receive the total amount of arrears;

- if the arrears of pay do not exceed the cap on their own they will be offset against the compensatory award.

In other words, the arrears of pay award is not freestanding - the arrears of pay, which by itself does not exceed the cap, should not be disregarded when applying the statutory cap (see *National Westminster Bank Plc v Parry* [2004] EWCA Civ 1563).

Mitigation: Any actual mitigation will be taken into account in identifying the loss suffered (s114(4) and s115(3)).

Tax: The arrears of pay sum is compensation for unfair dismissal and so is taxable only under s401 ITEPA 2003. The employer is expected to operate PAYE where the aggregate payments within that section exceed £30,000 (see EIM12960). If, unusually, there is as a matter of fact continuous employment between the dates of dismissal and reinstatement or re-engagement ordered by the tribunal, any payment for that period is taxable as earnings under Section 62 ITEPA 2003.

Recoupment: Arrears of pay up until the tribunal hearing will form part of the prescribed element for recoupment purposes.

Statutory authorities: ERA 1996 ss114 to 117 and s124

Relevant case law: National Westminster Bank Plc v Parry [2004] EWCA Civ 1563

Basic award

(see also Basic award, maximum; Basic award, minimum)

The basic award is a sum awarded to a claimant who has been unfairly dismissed and calculated on the same basis as statutory redundancy pay according to age and the number of complete years' continuous service.

There are circumstances where a maximum or minimum basic award can be paid - see the separate entries for more details.

Calculation of remedy: The total basic award is calculated as follows:

- 1 ½ weeks' gross pay for each year of employment in which they were not below the age of 41;

- 1 week's gross pay for each year of employment in which they were below the age of 41 but not below the age of 22; and

- ½ a week's gross pay for each year of employment in which they were below the age of 22.

Where an individual's continuous service straddles an age of 41 or 22, the individual only receives the higher rate for the complete years of service that have been worked after that age has been reached. In other words, an employee must have already reached his 42nd birthday for that year to qualify at the higher rate of 1 ½ weeks.

The maximum amount of a week's gross pay is currently £489. The definition of a week's pay (see *Week's pay*) can be found at ERA 1996 Part XIV Ch II.

The maximum number of years that can be taken into account is 20.

Thus, the current maximum basic award is 20 x 1.5 x £489 = £14,670.

Gross or net: Gross. A week's pay as defined in ss220 to 229 ERA 1996 applies (see *Week's pay*).

Limit on a week's pay: Currently £489 (see Table 1 for historical rates).

Limit on number of weeks: The limit depends on the age of the employee during his period of employment, and the maximum is the equivalent of 30 weeks, corresponding to 20 years' service all at the age of 41 or greater (1 ½ weeks for every year's service).

Any maximum or minimum: Maximum = £14,670; No minimum except in certain circumstances (see *Basic award, minimum* and *Basic award, maximum*).

Adjustments: The basic award can be reduced for contributory conduct (s122(2)) or for unreasonable refusal by the employee to accept an offer of reinstatement (s122(1)). This reduction will be the amount the tribunal considers is 'just and equitable', which is broader than the contributory conduct provision for the compensatory award and can take into account conduct which was not known to the employer at the time (see *Optikinetics Ltd v Whooley* EAT/1275/97 and *Parker Foundary Ltd v Slack* [1992] IRLR 11).

The award will not be reduced for contributory conduct in a redundancy dismissal, except where such a dismissal is for one of a number of specified reasons requiring a minimum basic award, when special statutory rules limit the ability to reduce the basic award (see s122(3) ERA 1996). If the minimum award of £5,970 has been made because the principal reason for a redundancy dismissal was one of those set out in s120(1) the figure may still be reduced for contributory conduct, but the percentage reduction is applied to the difference between what the claimant would have received under the standard case and the minimum £5,970. For example, if the claimant would otherwise have received £2,000 but does in fact qualify for the minimum £5,970, any contributory conduct will be applied to the difference, i.e. £3,970.

The basic award can be reduced by an amount that the tribunal considers to be just and equitable where the claimant has been awarded an amount under a designated dismissal procedures agreement (s122(3A)).

Where the dismissal is unfair by virtue of s104F (blacklists) the basic award will be reduced (or further reduced) by the amount of any basic award paid in respect of the same dismissal under s156 TULR(C)A (minimum basic award in case of dismissal on grounds related to trade union membership or activities).

Any redundancy payment that has been made to the employee must be deducted from the basic award first (see *Allmakes Ltd v Boorman* [1993] UKEAT/695/92). If, on the other hand the tribunal finds that the real reason for dismissal was not redundancy the claimant may be entitled to both payments. So if, for example, the employer mistakenly makes a redundancy payment in circumstances where the dismissal is automatically unfair under TUPE, then the employee will be entitled to recover a basic award despite having received a redundancy payment.

The basic award is not subject to any other adjustments such as for failure to mitigate loss, a failure to comply with a code of practice, or the chance of a future fair dismissal (see *Polkey*).

Mitigation: The award cannot be reduced for a failure to mitigate loss.

Tax: The basic award will be taxed under s401 ITEPA 2003 and goes to reduce the tax free amount at termination of £30,000 (see also *Grossing up*).

Recoupment: Recoupment does not apply to the basic award.

Statutory authorities: ERA 1996 ss119 to 122; TULR(C)A 1992 s156

Relevant case law: *Allmakes Ltd v Boorman* [1993] UKEAT/695/92; *Optikinetikcs Ltd v Whooley* EAT/1275/97; *Parker Foundary Ltd v Slack* [1992] IRLR 11

Example 1

An employee was 56 at EDT and had 20 years' continuous service, being paid £550 gross per week at an EDT of 10/04/2017. His basic award would be calculated as follows:

Number of years' service at or over the age of 41 = 56 - 41 = 15

Each of these years count for 1 ½ weeks' pay = 15 x 1.5 = 22.5

The other 5 years of service, i.e. 20 - 15, count for 1 week's pay = 5 x 1 = 5

The total number of weeks = 22.5 + 5 = 27.5

The total basic award is then 27.5 x £489 (the maximum gross weekly pay allowed as at 10/04/2017) = £13,447.50

Example 2

An employee was 35 at EDT and had 15 years' continuous service, being paid £330 gross per week at an EDT of 01/02/2016. His basic award would be calculated as follows:

Number of years' service at or over the age of 22 = 35 - 22 = 13

Each of these years count for 1 week's pay = 13 x 1 = 13

The other 2 years of service, i.e. 15 - 13, count for ½ a week's pay = 2 x 0.5 = 1

The total number of weeks = 13 + 1 = 14

The total basic award is then 14 x £330 = £4,620

Example 3

An employee was 55 at EDT and had 25 years' continuous service, being paid £600 per week at an EDT of 01/02/2016. His basic award would be calculated as follows:

Number of years' service over the age of 41 = 55 - 41 = 14

Each of these years count for 1 ½ week's pay = 14 x 1.5 = 21

The other 11 years of service, i.e. 25 - 14, are limited to 6 years, because the maximum number of years is 20. These 6 years each count for 1 week's pay = 6 x 1 = 6

The total number of weeks = 21 + 6 = 27

The total basic award is then 27 x £475 (the weekly limit as at 01/02/2016) = £12,825

See also the Statutory redundancy table, Table 25.

Basic award, maximum

(see also Basic award)

The statutory maximum where the reason for dismissal is redundancy but the employee is not entitled to a redundancy payment because they have unreasonably refused an offer of suitable alternative employment, or have had their contract renewed so that there is no dismissal, is 2 weeks' gross pay (s121 ERA).

Gross or net: Gross

Limit on a week's pay: £489 (see Table 1 for historical rates).

Limit on number of weeks: 2

Any maximum or minimum: Maximum is £978

Adjustments: Contributory conduct reduction applies (s122 ERA 1996).

Mitigation: The basic award cannot be reduced for failure to mitigate loss.

Tax: The basic award will be taxed under s401 ITEPA 2003 and goes to reduce the tax free amount at termination of £30,000 (see *Grossing up*).

Recoupment: Recoupment does not apply to the basic award.

Statutory authorities: ERA 1996 ss121 and 122

Basic award, minimum

(see also Basic award)

There is a statutory minimum basic award where dismissal is unfair by virtue of

- s100(1)(a) and (b) ERA 1996 (health and safety cases);
- s101A(d) (employee representative in working time cases);
- s102(1) (trustee of a relevant pension scheme);
- s103 (employee representatives);
- s104F (union blacklist); or
- s156 of TULR(C)A (union membership).

The minimum is currently £5,970 (s120(1) ERA 1996 and s156 TULR(C)A 1992), except for the s104F (blacklisting) dismissal, where the minimum is £5,000 (s120(1C) ERA 1996). The statutory minimum is ignored if the basic award exceeds this figure when calculated in the normal way.

Adjustments: Contributory conduct reduction applies. However, the percentage reduction is applied only to so much of the basic award as is payable because of s120 (s122(3) ERA 1996) or s156, i.e. the deduction only applies to the difference between what the claimant would have received under the standard case and the minimum £5,970 (or £5,000 in a blacklisting case). For example, if the claimant would only have received £2,000 but does in fact qualify for the minimum £5,970, any contributory conduct should be applied to the difference, i.e. £3,970.

Mitigation: The basic award cannot be reduced for failure to mitigate loss.

Tax: The basic award will be taxed under s401 ITEPA 2003 and goes to reduce the tax free amount at termination of £30,000 (see also *Grossing up*).

Recoupment: Recoupment does not apply to the basic award.

Statutory authorities: ERA 1996 ss120 and 122; TULR(C)A 1992 s156

Benefits: see Financial losses

Bonuses

Loss of earnings within an unfair dismissal award can include any commission, bonus or other benefit that the employee reasonably expected to receive had they remained in the employment (s123(2)(b) ERA 1996). The sums do not need to be contractual, provided that the reasonable expectation can be established. The same approach will apply in discrimination awards.

Where the value of a bonus is sought under the unlawful deduction from wages jurisdiction or for breach of contract, specific considerations apply (see *Unlawful deductions from wages*).

Gross or net: Such sums should be paid net of tax and NI and grossed up where appropriate.

Adjustments: Any bonus will be included in the compensatory award and adjusted alongside.

Mitigation: The mitigation rules applicable to the compensatory award apply to bonuses.

Tax: The compensatory award, which includes loss of benefits, is taxable and will fall to be grossed up under s401 if the award overall exceeds £30,000 (see also *Grossing up*).

Recoupment: The recoupment regulations state that 'any amount ordered to be paid and calculated under s123 [of the ERA 1996] in respect of compensation for **loss of wages** for a period before the conclusion of the tribunal proceedings' form part of the prescribed element. It is unclear whether a bonus would be defined as 'wages' but it is likely that any bonus payment awarded would be subject to the recoupment regulations.

Statutory authorities: ERA 1996) s123(2)(b)

Relevant case law: York Trailer Co Ltd v Sparkes [1973] IRLR 348

Breach of contract

The Employment Tribunal has a jurisdiction to hear breach of contract claims in certain limited circumstances (Employment Tribunals Extension of Jurisdiction (England and Wales) Order 1994 SI 1994/1623). Claims may be brought by employees where the claim *"arises on or is outstanding on"* the termination of the employee's employment (Reg 3). A counterclaim (but not a claim) may be brought by an employer similarly where it *"arises on or is outstanding on"* the termination (Reg 4). Claims on certain contractual terms are excluded by Reg 5, including terms as to living accommodation, intellectual property, an obligation of confidence and a restrictive covenant.

A claim for constructive dismissal will rely on conduct that amounts to a repudiatory breach of contract by the employer, but an unfair dismissal claim will be brought under that jurisdiction without invoking the breach of contract jurisdiction, unless the individual chooses to bring such a claim in addition.

Remedy: The remedy will be damages caused by the breach of contract. Typically, such claims are for unpaid notice pay and the value of discretionary bonuses.

Adjustments: Any failure to comply with the ACAS code of practice applies.

Limit: £25,000.

Calculation date: see Interest; Week's pay; Table 5

Cap on a week's pay

(see also Week's pay; Table 1)

For several awards referable to a definition of a 'week's pay' in s220-229 ERA 1996, a cap on the gross weekly pay is used in the calculations (see s186 and s227 ERA 1996). The current cap, as at 06/04/2017, is £489. The weekly pay cap applies to the following awards:

- Statutory redundancy pay (s162 ERA 1996);
- Basic award (s119-122 ERA 1996);
- Right to written particulars of employment (s38 EA 2002);
- Right to be accompanied at a disciplinary hearing (s11 ERelA 1999);
- Right to request flexible working (s80I(1)(b) ERA 1996);
- Right to be accompanied at a flexible working meeting (Reg 15 FW(PR) Regs 2002);
- Insolvency provisions (s186 ERA 1996);
- Additional award (s117(3)(b).

Cap on wrongful dismissal damages

The cap on wrongful dismissal damages is £25,000 if the claim is brought in the ET (Reg 10 Industrial Tribunals Extension of Jurisdiction (England and Wales) Order 1994). There is no cap if the claim is brought in the County Court or High Court.

Child care costs: see Financial losses

Commission: see Bonuses

Company cars: see Financial losses

Compensatory award

(see also Adjustments; Immediate loss of earnings: Future loss of earnings; Concurrent unfair and wrongful dismissal; Grossing up; Tax and termination payments; Recoupment; Protected disclosure; Unfair dismissal)

s123 of the ERA 1996 provides that the compensatory award shall be:

> '...such amount as the tribunal considers just and equitable in all the circumstances having regard to the loss sustained by the complainant in consequence of the dismissal insofar as that loss is attributable to action taken by the employer'.

Compensation for unfair dismissal should be awarded to *'compensate and compensate fully, but not to award a bonus'* according to Sir John Donaldson in *Norton Tool Co Ltd v Tewson* [1973] All ER 183. The object of the compensatory award is to compensate the employee for their financial losses as if they had not been unfairly dismissed - it is not designed to punish the employer for their wrongdoing.

Calculation of remedy: The calculation falls under two headings:

Immediate loss of earnings
This is the loss suffered between the EDT to the date of the remedies hearing. Loss of earnings will be calculated on the basis of net take home pay (that is, after deduction of tax and national insurance). The compensatory award can take into account any pay increase which would have been awarded in the previous employment up to the date of the hearing, including a back-dated pay rise. Conversely, if the claimant would probably have been paid less than their net earnings at the EDT in this period if they had not been dismissed (for example because of the financial constraints on the respondent at the time), the amount of loss of earnings can be correspondingly reduced.

The employer's liability will normally cease before the date of the remedies hearing if the employee has (or ought to have) got a new permanent job paying at least as much as the old job as there will no longer be a loss arising from the dismissal.

For claims relating solely to unfair dismissal the period of immediate loss is the number of weeks between the EDT and the remedies hearing, or the date of a new equivalent job, or the date by which the claimant should have found a new job, whichever is the soonest.

If a claim for wrongful dismissal has also been made, the number of weeks for the unfair dismissal immediate loss of earnings should be calculated from the date at which the wrongful dismissal damages period ends through to the date of the hearing, new job or expectation of a new job (see also *Damages for wrongful dismissal*).

Future loss of earnings
An employee may have on-going future losses if by the date of the remedies hearing they have not secured a new job or have obtained a job but with salary and benefits that are less valuable than their previous employment.

The future loss figure is based on the number of weeks for which it is calculated the particular loss will continue, and it may be that pay rises in the future will reduce the loss suffered in each of those years. The tribunal should take into account the personal characteristics of the employee such as age and health. They also need to take into account contingencies such as whether and for how long the employee would have remained in the original employment, whether there would have been a possibility of promotion and whether the level of earnings would have remained the same. A broad brush approach will be used, with Ogden tables usually used only where there is career long loss, in order to calculate loss based on various statistical contingencies.

Gross or net: Losses will be calculated on a basis net of tax and NIC and grossed up where appropriate (see *Grossing up*).

Limit on a week's pay: There is no limit - the award is based on actual net value of pay and benefits.

Limit on number of weeks: For dismissals occurring on or after 6 April 2017 the statutory cap (where it applies) is calculated as the lower of £80,541 or 52 weeks' gross pay (see *Statutory cap*).

Adjustments: (see also *Adjustments, Mitigation, Contributory conduct*)

Ex gratia payment: see *Ex gratia payment*

Earnings: A deduction of earnings which have mitigated the claimant's loss or a sum which reflects any failure by the claimant's failure to mitigate his/her loss.

Early payment of compensation: Any compensation paid to the employee before the tribunal hearing should be deducted from the compensatory award (see *Ex gratia payment*).

Polkey: A '*Polkey*' deduction (see also *Polkey*) to represent the chance the claimant may have been fairly dismissed in any event.

ACAS: A percentage increase or reduction up to a maximum of 25% to reflect an unreasonable failure by the employer or employee to comply with the ACAS code of practice on disciplinary and grievance procedures (see *ACAS*).

Protected disclosure not in good faith: Deduction, up to a maximum of 25%, if the award is under a s103A claim but the disclosure was not made in good faith (only for claims brought after 25 June 2013) (see *Protected disclosure*).

Written particulars: An increase for any failure by the employer to provide written particulars of employment (see also *Written particulars*).

Contributory conduct: A percentage reduction for any contributory conduct on the part of the employee (see *Contributory conduct*).

Enhanced redundancy: A deduction of any enhanced redundancy payment to the extent that it exceeds the basic award (see *Redundancy*).

Accelerated payment: A deduction for accelerated payment of compensation in respect of future loss (see *Accelerated/decelerated receipt*).

Interest: Any interest on the losses suffered (see also *Interest*).

Statutory cap: The cap, currently the lower of £80,541 or 52 weeks' gross pay, does not apply in all circumstances. If the reason for dismissal is on the grounds of discrimination (s13, s15, s16, s18, s19, s21, s26, s27 Equality Act 2010), uncapped compensation will be awarded under that statute, and if the dismissal is because of health and safety reasons or whistleblowing by virtue of sections 100 and 103A respectively (see s105(3) and s105(6A)) the cap will not apply.

The cap is applied **after** the grossing up calculation is applied (see *Hardie Grant London Ltd v Aspden* UKEAT/0242/11/RN).

If an additional award and arrears of pay are being claimed the statutory cap can be exceeded in certain circumstances (see *Arrears of pay* and *Additional award*).

Mitigation: The employee is under a duty to mitigate their loss and a deduction in compensation can be made if they have not fully done so.

Tax: If the combined sum of any basic and compensatory award is greater than £30,000 then the excess figure will be subject to tax (see *Grossing up*).

This is so even if the reason for termination is discriminatory (see *Tax and termination payments*).

Recoupment: Recoupment will apply to immediate loss of earnings only (see *Recoupment*). Note that the recoupment regulations do not apply if an award has been made under the Equality Act 2010.

Statutory authorities: EA 2010 ss13, 15, 16, 18, 19, 21, 26 and 27; ERA 1996 ss100, 103A, 105(3), 105(6A) and ss123 to 126

Relevant case law: *Hardie Grant London Ltd v Aspden* UKEAT/0242/11/RN; *Norton Tool Co Ltd v Tewson* [1973] 1 All ER 183 [1973] 1 All ER 183

Note on calculating with dates: There is a useful website called www.timeanddate.com, which calculates the number of days, weeks or months between two given dates. The calculator will also add a number of days, weeks or months to a fixed date.

Concurrent unfair and wrongful dismissal

(see also Compensatory award; Unfair dismissal)

It is often the case that unfair and wrongful dismissal claims are brought concurrently before an ET, for example where an employee has been summarily dismissed for gross misconduct. The wrongful dismissal claim falls within the tribunal's breach of contract jurisdiction which has a separate £25,000 cap.

However, it is important that awards are not double counted. In other words, damages for wrongful dismissal cannot be awarded for the same loss for which compensation for unfair dismissal is also awarded. As a corollary, where an individual's losses may be capped it is possible to take the losses during the notice period out of the (capped) compensatory award to maximise the value of the claims (or to take some of the (capped) wrongful dismissal losses into the compensatory award).

Where losses are compensated for under an award for damages the recoupment regulations will not apply, whereas they will apply to the compensatory award. Also, damages for breach of contract will not be reduced for contributory conduct or '*Polkey*'.

Two matters should be addressed when considering bringing both claims in the tribunal (rather than reserving the breach of contract claim for the High Court/ County Court):

- It is not possible to top up the £25,000 award from a tribunal by bringing a second claim in the civil courts as there will be no remaining cause of action (see *Fraser v HMLAD Ltd* [2006] EWCA Civ 738); and

- If a breach of contract claim has been started at a tribunal, it can be complicated to then withdraw it and bring it instead in the ordinary civil courts. Claimants should consider in which forum they wish to issue their claim at the outset, and if appropriate state explicitly in any ET1 that they *do not* intend to bring any breach of contract claim in the ET.

Calculation

There are two ways in which concurrent claims can be calculated and double counting avoided:

Either:

Calculate the damages for wrongful dismissal and then deduct this figure from the compensation awarded for unfair dismissal

Example
Damages = £5,000
Compensatory award = £6,000

The claimant would receive the damages figure of £5,000 plus (£6,000 - £5,000) = £6,000

Or:

Award the damages for wrongful dismissal, and then start the unfair dismissal period from the day after the damages period ended

Ordinarily both methods will produce the same outcome, but there will be different results where adjustments such as *Polkey*, contributory conduct, or an ACAS Code adjustment have to be applied. There are two potential advantages with the second method:

- there is no danger of the recoupment regulations being applied to the damages figure (see *Damages* and *Recoupment*) because the two awards have been calculated completely separately;

- if the compensatory award has to be adjusted, for example for contributory conduct, it is much easier to determine the figure that should be used in the calculation. Damages for wrongful dismissal are not subject to adjustment for contributory conduct or '*Polkey*'.

The EAT in *Shifferaw v Hudson Music Co Ltd* UKEAT/0294/15 cited a previous edition of this Handbook with approval and held that Employment Tribunals have a discretion over which of the above two methods it wishes to use.

Continuous employment: see Basic award; Effective date of termination; Qualifying period

Contractual notice period

(see also Actual notice period; Damages for wrongful dismissal; Effective date of termination; Statutory notice period)

An employee is entitled to be given notice of his dismissal in accordance with the terms of his contract, unless he has committed gross misconduct in which case dismissal can usually be effected summarily (subject to unfair dismissal and discrimination rights). Where a claimant has been dismissed without the appropriate contractual notice, the claimant is entitled to claim the damages which are equivalent to the wages which he would have earned between the time of the actual termination and the time at which the contract might lawfully have been terminated (by due notice), together with the value of any contractual fringe benefits which the employee would have received during the same period.

The damages are calculated by reference to the greater of the minimum period implied by section 86 ERA and "reasonable notice". The calculation of a period of reasonable notice takes account of all the circumstances of the case including the nature of the employment, the seniority and responsibilities of the employee. The minimum periods under section 86 ERA apply where a person who has been continuously employed for one month or more and are:

- one week's notice if his period of continuous employment is less than two years;

- one week's notice for each year of continuous employment if his period of continuous employment is two years or more but less than twelve years; and

- twelve weeks' notice if his period of continuous employment is twelve years or more.

Any provision for shorter notice in any contract of employment with a person who has been continuously employed for one month or more has effect subject to these provisions but they do not prevent the employee from waiving his right to notice on any occasion or from accepting a payment in lieu of notice (see *Damages for wrongful dismissal* and *Statutory notice period*).

Contributory conduct

(see also Adjustments; Basic award)

A number of awards available to the tribunal may be reduced due to the contributory conduct of the employee (also called *'contributory fault'*). The size of the reduction will be that which the tribunal considers to be just and equitable.

The wording of the test differs between that for the basic award and other awards. The basic award may be reduced where the tribunal *'considers that any conduct of the complainant before the dismissal (or, where the dismissal was with notice, before the notice was given) was such as it would be just and equitable to reduce or reduce further the amount of the award to any extent...'*. In respect of other awards *'where the tribunal finds that the [act] was to any extent caused or contributed to by any action of the complainant, [the tribunal] shall reduce the amount of the compensatory award by such proportion as it considers just and equitable...'*.

For the basic award (but not other awards), conduct which was not known to the employer and cannot have caused or contributed to the dismissal can still be taken into account (see *Optikinetics Ltd v Whooley* [1999] ICR 984 and *Parker Foundary Ltd v Slack* [1992] IRLR 11). For other awards the reduction will be a proportion (expressible as a percentage), whereas the reduction for the basic award may also be calculated to be a particular sum.

These different methods of calculation mean that the figure for contributory conduct can be different for the basic award and the compensatory award (see s122(2) and s123(6) ERA 1996). See in particular the cases of *Montracon Ltd v Hardcastle* UKEAT/0307/12/JO; *Optikinetics Ltd v Whooley* [1999] ICR 984; *Compass Group v Baldwin* UKEAT/0447/05/DM; *Rao v CAA* [1994] ICR 495.

To fall into this category, the claimant's conduct must be *'culpable or blameworthy'*. Save in respect of the basic award, such conduct must cause or contribute to the claimant's dismissal, rather than its fairness or unfairness.

Where there is a significant overlap between the factors taken into account when making a *Polkey* deduction and when making a deduction for contributory conduct, the ET should consider expressly, whether, in the light of that overlap, it is just and equitable to make a finding of contributory conduct, and if so, what its amount should be. This is to avoid the risk of a claimant being penalised twice for the same conduct (see *Lenlyn UK Ltd v Kular* UKEAT/0108/16/DM).

Reductions for contributory conduct apply to the following awards:

- Basic award (s122(2) ERA 1996) (but not in redundancy cases unless the reason for selecting the employee for dismissal was one of those specified in ss100(1)(a) and (b), 101A(d), 102(1) or 103, in which case the contributory conduct reduction applies only to the difference between the statutory minimum and the basic award that would otherwise have been received) (see *Basic award* and *Basic award, minimum*);

- Compensatory award (s123(6) ERA 1996);

- Award in respect of detriment (s49(5) ERA 1996, s149(6) TULR(C)A 1992 (but see s145E(6)) and Paragraph 159(5) Schedule A1 TULR(C)A 1992);

- Right not to be unjustifiably disciplined (s67(7) TULR(C)A 1992);

- Right not to be expelled or excluded from a union (s176(5) TULR(C)A 1992);

- Part time worker discrimination (Reg 8(13) PTW(PLFT) Regs 2000);

- Fixed term employee discrimination (Reg 7(12) FTE(PLFT) Regs 2002).

Grossing up should take place after all adjustments have been made (see also *Grossing up*).

The statutory cap will be applied after any grossing up has been applied.

Example
Basic award = £4,500

Financial loss = £8,000

Financial loss after contributory fault assessed as 25% on the compensatory award only = £8,000 x 0.75 = £6,000

Award = £4,500 + £6,000 = £10,500

Statutory authorities: ERA 1996 ss49(5), 100(1)(a) and (b), 101A(d), 102(1), 103, 120, 122(2) and 123(6); PTW(PLFT) Regs 2000 Reg 8(13); TULR(C)A 1992 Paragraph 159(5) Schedule A1 and ss67(7), 149(6) and 176(5)

Relevant case law: *Compass Group v Baldwin* UKEAT/0447/05/DM; *Lenlyn UK Ltd v Kular*

UKEAT/0108/16/DM; *Montracon Ltd v Hardcastle* UKEAT/0307/12/JO; *Optikinetics Ltd v Whooley* [1999] ICR 984; *Parker Foundary Ltd v Slack* [1992] IRLR 11; *Rao v CAA* [1994] ICR 495

Costs and wasted costs

(See also Fees)

The Employment Tribunals (Constitution and Rules of Procedure) Regulations 2013, Schedule 1, Rules 74 to 84 set out the tribunal's approach and powers to award costs incurred by a party to a tribunal claim. Unlike in the ordinary civil courts, the successful party's costs are not as a matter of course ordered to be paid by the losing party. The costs of one party will only be borne by another party in specified circumstances.

Discretionary orders
By rule 76(1) a tribunal may make a costs order or a preparation time order, and shall consider whether to do so, where it considers that:

a) a party (or that party's representative) has acted vexatiously, abusively, disruptively or otherwise unreasonably in either the bringing of the proceedings (or part) or the way that the proceedings (or part) have been conducted; or

b) any claim or response had no reasonable prospect of success.

A tribunal may also make a costs order or a preparation time order where a party has been in breach of any order or practice direction or where a hearing has been postponed or adjourned on the application of a party (Rule 76(2)). From April 2016, tribunals will be obliged to consider the imposition of a costs order or a preparation time order against a party that is granted a late postponement, i.e. one which is applied for less than seven days before the hearing. A party does not have to prove unreasonable behaviour to obtain a cost order in respect of a postponement (although the reasonableness of such behaviour may be relevant to whether the tribunal exercises its discretion in favour of granting such an order).

Costs that have been incurred in respect of the work undertaken by in-house lawyers are recoverable (see *Ladak v DRC Locums Ltd* UKEAT/0488/13/LA).

A tribunal may make an order that a party pay the expenses incurred by a witness in attending, and this order may be made at the request of the witness (Rule 76(5)).

Mandatory orders

A tribunal must make a costs order against the respondent where at a final hearing for unfair dismissal a claimant has given the respondent 7 days' notice that he wishes to be reinstated or re-engaged, but the hearing is postponed or adjourned because the employer has not provided reasonable evidence of the availability of the claimant's job without a special reason (Rule 76(3)).

Where a party has been subject to a deposit order due to a specific allegation or argument in the claim or response having little reasonable prospect of success (of up to £1,000) and the tribunal decides that issue against the paying party for substantially the reasons set out in the deposit order, the paying party is presumed to have acted unreasonably in pursuing that allegation, unless he shows the contrary, and the deposit will be paid to the other party (this sum will count towards any other costs award).

Costs orders

Rule 74 defines costs as fees, charges, disbursements or expenses incurred by or on behalf of the receiving party.

Limit: The amount of a costs order where the amount costs is determined by the tribunal under its basic jurisdiction is limited to £20,000. However, the tribunal can order that the amount of costs be determined by way of detailed assessment at the County Court, or by an Employment Judge applying the same principles, (and the equivalent in Scotland), in which case there is no cap on the costs awardable. The limit of £20,000 can also be exceeded if the tribunal orders the losing party to pay back any fee paid by the successful party, or for witness expenses reasonably incurred or if both parties agree to a figure which is higher.

Where the costs are that of a lay representative, the maximum hourly available rate is the figure used for preparation time awards (currently £36) (Rule 78(2)).

Preparation time orders

Preparation time orders award an amount to a party to reflect their preparation time whilst not legally represented. A preparation time order and a costs order cannot both be awarded in favour of the same party in the same proceedings, though a party may apply for both, pending the tribunal's determination of entitlement (Rule 75(3) and also see *Duhoe v Support Services Group Ltd - In Liquidation* UKEAT/0102/15/MC). The number of hours in respect of which a preparation time order can be made will be determined by the ET according to the actual time spent and the tribunal's own assessment of what it considers to be a reasonable and proportionate amount of time to spend on such preparatory work (Rule 79).

Hourly rate: the hourly rate is £37 (as at 6 April 2017) and increases by £1 on 6 April each year.

Calculation: Amount of preparation time order = number of hours assessed by the ET x 37

Wasted costs orders

Wasted costs orders require a party's representative rather than a party itself to pay an amount of costs. A tribunal may make a wasted costs order against a representative in favour of any party ('the receiving party') where that party has either:

a) incurred costs as a result of any improper, unreasonable or negligent act or omission on the part of the representative; or

b) incurred costs which, in the light of any such act or omission occurring after they were incurred, the tribunal considers it unreasonable to expect the receiving party to pay.

An award can be made against a representative in favour of his own client.

Allowances

Where a tribunal has made any of the above orders, it may order the paying party to reimburse the Secretary of State for any allowances paid for example witness attendance (see Rule 84).

Ability to pay

In deciding whether to make a costs, preparation time, or wasted costs order, and if so in what amount, the tribunal may have regard to the paying party's (or, where a wasted costs order is made, the representative's) ability to pay (Rule 84). Any insurance policy that may have been taken out by the recipient of a costs award however is not a relevant consideration, nor is the fact that the paying party is a volunteer or trustee (see *Mardner v Gardner & Ors* UKEAT/0483/13/DA MC).

VAT

In *Raggett v John Lewis Plc* UKEAT/0082/12/RN it was confirmed that, if the receiver can claim back the VAT element of any costs incurred as input tax, then those costs should be calculated net of VAT because the receiver will otherwise receive a windfall. On the other hand, if the receiver is not VAT registered, the costs award should be calculated gross (see also Paragraph 5.3 of the Costs Practice Direction which supplements part 43 and Rule 38(3) of The Employment Tribunals (Constitution and Rules of Procedure) Regulations 2004).

Time limit

A party may apply for a costs order or preparation time order at any stage up to 28 days from which the judgment finally determining the proceedings in respect of that party was sent to the parties (Rule 77).

ET and EAT fees

In a provision that brings the tribunal regime closer to the costs availability in small claims in the civil courts, where a party has succeeded on a contract claim or counterclaim an employment tribunal may order the unsuccessful party to pay the tribunal fee paid by the successful party (Employment Tribunals (Constitution and Rules of Procedure) Regulations 2013, Schedule 1, Rule 76(4)).

If the Employment Appeal Tribunal allows an appeal, in full or in part, it has a broad discretion to make a costs order against the respondent specifying that the respondent pay to the appellant an amount no greater than any fee paid by the appellant (Rule 34A(2A) Employment Appeal Tribunal Rules 1993) (see *Sefton Borough Council v Wainwright* UKEAT/0168/14/LA and *Look Ahead Housing & Care Ltd v Chetty & Anor* UKEAT/0037/14/MC). However, where an appeal has only been partly successful the EAT may have to exercise its discretion with more care, and consider only allowing part (or even disallowing entirely) the recovery of fees from the other side (*Itulu v London Fire and Emergency Planning Authority* UKEAT/0055/16).

If the appeal fee is paid not by the appellant but by the union representing them, *Goldwater & Ors v Sellafield Ltd* UKEAT/0178/14/DXA says that no costs order will be made. However, the EAT in *Ibarz v University of Sheffield* UKEAT/0018/15/JOJ disagreed saying that the rules on payment of fees only made sense as a matter of practicalities if the wording 'by the appellant' were read as including 'or on his behalf'. It is the opinion of the author that *Ibarz* should be followed.

Damages for wrongful dismissal

(see also Adjustments; Contractual notice period; Concurrent unfair and wrongful dismissal)

Damages can be awarded if the employee has been dismissed without the appropriate length of notice.

Calculation of remedy: The damages will cover the lost remuneration and benefits that would have been received during the full notice period.

Damages are only awarded for payments and benefits to which the claimant is contractually entitled. Where the contractual entitlement is discretionary, damages for the loss of that benefit will be assessed on the basis that the discretion would have been exercised rationally and in good faith (see *Cantor Fitzgerald International v Horkulak* [2004] EWCA Civ 1287).

Gross or net: Net

Limit on a week's pay: There is no limit on a week's pay, and the statutory definition of a week's pay does not apply.

Any maximum or minimum: None

Adjustments: Damages can be reduced for mitigation or failure to mitigate, reduced/increased for accelerated/decelerated receipt (see *Accelerated/decelerated receipt*), and for failure by the employer/employee to comply with the ACAS code of practice (TULR(C)A s207A and Schedule A2). Interest may be awarded in the County Court and High Court, but not in the Employment Tribunal.

Cap on award: £25,000 if the claim is brought to the ET, no cap if brought in the County Court or High Court.

Mitigation: The employee has a duty to take reasonable steps to mitigate their loss.

Tax: The award for damages for wrongful dismissal is taxable under s401 ITEPA 2003 and will fall to be grossed up to the extent it causes the £30,000 allowance to be exceeded.

Recoupment: Recoupment does not apply to damages for wrongful dismissal.

Statutory authorities: ERA 1996 s86

Relevant case law: *Cantor Fitzgerald International v Horkulak* [2004] EWCA Civ 1287

Damages period: see Damages for wrongful dismissal

Decelerated receipt: see Accelerated/decelerated receipt

Deductions: see Adjustments

Deductions from wages: see Unlawful deductions from wages

Deferred pension

This is the pension entitlement built up by an employee who left employment before normal retirement date (see also *Pension loss*).

Defined benefit: see Pension loss

Defined contribution: see Pension loss

Deposit order: see Costs and wasted costs

Detriment

There are a large number of employment rights which can themselves be enforced by bringing a direct claim, including the right not to be unfairly dismissed. In addition to this type of right, there are rights protecting employees from suffering detriment because of certain protected behaviour and rights to protection from dismissal because of certain protected behaviour (see *Unfair dismissal*). This section deals with the statutory protections from detriment - some rights apply only to employees; some also apply to the broader class of workers.

An **employee** has the right not to be subjected to a detriment because of them:

- having to attend jury service (s43M ERA 1996);

- acting as a health and safety representative (s44);

- refusing to work on Sundays (s45) or refusing to work additional hours on a Sunday (s45ZA), if the employee is a shop or betting worker;

- being a pension scheme trustee (s46);

- being an employee representative (s47);

- exercising right to time off work for education, study or training (s47A and s47AA);

- exercising their right to take leave for family or domestic reasons (including ordinary and additional maternity leave, ordinary and additional adoption leave, parental leave, shared parental leave; rights during and after parental leave, ordinary and additional paternity leave (pre 5 April 2015) for birth, ordinary and additional paternity leave for adoption (pre 5

April 2015), rights during and after paternity leave) (s47C);

- exercising rights in connection with tax credits (s47D);

- exercising rights under the flexible working regulations (s47E);

- exercising rights to request study and training (s47F);

- exercising the right to be accompanied or to accompany someone else to a disciplinary or grievance meeting (ERelAct 1999 s12);

- exercising rights in relation to part-time workers (Reg 7(2) PTW(PLFT) Regs 2000).

A **worker** (which includes an employee) has the right not to be subjected to a detriment because of them:

- exercising working time rights (s45A);

- making a protected disclosure (s47B);

- exercising rights in relation to fixed-term employees (FTE(PLFT) Regs 2002);

- exercising rights related to trade union membership (s146 TULR(C)A 1992); or

- exercising rights related to trade union recognition (Paragraph 156 to Schedule A1 TULR(C)A 1992);

- exercising rights under the Exclusivity Terms in Zero Hours Contracts (Redress) Regulations 2015 (Reg 2) (see *Zero-hours contracts*);

- exercising rights under the Agency Workers Regulations 2010 (see Agency workers).

Remedy: If a claim is well founded the tribunal must make a declaration and may make an award of such an amount as it considers is just and equitable having regard to:

1) the infringement to which the complaint relates;

2) any loss which is attributable to the act, or failure to act, which infringed the claimant's right (s49(2) ERA 1996, s149(2) and Paragraph 159(2) to Schedule A1, TULR(C)A 1992).

The loss shall be taken to include: any expenses reasonably incurred by the claimant in consequence of the act, or failure to act, to which the complaint relates; and loss of any benefit which the claimant might reasonably be expected to have had but for the act or failure to act (s49(3) ERA 1996, s149(3) and Paragraph 159(3) to Schedule A1, TULR(C)A 1992).

The award may also include compensation for injury to feelings. Where a worker has brought the claim under s45A, 47B or 47D and the detriment is termination of the contract, which is akin to a claim for unfair dismissal of an employee, it is arguable that injury to feelings may be awarded, but only up to the amount of a basic award (see *Injury to feelings*).

In determining the amount of compensation to be awarded in relation to detriment for exercising rights related to trade union membership, no account can be taken of any pressure which was exercised on the employer by calling, organising, procuring or financing a strike or other industrial action, or by threatening to do so. The question must be determined as if no such pressure had been exercised (s146) TULR(C)A 1992).

Any maximum or minimum:

- For claims under ss43M, 44, 45, 46, 47, 47A, 47C, 47E, and 47F ERA 1996, and for s12 ERelA 1999, the compensation is unlimited;

- For a claim under s45A ERA 1996, if a worker has brought the claim and detriment is termination of the contract, the cap relevant to being dismissed under s101A (currently none) will apply;

- For a claim under s47B ERA 1996, if a worker has brought the claim and detriment is termination of the contract, the cap relevant to being dismissed under s103A (currently none) will apply;

- For a claim under s47D ERA 1996, if a worker has brought the claim and detriment is termination of the contract, the cap relevant to being dismissed under s104B (currently none) will apply;

- For a claim under the zero-hours contracts regulations, any award is limited to the sum of a basic award and compensatory award which would have been awarded if the worker had been an employee and had been dismissed (Reg 4(6));

- For a claim under the Agency Workers Regulations, the minimum award is 2 weeks' pay and an additional sum of £5,000 where Reg 9 applies.

Adjustments: Contributory conduct (s49(5) ERA 1996, s149(6) and Paragraph 159(5) to Schedule A1, TULR(C)A 1992) and a failure to comply with the

ACAS code of practice apply (see TULR(C)A s207A and Schedule A2). Also, for claims brought on or after 29 July 2013, the tribunal can reduce any award by up to 25% if a protected disclosure has been made but not in good faith (s49(6A) (see *Adjustments*).

Mitigation: The tribunal may reduce the award if the claimant has failed to mitigate their loss (s49(4) ERA 1996, s149(4) and Paragraph 159(4) to Schedule A1 TULR(C)A 1992).

Tax: The tax treatment will depend on the nature of the loss awarded (see *Tax and termination payments*).

Recoupment: N/A

Statutory authorities: ERA 1996 ss43M, 44, 45, 46, 47, 47A, 47C, 47E, and 47F; ERelA 1999 s12; TULR(C)A 1992 s149 and Paragraph 159 to Schedule A1

Direct discrimination: see Discrimination

Discrimination

(see also Aggravated damages; Compensatory award; Contributory conduct; Exemplary Damages; Financial Losses; Incapacity benefit; Injury to feelings; Physical and psychiatric injury; Sex Equality Clause)

The Equality Act 2010 creates the right not to be discriminated against where the reason for the discrimination is one of a number of protected characteristics. These are: age; disability; gender reassignment; marriage and civil partnership; pregnancy and maternity; race; religion or belief; sex; and sexual orientation (s4 and ss5 to 12 EA 2010).

Discrimination may take different forms, and the types of conduct prohibited by the Equality Act 2010 are:

- direct discrimination (s13 EA 2010);

- discrimination arising from disability (s15);

- gender reassignment discrimination in cases of absence from work (s16);

- pregnancy and maternity discrimination (s18);

- indirect discrimination (s19);

- failure to comply with the duty to make reasonable adjustments (ss20 and 21);

- harassment (s26); and

- victimisation (s27).

The Equality Act 2010 consolidated a number of different strands of discrimination found in SDA 1975 (sex), RRA 1976 (race), DDA 1995 (disability), EE(RB)R 2003 (religion or belief), EE(SO)R 2003 (sexual orientation) and EE(Age)R 2006 (age). Many of the authorities relevant to discrimination under EA 2010 relate to the earlier statutory provisions.

The right to equality of terms, formerly called equal pay, is contained in the EA 2010 (ss64 to 80 and ss127 to 135). The remedies for breach of the right to equality of terms is addressed in the *Sex Equality Clause* entry.

There are other employment rights that protect individuals against less favourable or detrimental treatment on the grounds of the individual having certain characteristics or satisfying certain conditions. These are not strictly speaking prohibitions on 'discrimination', though the prohibitions may take similar forms and the remedies may be calculated in similar ways, for example, the protections against suffering detriment in Part V ERA 1996, the Fixed-Term Employees (Prevention of Less Favourable Treatment) Regulations 2002 and the Part-Time Workers (Prevention of Less Favourable Treatment) Regulations 2000 which both give an employee a right not to be treated 'less favourably' than a comparator employee. Further, the remedy for breach of the right not to be subjected to a detriment under ERA 1996 s47B, and probably other similar protections in Part V ERA 1996 may include not just compensation for financial loss but also an award for injury to feelings.

Remedy: If a tribunal finds that an employer has discriminated against an employee, there are three types of remedy available (s124 EA 2010). The tribunal may:

a) make a declaration as to the rights of the complainant and the respondent in relation to the matters to which the proceedings relate;

b) order the respondent to pay compensation to the complainant;

c) make a recommendation that the respondent take specified steps for the purpose of obviating or reducing the adverse effect of any matter to which the proceedings relate on the complainant or any other person.

Each of the remedies is discretionary, and though it is highly unusual for a remedy not to be awarded, under previous statutory provisions the motive and intention of the discriminator was relevant to the issue of remedy, in particular the value of any injury to feelings award (though not to the issue of whether discrimination had occurred) (see *O'Neill v Governors of St Thomas More Roman Catholic Voluntary Aided Upper School* [1997] ICR 33 and *Chief Constable of Manchester v Hope* [1999] ICR 338). It may be that tribunals can apply a similar approach under EA 2010.

Where the tribunal has found indirect discrimination under s19 EA 2010, and where the tribunal is satisfied that the provision, criteria or practice was not applied with the intention of discriminating against the claimant, the tribunal must consider making either a declaration or a recommendation before it awards compensation (see s124(4) and (5) EA 2010).

The remedy most frequently obtained by claimants is compensation and the principles to be applied are outlined below, with detailed analysis set out elsewhere under the specific headings where appropriate.

Failure to comply with recommendation: Where the tribunal has made a recommendation under s124(2)(c) EA 2010, but so far as it relates to the claimant it has without reasonable excuse failed to comply with the recommendation, the tribunal may increase any award for compensation or make an award of compensation where it has not already done so (see s124(7) EA 2010).

Compensation: Any award of compensation will be assessed under the same principles as apply to torts (see s124(6) and s119(2)). The central aim is to put the claimant in the position, so far as is reasonable, that he or she would have been had the tort not occurred (*Ministry of Defence v Wheeler* [1998] IRLR 23 and *Chagger v Abbey National plc* [2010] IRLR 47). The sum is not determined by what the tribunal considers just and equitable in the circumstances as it would do in an unfair dismissal award (*Hurley v Mustoe (No 2)* [1983] ICR 422), though the two approaches will often generate the same result. One impact is that certain items for which credit must be given by an employee are treated differently under the two awards, such as earnings from a new job during a notice period.

Causation and remoteness limit the damages available to a claimant; only those losses caused by the unlawful act will be recoverable, so for example where an individual would have lost their job at some point in any event, and if the discriminatory dismissal they have suffered has not altered their job prospects, the losses suffered after the date when the individual would have been dismissed anyway have not been caused by the discriminatory dismissal. Further, in the general law of tort losses that are too remote and unforeseeable will not be recoverable. However, in *Essa v Laing Ltd* [2004] ICR 746 the Court of Appeal held that this principle does not apply to all statutory torts including discriminatory harassment, such that any loss proved to flow directly from the discriminatory act will be recoverable. It may be that the principle applies to other forms of discrimination.

Awards may be made not just against employers, but also against individual respondents where these have been named in the ET1 (see *Individual respondents*).

Non-financial losses are also recoverable (see *Aggravated damages; Exemplary damages; Injury to feelings; Physical and psychiatric injury*).

The types of financial loss that are recoverable are in general the same as for an unfair dismissal compensatory award, and will include the value of lost earnings and benefits. The calculation of the financial losses the claimant has suffered will also be broadly similar to awards for unfair dismissal (see *Financial losses*).

The central matters the tribunal will need to determine are the 'old job' facts and the 'new job' facts. It will need to compare the financial benefits had the claimant not been treated unlawfully with the financial benefits the claimant has been able to obtain or will be able to in the future (see *Chagger v Abbey National plc* [2010] IRLR 47). Factors that will be considered include whether the employment would have terminated anyway, whether the individual would have been promoted or received a pay rise, what employment has been or will be obtained, what the financial rewards will be and whether these will increase to meet the losses currently being suffered at some point in the future.

The tribunal can take into account the chance of the original employment not continuing, and the chance of any particular employment arising in the future (see *Loss of chance* and *Polkey*).

Gross or net: Net for the compensatory element.

Limit on a week's pay: There is no limit on a week's pay - the claimant's actual net pay will be used in the calculation of loss.

Limit on number of weeks: There is no statutory limit to the number of weeks' loss that can be awarded.

Any maximum or minimum: None

Adjustments

Contributory conduct: Discrimination is a statutory tort and awards may be reduced for contributory fault, though this is unusual (see *Contributory conduct*).

ACAS: An adjustment for failure by the employer/employee to comply with the ACAS Code of Practice for Grievance and Disciplinary Procedures can also be made (Schedule A2 TULR(C)A).

Failure to comply with recommendation: Where the tribunal has made a recommendation under s124(2)(c) EA 2010, but so far as it relates to the claimant the respondent has without reasonable excuse failed to comply with the recommendation, the tribunal may increase any award for compensation or make an award of compensation where it has not already done so (see s124(7) EA 2010).

Grossing up: Where an award will attract a tax liability on the claimant who receives the award, the award will be increased to reflect the net sum the claimant ought to receive (see *Grossing up*).

Interest: Interest can also be added to the sum awarded (see *Interest*).

Cap: There is no statutory cap on compensation for discrimination.

Mitigation: The claimant is under the usual duty to mitigate their loss (see *Mitigation*).

Tax: s401 ITEPA 2003 will apply to the compensatory element of the award if there has been a discriminatory dismissal but an award of injury to feelings will generally not be taxed unless, possibly, it is in connection to termination (see in particular *Injury to feelings; Tax and termination payments*).

Recoupment: Recoupment does not apply to compensation for discrimination.

Statutory authorities: Equality Act 2010 ss15 to 27, s119 and s124

Relevant case law: Carmelli Bakeries Ltd v Benali UKEAT/0616/12/RN; *Chagger v Abbey National Plc & Anor* [2009] EWCA Civ 1202; *Way & Anor v Crouch* UKEAT/0614/04/CK

Early conciliation

Before a claimant can bring certain claims in the tribunal (set out at section 18(1) Employment Tribunals Act 1996), they must contact ACAS and provide them with basic information to see if it is possible to resolve the claim without litigation.

Although the requirement to contact ACAS is mandatory, the scheme itself is voluntary. Upon conclusion of the early conciliation process (either through unsuccessful negotiations or a lack of desire to participate), ACAS issues a certificate containing a start date and an end date.

Time Limits

In calculating time limits for any claim, time spent on Early Conciliation (defined as running from the day after contacting ACAS to the date of the claimant receiving an Early Conciliation certificate) 'is not to be counted' (s207B(3) Employment Rights Act 1996).

Any time spent in Early Conciliation prior to the start of a time limit (e.g. prior to the Effective Date of Termination in an unfair dismissal claim) does not operate to extend time limits: the scheme is a 'stop the clock' provision, rather than a general extension of time. It cannot stop a time limit clock that has not started (*HMRC v Garau* UKEAT/0348/16).

Where, however, a time limit would expire during the period from the beginning of Early Conciliation to one month after receipt of the Early Conciliation certificate, the time limit is then extended to expire a further month after the receipt of the certificate.

Early payment of compensation: see Ex gratia payment

Effective date of termination

(see also Basic award; Cap on a week's pay; Compensatory award; Statutory cap)

The 'effective date of termination' (see s97 ERA 1996) or 'EDT' is a statutory concept necessary for the following calculations:

1) identifying the number of years of continuous service necessary to bring a claim (claims of normal unfair dismissal and claims for a redundancy payment can only be brought after 2 years of continuous service (subject to the exceptions listed in s108(3)) (see s108 ERA 1996);

2) determining whether a claim for unfair dismissal has been brought within the time limit (the claim must be presented to the tribunal before the end of the period of 3 months beginning with the EDT unless the time limit is extended by the tribunal: for example, if the EDT is 5 July, the claim must be brought by 4 October) (see s111 ERA 1996); and

3) calculating the basic award, since this is based on the number of continuous years of service (see s119).

Often the EDT is the actual date of termination of the employment contract, and there is extensive case law surrounding exactly when the termination of employment takes place (for example where an employee is dismissed during a heated argument but the employer quickly attempts to withdraw the dismissal, or where the dismissal is communicated by a third party and only on a later date communicated directly by the employer). This is often critical to determine whether a claim has been brought in time, but can also be relevant to establishing an employee's length of service (for example because the right to bring a claim of unfair dismissal, and the amount of any basic award or redundancy payment, depends on the number of *complete* years' service).

Usually, where notice of termination of employment has been given either by the employee or the employer, the EDT will be the date on which notice expires. If the notice given is greater than that required by s86 ERA 1996, the former date is the EDT.

However, there are two situations where an EDT is 'deemed' to be a particular date. If the employer gives no notice or less than the minimum guaranteed by s86 ERA 1996, the EDT will be the date on which statutory notice would have expired if it had been given (see s97(1) to (3)). If the employee resigns where he is not already under notice, the EDT will be the date the employment terminates, but if that notice period is less than the employer would have had to give the employee under s86 ERA 1996, then the EDT will be the date of the expiry of that notional notice. By s86(6) there is no statutory minimum notice period where either party terminates the contract for repudiatory breach by the other party.

The period of notice begins on the day after the day on which notice was given unless the contract provides otherwise (see *Wang v University of Keele* [2011] IRLR 542 and *West v Kneels Ltd* [1986] IRLR

430).

Some examples
The claimant is given notice and it is worked out in full
The EDT is the date of expiry of the contractual notice period, or the statutory notice period, whichever is the later (s97(1)(a)).

Contractual notice has been given, the claimant is working during the notice period and then is summarily dismissed before the expiry of the contractual notice period, but after the statutory notice period would have expired
The EDT is the date of dismissal, and not the date when contractual notice would have ended. Relevant authorities dealing with a range of such factual circumstances include: *M-Choice UK Ltd v A* UKEAT/0227/11/DA, *Harper v Virgin Net Ltd* [2004] EWCA Civ 271 and *Parker Rhodes Hickmott Solicitors v Harvey* UKEAT/0455/11/SM.

The claimant is summarily dismissed, but the employer was not entitled to do so and the claimant is entitled to statutory notice under s86
The EDT is the date that the statutory notice would have ended (s97(2) ERA 1996). **Note:** the EDT is only extended by the statutory notice period, not any contractual notice period.

The claimant is summarily dismissed and the employer was entitled to do so due to the conduct of the employee
The EDT is the date on which termination takes effect (s97(1)(b)).

The claimant has been put on garden leave
The EDT is the date the notice period expires.

The claimant is dismissed with a payment in lieu of notice
The contract ends when the PILON clause is successfully put into effect, with the EDT being the date of termination of the contract (see *Société Générale, London Branch v Geys* [2013] IRLR 122).

The employee resigns in response to a repudiatory breach by the employer
The EDT will normally be the date of expiry of the statutory notice period which the employer would have had to give if they had given the employee notice of termination on the day the employee resigned.

The claimant resigns on notice following which there is correspondence/ discussions between the parties
The EDT is the date on which the notice period expires. The claimant's unequivocal notice of resignation is unaffected by subsequent discussions/ correspondence between the parties and the claimant cannot subsequently unilaterally withdraw or extend the notice period (see *Wallace v Ladbrokes Betting and Gaming Limited* UKEAT/0168/15/JOJ).

The employer and employee agree on a date when the employment will terminate
The EDT will be the date of the agreed termination, even if the employee had already received notice but then later agreed to an earlier termination date (*Palfrey v Transco Plc* [2004] IRLR 916).

The employer summarily dismisses an employee but on appeal varies the date of dismissal to a later date
The EDT will be the later date as varied by the appeal decision (see *Hawes & Curtis Ltd v Arfan & Anor* UKEAT/0229/12/JOJ; [2012] ICR 1244).

The dismissal was without notice but the employer pays PILON
The EDT is the date of the summary dismissal (see *Rabess v London Fire & Emergency Planning Authority* UKEAT/0029/14/JOJ). The EDT is not extended by the PILON.

Termination of fixed term contract which is not renewed
The EDT is the last day of the fixed term.

Statutory authorities: ss86, 97, 108 and 119 ERA 1996

Relevant case law: *Gisda Cyf v Barratt* [2010] UKSC 41; *Harper v Virgin Net Ltd* [2004] EWCA Civ 271; *Hawes & Curtis Ltd v Arfan & Anor* UKEAT/0229/12/JOJ; *M-Choice UK Ltd v A* UKEAT/0227/11/DA; *Martin v Yeoman Aggregates Limited* [1983] ICR 314; *Palfrey v Transco Plc* [2004] IRLR 916; *Parker Rhodes Hickmott Solicitors v Harvey* UKEAT/0455/11/SM; *Rabess v London Fire & Emergency Planning Authority* UKEAT/0029/14/JOJ; *Robinson v Bowskill & Ors Practising as Fairhill Medical Practice* UKEAT/0313/12/JOJ; *Société Générale, London Branch v Geys* [2013] IRLR 122; *The Governing Body of Wishmorecross School v Balado* UKEAT/0199/11/CEA; *The Secretary of State for Justice v Hibbert* UKEAT/0289/13/GE; *Wallace v Ladbrokes Betting and Gaming Limited* UKEAT/0168/15/JOJ; *Wang v University Of Keele (Jurisdictional Points: Claim in time and effective date of termination)* [2010] UKEAT/0223/10; *West v Kneels Ltd* [1986] IRLR 430

Employment and Support Allowance (ESA)

(see also Housing benefit; Recoupment)

Employment and Support Allowance (formerly Incapacity benefit) may be paid if the individual cannot work because they are ill or disabled.

Damages for wrongful dismissal
Credit must be given for the receipt of state benefits during the damages period. However, some state benefits are excluded. It is not clear whether ESA will always be deducted since it will depend on the facts of the case and how remote or otherwise the benefit is. It could also be argued that state benefits received during the statutory notice period should not be deducted in full (*see Westwood v Secretary of State for Employment* [1984] 1 All ER 874 where the employee was dismissed without the statutory notice period or payment in lieu) because the employee would exhaust their entitlement to state benefits earlier than they would have done if they had been given the statutory notice.

Compensatory award
ESA can be deducted from the compensatory award if, but for the dismissal, the benefit would not have been obtained. *Morgans v Alpha Plus Security Ltd* [2005] ICR 525 confirms this position, where the claimant was dismissed and then was unable to work because of his psychological state attributable to the respondent's action in dismissing him. The EAT held that there is no jurisdiction to disregard receipts, or to claim and recover a sum in excess of the actual loss. Where a claimant has suffered a lesser loss by virtue of his receipt of benefits, which would not have been paid had they remained employed, credit must be given for them.

However, credit need not be given for benefits that are too remote. Often, the decision as to whether the benefits are deductible or not is up for argument.

Relevant case law: *Morgans v Alpha Plus Security Ltd* [2005] ICR 525; *Westwood v Secretary of State for Employment* [1984] 1 All ER 874

Enhanced redundancy: see Redundancy

Enhancement of accrued pension rights: see Pension loss

Equal pay: see Sex Equality Clause

Equality of terms: see Sex Equality Clause

Ex gratia payment

(see also Adjustments; Tax and termination payments)

An employee may receive an ex gratia payment from his employer following his dismissal. There are various reasons why any such payment may be made, and the sum may be viewed as compensation for the losses suffered, advance payment of any liability caused by the dismissal, or as a payment unrelated to the dismissal. An ex gratia payment is made where there is no legal obligation to do so.

The claimant will normally be required to give credit for the ex gratia payment (see *Digital Equipment Co Ltd v Clements (No 2)* [1998] IRLR 134 (CA)).

The particular reason for the payment dictates how it is factored into the tribunal's calculation of the sum to be paid by the ex-employer. If the payment is taken to reduce the loss suffered by the claimant flowing from the dismissal, credit will be given before the application of any adjustments such as contributory conduct. However, if the payment is treated as reducing the ultimate liability of the employer, then the credit will apply to the award before the cap has been imposed. The employee will likely benefit if the former approach is applied, and the employer if the latter approach is applied. Full benefit to the employer will only occur if the award is less than the statutory cap. The following principles apply:

- Payment made under a legal obligation, such as pay in lieu of notice, will be taken to reduce the loss sustained (see *Heggie v Uniroyal Ltd* [1999] IRLR 802);

- Payment of a contractual enhanced redundancy payment is dealt with by s123(7) ERA 1996 (see *Adjustments*);

- Ex gratia payments will usually be taken to reduce the loss suffered (see *Horizon Holiday Ltd v Grassi* [1987] IRLR 371 and *Babcock FATA Ltd v Addison* [1987] IRLR 173);

- Payments made by mistake will usually be taken to reduce the loss suffered (see *Boorman v Allmakes* [1995] IRLR 553);

- Where the payment is expressly made by reference to liability for compensation for an unfair dismissal, it may be set off against any basic award and compensatory award (see

Chelsea Football Club & Athletic Co Ltd v Heath [1981] IRLR 73);

• Where the employee receives an ex gratia payment that he would have received had he not been unfairly dismissed it will not factor into reducing the losses suffered by the claimant (see *Babcock FATA Ltd v Addison* [1987] IRLR 173 and *Roadchef v Hastings* [1988] IRLR 142).

Adjustments: The ex gratia payment, where it is taken to reduce the losses suffered by the claimant, should be deducted before any reduction/increase for contributory conduct, *Polkey*, ACAS, interest and accelerated payment (see *Digital Equipment Co Ltd v Clements (No 2)* [1997] IRLR 140 (EAT)). Credit for the ex gratia payment will be made before the statutory cap is applied (see *McCarthy v British Insulated Callenders Cables Plc* [1985] IRLR 94).

Tax: Assuming that the ex gratia payment has been deducted from the calculation of financial loss, any sums awarded exceeding £30,000 will be taxed under ITEPA 2003 s401. Whether or not the employer should have taxed the ex gratia payment when it was made will depend on the nature of the payment - see HMRC NIM02510 for further information, although this point would not be an issue for the tribunal to decide.

Relevant case law: *Babcock FATA Ltd v Addison* [1987] IRLR 173; *Boorman v Allmakes* [1995] IRLR 553; *Chelsea Football Club & Athletic Co Ltd v Heath* [1981] IRLR 73; *Digital Equipment Co Ltd v Clements (No 2)* [1997] IRLR 140; *Heggie v Uniroyal Ltd* [1999] IRLR 802; *Horizon Holiday Ltd v Grassi* [1987] IRLR 371; *McCarthy v British Insulated Callenders Cables Plc* [1985] IRLR 94; *Publicis Consultants UK Ltd v O'Farrell* UKEAT/0430/10; *Roadchef v Hastings* [1988] IRLR 142

Exemplary damages

Exemplary damages are available in discrimination claims but are very rarely awarded. In contrast to the usual awards made by tribunals, exemplary damages are punitive not compensatory. They will only be awarded if compensation is insufficient to punish the wrongdoer and if the conduct is either:

• oppressive, arbitrary or unconstitutional action by the agents of government; or

• where the defendant's conduct has been calculated to make a profit which may well exceed the compensation payable to the claimant.

The EAT in *MOD v Fletcher* [2010] IRLR 25 has stated

that exemplary cases are reserved for the worst cases of the oppressive use of power by public authorities, where the wrongdoing was '*conscious and contumelious*'.

Remedy: Damages. There is no formulaic calculation.

Any maximum or minimum: None. However, in *MOD v Fletcher*, the EAT held that an award of £50,000 was excessive, it reflected the type of award for false imprisonment, and that had an award been appropriate a sum of £7,500 would have been awarded by the EAT. Such a figure would have reflected the level of award in other torts.

Adjustments: None

Tax: It is unlikely that such an award will be taxable, due to its punitive rather than compensatory nature.

Recoupment: N/A

Relevant case law: *Kuddus v Chief Constable of Leicestershire Constabulary* [2002] 2 AC 122, HL; *London Borough of Hackney v Sivanandan and Ors* [2001] IRLR 740; *MOD v Fletcher* [2010] IRLR 25, UKEAT/0044/09

Expenses

(see also Compensatory award)

Expenses incurred as a result of being unfairly dismissed or discriminated against can be claimed as part of the financial losses suffered. These may include the following costs: looking for alternative work; starting up a new business; extra child or dependant care; accommodation; medical expenses etc. In all cases, the expenses should have been reasonably incurred as a result of the dismissal/discrimination/detriment and the sums claimed should be reasonable. Any such expenses will have to be proved by evidence in the usual way.

Fees

(see also Costs and Wasted Costs; Tables 6 to 14)

Fees are payable by those bringing employment tribunal claims and appeals to the EAT from 29 July 2013 (although full and partial help with fees (formerly called fee remission) is available in certain circumstances - see Tables 6 to 14 for more information). There have been several unsuccessful attempts to have the fees regime declared unlawful in England and Wales. However, on 26 February 2016, the Supreme Court granted permission for

Unison to appeal the Court of Appeal's decision in *R (On the Application of Unison) v The Lord Chancellor* [2015] EWCA Civ 935. The case was heard on 27 and 28 March 2017 and judgment is awaited.

In Scotland, tribunal powers in relation to administration and management of tribunals are expected to be devolved to the Scottish Parliament. The Scottish Government's Programme for Government says: 'We will abolish fees for employment tribunals when we are clear on how the transfer of powers and responsibilities will work'. The timescale for the abolition is currently unclear.

Final salary pension scheme

(see also Pension loss; Ogden Tables 15 to 27)

This is a pension scheme where the value of a person's pension on retirement is calculated by reference to their final salary. Sometimes, the pension may be calculated according to the average of the last few years' salary. The value of the pension will also be calculated according to the number of years' service - typically entitlement will increase by a particular fraction of final salary for each year of employment. Some pension fractions are more generous than others - a pension fraction of 1/60 is more generous than a pension of 1/80 for example. A person who works for 30 years with a pension fraction of 1/60 will retire on half their final salary, whereas a person with a pension fraction of 1/80 will have to work for 40 years to retire on half their salary.

Financial losses

Financial losses suffered from unfair dismissal and discrimination that an employee can claim will generally include loss of any benefits that have a monetary value as well as loss of actual income. Such benefits could include: bonus; commission; holiday pay for lost holiday leave; stock options and profit related pay; enhanced redundancy pay; company car allowance; accommodation; company loan; food allowance; travel allowance; free telephone; private medical insurance; childcare benefits; share ownership; pensions (see also *Pension loss*).

Calculation: The calculation of the value of lost benefits will often take a broad brush approach unless, for example with a company car, it can easily

be ascertained exactly the value of the benefit the employee has lost. Such losses have to represent the *personal* loss to the employee, rather than just the value of the benefit generally.

Bonuses and commission: financial losses can include loss of bonus and commission, and it is not necessary to show that the employee had a contractual right to them. s123(1) of the ERA 1996 states that: *'the amount of the compensatory award shall be such amount as the tribunal considers just and equitable in all the circumstances having regard to the loss sustained by the complainant in consequence of the dismissal in so far as that loss is attributable to action taken by the employer.'* s123(2) states that the amount may include: *'loss of any benefit which he might reasonably be expected to have had but for the dismissal.'* The claimant needs to show on the balance of probabilities that he had an expectation of receiving the payment and that that expectation was reasonable. It may be difficult to quantify a bonus where it is discretionary, and tribunals may make an award for the loss of a chance of a particular level of bonus, following from the approach taken in *Allied Maples Group Ltd v Simmons & Simmons* [1995] WLR 1602.

Loss of holiday pay: If the claimant obtains another job with less generous holiday benefits, he may seek compensation for the value of those benefits.

Stock options and profit related pay: Such schemes are common for senior staff and may take a number of forms. The valuation of the lost benefits will depend on the terms of the scheme. One simple way in which to value the lost options is to calculate the value of the shares to the employee at the date of termination, and then to calculate the profit, if any, that the employee might have made if they remained part of the scheme. In addition, if the employee is forced to sell their shares as a result of the dismissal and the share price rises, they may be able to claim the difference in valuation between dismissal and a future date. The valuation of share options can be difficult and tribunals will generally base their assessment on an estimate of what appears just and equitable in the circumstances.

Enhanced Redundancy Payments: Compensation for the loss of any redundancy payment in excess of the statutory redundancy can be claimed (see s123(3)), whether contractual or whether the employee would merely have an expectation of such payment.

Arguably there is a loss that can be claimed where the employee might have been dismissed as redundant during the period covered by the compensatory award.

Company car: Compensation can only be awarded for the private use of a company car and also any loss of free fuel, insurance etc.

Several methods are available to calculate the loss as follows:

• Consider the AA or RAC estimates for the weekly running costs of a particular car (see http://www.theaa.com/motoring_advice/runnin g_costs/index.html for more information). Then the cost should be adjusted to take into account the proportion of private use as opposed to business use, and again reduced if the employee had to contribute to the running of the car. If the employer has a different method of valuing the company car benefit, this may be used instead;

• HMRC have an online calculator which can be used to calculate the value of company cars (see https://www.gov.uk/expenses-and-benefits-company-cars/work-out-the-value). This is HMRC's method of valuing the company car benefit for tax purposes but this may not be an appropriate way to value the actual benefit lost by the claimant;

• Calculate the cost of buying a car or the hire of a car and claim a proportion of the cost from the employer;

• For cars bought on hire purchase in the employee's name and where the employer paid part or all of the repayments the tribunal could award the employee a proportion of the outstanding amount.

Accommodation: one method to assess the value of free or subsidised accommodation is to find evidence of the open-market value of similar accommodation. Alternatively, if the employee has found somewhere else similar to live, the loss could be calculated as the difference between what he would have been paying to the employer and what he is paying now. If the employee had bought their new accommodation, the loss could be calculated on the basis of a proportion of the interest paid on a mortgage (but not the capital).

Company loans: the value of such a benefit can be calculated as the difference between the cost to the employee whilst still in employment and the comparable market rate.

Free food: the loss may be calculated by finding out the value of the food and drink to which the employee was entitled.

Travel allowances: the loss is the value of the travel allowance.

Telephone: the loss is again the value of the telephone, including line rental and actual call charges.

Medical insurance: this can be calculated by finding out the equivalent cost to the employee of obtaining private medical insurance.

Childcare benefits: the loss can be calculated by working out the cost of equivalent child care that was provided by, or subsidised by, the employer. In the case of a subsidy, the difference between the costs can be claimed.

Pensions: the employee may be able to claim for the value of their lost occupational pension (either defined benefit or defined contribution) as well as loss of enhancement of accrued pension rights.

Consequential losses: In *Timbulas v The Construction Workers Guild Ltd* UKEAT/0325/13/GE, the claimant won his claim of unpaid holiday pay and also argued that, because his holiday pay was not paid at the date it should have been, he was unable to take advantage of an offer from his mortgage company to pay off his mortgage without incurring a penalty. In consequence, he paid interest on the outstanding mortgage which would not have been payable if he had paid the mortgage off in full. The ET ruled that interest at 5% above base should be added to the holiday pay award.

Gross or net: Any tax deductible benefits should be calculated net of tax and NI.

Adjustments: Any benefits will be included within the compensatory award and adjusted in the normal way (see *Compensatory award*).

Cap: The loss of benefits will be included in the compensatory award and the statutory cap (where applicable) will be applied to the total.

Mitigation: Normal mitigation expectations apply.

Tax: The compensatory award, including benefits, is taxable above £30,000 and will fall to be grossed up under s401 ITEPA 2003 if the award overall exceeds this figure (see also *Grossing up*).

Recoupment: Loss of benefits are not subject to the recoupment regulations. Recoupment applies only to immediate loss of earnings, so loss of benefits during the time between dismissal and the hearing should not be included in the calculation.

Statutory authorities: ERA 1996 s123

Financial penalties on employers

(See also Interest on unpaid compensation)

There are two financial penalties that can be imposed on employers.

Breach of worker's rights with aggravating features

From 6 April 2014 employment tribunals have had a discretionary power to impose a financial penalty on a losing employer if they find the employer has breached a worker's rights and the employer's behaviour has *'one or more aggravating features'* (see section 16 of the Enterprise and Regulatory Reform Act 2013 which inserted s12A into the ETA 1996) .

A penalty may be ordered even if no financial award is made to the claimant, e.g. where the tribunal makes a declaration. The payment is made from the employer to the Secretary of State, not to the claimant.

Calculation: The penalty is calculated as a fixed 50% of the compensation awarded with a 50% discount where the employer pays within 21 days of the tribunal's decision. Only one penalty will be imposed where there are two or more claims in respect of the same act and worker, e.g. overlapping claims of wrongful and unfair dismissal.

Any maximum or minimum: Minimum is £200 (but if the award is less than £200, the penalty will be £100); Maximum is £5,000

Financial penalty for failure to pay sums ordered by the ET

Section 150 of the Small Business, Enterprise and Employment Act 2015 came into force on 6 April 2016 and inserted a new Part 2A into the Employment Tribunals Act 1996 to allow financial penalties to be imposed on employers who do not pay workers the award that the ET has ordered (or awards ordered on a relevant appeal) including costs and sums to cover preparation time as awarded by an ET. Employers who do not pay costs awarded against them to cover a worker's ET fee can also be required to pay a penalty under the new provisions, as can employers who fail to pay sums due under ACAS conciliated settlements (sections 37A to 37D in Part 2A ETA 1996). The financial penalty regime will be operated by enforcement

officers appointed or authorised by the Secretary of State (section 37M).

Penalties will be payable to the Secretary of State not to the employee.

Calculation: The amount of the penalty will be based on the total amount that remains unpaid to the worker, including interest on the award payable on the last date for responding to the warning notice, as well as any amount the employer has been told to pay in respect to employment tribunal fees: it will be 50% of the sum owed. In cases where an employer has defaulted on an agreement to pay by instalments, the penalty will be based on the whole unpaid amount. The penalty can be reduced by 50% if both the penalty and the whole unpaid amount are paid within 14 days of the penalty notice.

Any maximum or minimum: Minimum is £200 (but if the award is less than £200, the penalty will be £100); Maximum is £5,000.

Fixed term contract

(see also Damages for wrongful dismissal)

When determining damages for wrongful dismissal, it is important first to identify whether the claimant was employed on a permanent or fixed term contract since the period of loss as calculated depends on the period of notice (see *Damages for wrongful dismissal*).

If the contract is for a fixed term and there is no right to terminate on notice, the earliest date at which the employer can end the contract is at the end of the term. If the contract is terminable by notice, the earliest date at which the contract can be brought to an end is the end of the notice period.

Fixed-term employee protection

An employee working under a fixed-term contract has the right not to be treated by his employer less favourably than the employer treats a comparable permanent employee for the following reasons (see Reg3 FTE(PLFT) Regs 2002 SI 2002/2034):

- as regards the terms of his contract; or

- by being subjected to any other detriment by any act, or deliberate failure to act, of his employer.

Particular reference is made in the FTE(PLFT) Regs

2002 to less favourable treatment in relation to qualification for benefits on the basis of periods of service, the opportunity to receive training and the opportunity to secure a permanent position (including being informed of any vacancies).

Less favourable treatment will be permitted where it can be objectively justified (Reg 3(3)(b) and Reg 4).

The employee has a right to written reasons for his treatment from his employer (see Reg 5).

The employee has the right to not be unfairly dismissed or be subject to detrimental treatment in relation to exercising the rights of a fixed term employee (see Reg 6).

Remedy: Where a tribunal finds that an employee has been subject to less favourable treatment or detriment as set out above, the tribunal (Reg 7(7)):

"shall take such of the following steps as it considers just and equitable:

(a) making a declaration as to the rights of the complainant and the employer in relation to the matters to which the complaint relates;

(b) ordering the employer to pay compensation to the complainant;

(c) recommending that the employer take, in all the circumstances of the case, for the purposes of obviating or reducing the adverse effect on the complainant of any matter to which the complaint relates."

There are specific provisions providing for the calculation of compensation awarded under Reg 7 and 7(b) (see Regs 7(8) to (12)):

• The amount of compensation awarded shall be such as the tribunal considers just and equitable in all the circumstances (this phrase is used in the assessment of the compensatory award for unfair dismissal and similar principles will apply);

• The tribunal will have regard to the infringement to which the complaint relates and any loss which is attributable to the infringement;

• The loss will include any expenses reasonably incurred by the claimant as a consequence of the infringement and any loss of any benefit he has suffered as a result;

• Compensation for infringement of the right not to be less favourably treated under Reg 3 will not include an award to injury to feelings (although an award for detriment under Reg 6 may include such an award – see *Detriment* and *Injury to feelings*); and

• Where there has been contributory fault by the claimant, the amount of compensation will be reduced by such proportion as the tribunal considers just and equitable having regard to that failing.

Failure to comply with recommendation: Where the tribunal has made a recommendation under Reg 7(c), but the employer has without reasonable excuse failed to comply with the recommendation, the tribunal may increase any award for compensation under Reg 7(7)(b) or make an award of compensation where it has not already done so (see Reg7(13)).

Gross or net: This will depend on whether the sums paid are treated as suppressed wages, an award for discrimination or injury to feelings (see *Tax* below, within this entry). Where a sum is paid to represent a net loss it will be calculated on the net figure and grossed up where appropriate to make the final award. Where the sum is viewed as suppressed wages the award will be calculated on gross earnings, with the employer deducting tax and NI.

Any maximum or minimum: No, the award is unlimited.

Adjustments: A percentage deduction for contributory conduct can be applied (Reg 7(12)). Also, if the employer fails to comply with a tribunal's recommendation, the award can be increased to a level that the tribunal considers is just and equitable (Reg 7(13)).

Mitigation: The usual rules on mitigation apply.

Tax: Any payment to compensate for an employee's reduced wages or benefits would probably be classed as arrears of pay and taxed under s62 ITEPA 2003 in the normal way (see EIM02550 and EIM02530, HMRC). The tax to be paid should be calculated according to the tax year in which the pay was withheld, not the tax year in which the repayment is made.

However, EIM12965 of the Employment Income Manual states that payments of compensation for discrimination which occurs before termination is not employment income for the purposes of s401 and that they are therefore not taxable. It is therefore arguable that the award for infringement of Reg 3 or Reg 6 FTE would not be subject to tax as they are compensation for discrimination (in its broadest sense).

Injury to feelings awards arising other than from dismissal are not taxable.

Statutory authorities: FTE(PLFT) Regs 2002 (SI 2002/2034) Regs 3, 6 and 7

Flexible working

A qualifying employee may apply to his employer for a change in his terms and conditions of employment (s80F ERA 1996) to enable flexible working.

From 30 June 2014 every employee has the statutory right to request flexible working after 26 weeks' employment service. Before 30 June 2014, the right only applied to parents of children under the age of 17 (or 18 if the child is disabled) and certain carers.

Section 80G identifies procedural and substantive rules for how an employer must deal with a request.

Remedy: Where an employee succeeds in a complaint that the employer has failed to comply with the requirements of s80G ERA 1996, or that a decision to reject the application was based on incorrect facts, the tribunal must make a declaration to that effect, may make an order for reconsideration of the application and may make an order that compensation be paid (s80I ERA 1996).

The amount of compensation is the sum the tribunal considers just and equitable, up to the permitted maximum (s80I(2)).

The maximum award is 8 weeks' pay, capped at £489 per week (see Reg 7 FW(ECR) Regs 2002/3236 and s227(za) ERA 1996).

Gross or net: The maximum is calculated according to a week's pay, which is a gross figure.

A week's pay as defined in ss220 to 229 ERA 1996 applies (see *Week's pay*).

Limit on a week's pay: £489 (see Table 1 for historical rates).

Limit on number of weeks: 8

Any maximum or minimum: No minimum; Maximum is 8 x a week's pay (capped at £489 per week) = £3,912.

Adjustments: None, although any compensation ordered will be the sum which the tribunal considers just and equitable. This will include considerations such as the loss actually suffered and attempts to mitigate.

Mitigation: Within the tribunal's consideration of what sum is just and equitable to award.

Tax: The tax treatment is not clear. To the extent that any sum awarded is compensation for lost

earnings, it is likely to be taxed under s62 ITEPA 2003 (see *Tax and termination payments*).

Recoupment: N/A

Statutory authorities: ERA 1996 s80G to 80I and s220-229 ERA 1996; FW(ECR) Regs 2002/3236

Future loss of earnings

(see also Compensatory award; Financial losses; Mitigation)

Where the remedy available to a claimant includes compensation for losses suffered as a result of the unlawful conduct, the losses may still be continuing at the date of the tribunal hearing. A frequently occurring example is an individual found to have been unfairly dismissed who has not obtained employment at the same level of pay as their old job. The tribunal must assess the losses that the employee will suffer in the future, and the period over which these will continue.

The tribunal will compare the financial circumstances of the claimant, had the unlawful act not occurred, with the circumstances in which they continue to find themselves. Both require the tribunal to assess uncertain scenarios: would the claimant have remained employed or would he have been dismissed in any event; if so would he have found equivalent employment or would he have suffered the same difficulties as he is currently experiencing, or might he have been promoted and received higher pay; when will the claimant obtain equivalent remuneration, or when ought he to? The tribunal will take into account the personal characteristics of the employee such as age and health.

The tribunal's assessment will be based on findings of fact, and will then go on *'to assess the loss flowing from the dismissal, using its common sense, experience and sense of justice'* (see *Software 2000 Ltd v Andrews* [2007] IRLR 568, per Elias P). As HHJ Hand QC said in *Stroud Rugby Football Club v Monkman* UKEAT/0143/13/SM, the assessment of future loss is a *'rough and ready matter. It always has been and it always will be'*.

However, in order to make a judgement of the extent of future loss, the tribunal must have any relevant information that will help it to make its decision. This includes disclosure of information relating to the claimant's pension entitlement from other sources since this would be clearly relevant to an assessment of the chance that the claimant would have remained in employment until a future date (see *Essex County Council v Jarrett*

UKEAT/0087/15/MC).

The tribunal will also assess the relevant weekly loss figure for the purpose of the loss of earnings calculation. This may not be the same as the weekly loss at the date of dismissal (for example, if the claimant would only have been paid sick pay as a result of a condition unrelated to the dismissal - see *The Royal Bank of Scotland v O'Doherty* UKEAT/0307/14/RN).

Whole career loss

In exceptional cases a tribunal may be able to award whole career loss. Such cases are rare and only suitable where there is no real prospect of an employee ever obtaining an equivalent job. Otherwise, a tribunal should stick to the usual approach, suitable for the vast majority of cases, of assessing when it is likely that an employee will get an equivalent job (*Wardle v Credit Agricole* [2011] EWCA Civ 545; *Lennon-Knight v Yakira Group Ltd* UKEAT/0186/16).

Garden leave

(see also Effective date of termination; Tax and termination payments)

The employment contract of an employee who possesses or has access to the employer's confidential information and/or through whom the employer's customer connections are maintained and developed may well have a "garden leave" or "gardening leave" clause which empowers the employer to withdraw all or some of the employee's duties during the period of notice given by either party to the other. Such a power may be implied but this runs up against arguments that the employee has a countervailing (implied) right to work during the period of the contract. During a period of garden leave the employee's express or implied duties of fidelity, and in particular constraints on working for other employers, will continue to apply and may be enforced by an injunction. Frequently employees will contend that their employer has repudiated the employment contract, entitling them to be discharged from compliance with its terms (including as to garden leave and any restrictive covenants).

A case considering the extent to which the public policy against clauses in restraint of trade applies to garden leave is *JM Finn & Co Ltd v Holliday* [2013] EWHC 3450 (QB), [2014] IRLR 102.

Workers on garden leave are not entitled to payment in lieu of any accrued holiday they could have taken when on such leave, save when they are unable to use up that entitlement due to illness (*Maschek v Magistratsdirektion der Statdt Wien – Personalstelle Wiener Stadtwerke* [2016] EUECJ C-341/15; [2016] IRLR 801).

Gourley principle

(see also Tax and termination payments)

The *Gourley* principle is that damages awarded for loss suffered to the claimant should put him in the same position as he would have been in if he had not suffered the unlawful conduct. Where his remuneration would have been subject to tax and NI, the award will be based on his net loss.

The *Gourley* principle was established in the case of *British Transport Commission v Gourley* [1955] UKHL 4 where a civil engineer was awarded damages by the British Transport Commission in respect of a railway accident. The award included an amount for loss of earnings. The question was whether the amount of damages should be paid to the recipient gross or net of deductions that would have been suffered by the individual had he remained in employment.

The court held that '*the broad general principle which should govern the assessment of damage in cases such as this is that the tribunal should award the injured party such a sum of money as will put him in the same position as he would have been in if he had not sustained the injuries … to ignore the tax element at the present day would be to act in a manner which is out of touch with reality*'. The significance of the *Gourley* principle is that damages will be calculated on the basis of the loss suffered after tax and NI had been deducted from his earnings.

However, where the claimant will have to pay tax on the award, or where the employer will have to deduct tax and NI, the tribunal must 'gross up' the award to ensure that the claimant's net loss is compensated for by an equivalent net sum (see also *Grossing up*). For example, where an award for unfair dismissal exceeds the tax free £30,000, the tribunal will calculate the net loss suffered by the claimant and increase the sum awarded to reflect any tax that the claimant will have to pay on receipt of the award. The two incidences of tax are set off against each other - see *Parsons v BNM Laboratories Ltd* [1963] 2 All ER 658, and *Shove v Downs Surgical Plc* [1984] 1 All ER 7.

Government Actuary Department

(see also Pension loss)

The Government Actuary Department produced guidance on how to calculate pension loss after termination of employment (Compensation for Loss of Pension Rights - Employment Tribunals 3rd Edition, TSO). Tribunals were not obliged to apply the guidance or the tables within but would often at least use them as a guide. However, this guidance has now been withdrawn pending a review of the way in which pension loss should be calculated in the future. Presidential guidance is expected later in 2017.

Grievance procedure

(see also ACAS; Adjustments)

Employers will often have written procedures for considering grievances raised by employees. The core principles upon which a grievance should be considered have been set out by ACAS in the ACAS *Code of Practice 1: Code of Practice on Disciplinary and Grievance Procedures*. This code provides basic practical guidance to employers, employees and their representatives and sets out principles for handling disciplinary and grievance situations in the workplace. The Code is issued under section 199 of the Trade Union and Labour Relations (Consolidation) Act 1992 and came into effect on 11 March 2015 (replacing the code issued in 2009). In a number of types of tribunal claims, if an employee or employer has unreasonably failed to follow the guidance set out in the code relating to the grievance procedure a tribunal may reduce or increase any award they have made by up to 25% (see *ACAS*).

Gross weekly pay

(see also Week's pay)

This is to be contrasted with net weekly pay. Gross weekly pay is the total sum payable under the contract of employment before the deduction of tax, NI or pension contributions.

Gross weekly pay is used in the calculation of the following claims:

- Additional award;
- Basic award;
- Guarantee pay;
- Insolvency;
- Protective award;
- Suspension;
- Right for union member not to be unjustifiably disciplined/expelled;
- Time off for looking for work/training after redundancy; antenatal care; employee representatives; pension trustees; union duties, activities and union learning reps; study or training; young person for study or training; members of a European Council;
- TUPE claims;
- Right to be accompanied;
- Flexible working;
- Written reasons for dismissal;
- Redundancy payments.

Gross weekly pensionable pay

(see also Pension loss)

The pensionable pay is that part of the employee's salary which will be used to calculate employer and employee pension contributions and may not be the same as their gross weekly pay. If pension loss has to be calculated according to the GAD guidelines, the employee's gross weekly pensionable pay will first have to be ascertained, usually from the pension provider or the employer.

Grossing up

(see also *Gourley* principle; Marginal tax rate; Tax and termination payments)

Awards will be 'grossed up' by a tribunal where the sum to be received by the claimant will be taxed. The purpose is to place in the claimant's hands the sum he would have held had he not been treated unlawfully, i.e. to compensate for the true net loss.

Where the award will be taxed by the employer before payment is made to the claimant, such as where the award is for unpaid wages, the tribunal will award the true gross sum. Grossing up therefore applies to awards where s401 ITEPA 2003 operates to tax the sum in the claimant's hands.

Section 401 applies to payments and other benefits which are received directly or indirectly in consideration or in consequence of, or otherwise in connection with:

a) the termination of a person's employment;

b) a change in the duties of a person's employment; or

c) a change in the earnings from a person's employment, by the person, or the person's spouse, blood relative, dependant or personal representatives.

In this case the recipient enjoys a tax free amount of £30,000 in any particular tax year and will then pay tax at their marginal tax rate on sums in excess of this figure. Neither the tax free sum nor the excess is subject to employee national insurance, but, from 2018, employer national insurance will be payable on any amount above the £30,000 threshold.

To avoid disadvantage to the claimant, the tribunal should 'gross up' any award it makes over £30,000. This requires the tribunal to estimate the tax the claimant will have to pay on receipt of the award and add a sum for that tax back on to the award, thus cancelling out the tax burden to the claimant. In other words, where the tribunal has determined the sum a claimant is to be awarded, the tribunal will consider the likely tax consequences and increase the award to ensure that the claimant retains the sum to which the tribunal has determined he is entitled.

It is the responsibility of the claimant or their representative to raise the question of grossing up at the ET. If they do not, the point may not be raised at the EAT (see *Bethnal Green & Shoreditch Education Trust v Dippenaar* UKEAT/0064/15/JOJ).

Before the £30,000 threshold (see EIM13505) is applied to an award, it is necessary to add together all the payments and benefits within s401 ITEPA 2003 that are made to, or are in respect of, the same person in connection with:

• the same office or employment; and

• different offices or employments with the same employer; and

• different offices or employments with associated employers (see EIM13540).

The threshold is then applied to the total. This ensures that all sums fall within just the one £30,000 threshold.

For example, a director is dismissed from two separate employments with associated employers within the same tax year, receiving payments and benefits worth £25,000 in each case which all fall within s401 ITEPA 2003. He also receives a tribunal award of £40,000 for unfair dismissal. The aggregated total received in connection with the terminated employments is £90,000 and only one £30,000 threshold is available against that total.

The tribunal will gross up the sum in excess of £30,000 taking into account the employee's personal allowance and tax banding (*Shove v Downs Surgical Plc* [1984] 1 All ER 7). This tax rate that should be applied is called the claimant's marginal tax rate and may be difficult to ascertain. Further, different marginal tax rates may be applied to different elements of the award (see *Yorkshire Housing Ltd v Cuerden* UKEAT/0397/09).

Awards to be grossed up
The only awards that should be grossed up are those that are calculated using net weekly pay and which will be taxed in the recipient's hands i.e:

• Compensatory award;

• Damages for wrongful dismissal;

• Financial losses suffered as a result of unlawful discrimination.

The following heads of loss will not be grossed up:

1) any awards that have been calculated as a gross figure and tax will be deducted either before the claimant receives the payment (for example, accrued holiday pay and the claimant is still employed); or on the claimant's self-assessment (if they are no longer employed);

2) any other awards calculated as a gross figure (such as the basic award or additional award);

3) awards which will not be taxed (see *Injury to feelings*).

An award for pension loss also falls to be grossed up – see *Yorkshire Housing Ltd v Cuerden* UKEAT/0397/09. The pension loss figure should therefore be the *net* loss (see *Chief Constable of Northumbria Police v Erichsen* UKEAT/0027/15/BA).

In what order should grossing up be applied?
Calculations should be performed in the following order:

1) Adjustments, including the addition of interest (see *Adjustments and order of adjustments*);

2) Grossing up;

3) Statutory cap applied (see *Hardie Grant London Ltd v Aspden* UKEAT/0242/11/RN).

Recoupment: There is no information to explain whether the prescribed element should be calculated before grossing up or after. However, it is likely that the sums involved would render the distinction of no relevance.

Relevant case law: *Bethnal Green & Shoreditch Education Trust v Dippenaar* UKEAT/0064/15/JOJ; *Chief Constable of Northumbria Police v Erichsen* UKEAT/0027/15/BA; *Hall v Durham County Council & Ors* UKEAT/0256/14/MC; *Hardie Grant London Ltd v Aspden* UKEAT/0242/11/RN; *Shove v Downs Surgical Plc* [1984] 1 All ER 7; *Yorkshire Housing Ltd v Cuerden* UKEAT/0397/09/SM

Examples

It is important to understand that the percentage by which the claimant will be taxed should **not** just be 'added back' to the award (see *Hall v Durham County Council & Ors* UKEAT/0256/14/MC). The following examples demonstrate how the calculation should be performed.

All examples assume that the claimant's marginal tax rate is 20% and the maximum statutory cap on an unfair dismissal award as at 6 April 2017, which is £80,541. The calculation for grossing up the award is:

(Grossed up sum) x (1 – marginal tax rate) = true net loss

Therefore:

Grossed up sum = (true net loss) / (1 – marginal tax rate)

Example 1
Basic award = £11,000 (Taxable)

Compensatory award = £70,000 (Taxable)

Tax free element = £30,000

Calculation
Amount of compensation up to the £30,000 tax free element = £30,000 - £11,000 = £19,000

Amount of compensation award that should be taxed = £70,000 - £19,000 = £51,000

The grossed up compensation of £51,000 = £51,000 ÷ 0.8 = £63,750

Total compensation = £19,000 + £63,750 = £82,750

Compensation cap = £80,541

Total award = £11,000 (basic) + £80,541 (statutory cap) = £91,541

Example 2
Basic award = £11,000 (Taxable)

Injury to feelings = £25,000 (Non-taxable)

Compensation for financial loss = £70,000 (Taxable)

Tax free element = £30,000

Calculation
Basic award = £11,000

Amount of compensation up to the £30,000 tax free element = £30,000 - £11,000 = £19,000

Amount of compensation award that should be taxed = £70,000 - £19,000 = £51,000

The grossed up compensation of £51,000 = £51,000 ÷ 0.8 = £63,750

Total compensation = £19,000 + £63,750 = £82,750 (the statutory cap does not apply to awards for discrimination).

Injury to feelings = £25,000 and is not grossed up because it is not taxable.

Total award = £11,000 (basic) + £25,000 (untaxed injury to feelings award) + £82,750 (uncapped compensation) = £118,750

Example 3
Basic award = £11,000 (Taxable)

Detriment award = £25,000 (Taxable)

Compensation award = £10,000 (Taxable)

Tax free element = £30,000

Calculation
Basic award = £11,000

Detriment award = £19,000 plus £6,000, of which £6,000 should be grossed up

Grossed up detriment award = £6,000 ÷ 0.8 = £7,500

Compensation award = £10,000 which will be taxed in full

Grossed up compensation = £10,000 ÷ 0.8 = £12,500

Total award = £11,000 (basic) + £19,000 (untaxed detriment award) + £7,500 (grossed up detriment award) + £12,500 (grossed up compensation) = £50,000

Example 4
Basic award = £11,000 (Taxable)

Compensation award = £40,000 (Taxable)

Tax free element = £30,000

Calculation
Compensation award exceeding the tax free element = £40,000 – (£30,000 - £11,000) = £21,000

Grossed up compensation = £21,000 ÷ 0.8 = £26,250

Total award = £11,000 (basic) + £19,000 (compensation up to tax free limit) + £26,250 (grossed up compensation) = £56,250

Guarantee payment

(see also Week's pay; Table 3)

Employees are entitled to be paid a minimum amount where throughout a day during any part of which an employee would normally be required to work in accordance with his contract of employment the employee is not provided with work by his employer, and the reason is:

a) a diminution in the requirements of the employer's business for work of the kind which the employee is employed to do; or

b) any other occurrence affecting the normal working of the employer's business in relation to work of the kind which the employee is employed to do.

That minimum sum is called a guarantee payment (s28 ERA 1996).

An employee may bring a complaint to a tribunal that his employer has failed to pay the whole or any part of a guarantee payment to which he is entitled (s34 ERA 1996).

Remedy: The remedy is an order from the tribunal that the employer must pay to the employee the amount of guarantee payment that the tribunal has found to be due.

Calculation of remedy: Guarantee pay for a particular day = normal working hours on that day x guaranteed hourly rate

where:

Guaranteed hourly rate = 1 week's pay ÷ number of normal working hours in a week for that employee when employed under the contract of employment in force on the particular day (s30(1) ERA 1996).

If the number of hours the employee works differs from week to week, the number of normal working hours is calculated by taking the total number of the employee's normal working hours during the period of 12 weeks ending with the last complete week before the day in respect of which the guarantee payment is payable, and dividing that by 12. Where the employee has not been employed for a sufficient period to enable the calculation to be made, a number which fairly represents the number of normal working hours in a week will be used (s30(3) and (4) ERA 1996).

Gross or net: Gross. Any guarantee pay, either paid by the employer or awarded by the tribunal, should be added to other gross pay in that period and PAYE and NI deducted in the normal way.

Limit on guarantee payment: The limit on the guarantee payment for a particular day is £27 from 06/04/2017 (s31(1) ERA 1996).

Limit on number of days: A tribunal can order a guarantee payment to be paid for a maximum of 5 days in any 3 month period (s31(2) and (3) ERA 1996).

Any maximum or minimum: No minimum; Maximum will be £135 in any 3 month period.

Adjustments: None

Mitigation: N/A

Tax: Taxed under s62 ITEPA 2003 (see EIM02550, HMRC)

Recoupment: Any amount found to be due to the employee and ordered to be paid under section 34(3) for a period before the conclusion of the tribunal proceedings will form part of the prescribed element.

Statutory authorities: ERA 1996 ss28 to 35; ITEPA 2003 s62; EP(RJAIS) Regs 1996

Harassment: see Discrimination

Holiday pay

(see also Insolvency; Table 15; Appendix 3: Calculating holiday entitlement)

The Working Time Regulations 1998 provide workers with a minimum entitlement to paid leave. The minimum entitlement, subject to certain exclusions, is 5.6 weeks paid holiday per year subject to a cap of 28 days. The 5.6 weeks are made up of 4 weeks basic annual leave under Reg 13 and 1.6 weeks additional leave under Reg 13(A). 28 days corresponds to 5.6 weeks for a worker working 5 days per week, but if a working week is longer, the statutory minimum remains capped at 28 days even though the full 5.6 weeks of holiday will thereby not be guaranteed. Workers may in addition to the guaranteed minimum holiday be entitled under their contractual terms to enhanced holiday entitlement.

For a typical worker calculating holiday entitlement and the corresponding holiday pay may not be straightforward. Difficulties can arise for example where workers start, or leave, part way through a holiday year, where workers seek to carry over leave from one year to another, or where a worker's working time is non-standard. Special rules apply to calculating statutory holiday entitlement for part time workers, workers working atypical days and hours, and workers absent on sick leave or family related leave.

Where a part time worker's hours are increased there is no retrospective recalculation of the amount of holiday that has accrued (*Greenfield v The Care Bureau* [2016] IRLR 62).

Holiday and holiday pay claims may arise in a number of circumstances including where:

- the worker has been denied the right to take holiday;

- the worker has not been paid for the holiday they have taken;

- the worker has left their employment without having taken the leave to which they were entitled and seeks pay in lieu of that holiday; or

- the worker may have been subject to a detriment or dismissed for conduct relating to seeking to take holiday or enforce the right to paid holiday.

Claims for unpaid statutory holiday pay may be made under Reg 30 WTR 1998 and, where the right is contractual, under s13 ERA 1996 (see *Revenue and Customs Commissioners v Stringer* [2009] ICR 985). Where the right is contractual, a claim for unpaid holiday pay may be made under s13 ERA 1996. It is also possible to bring such a contractual claim in the ordinary civil courts, or where the contract has been terminated, in the employment tribunal under its limited contractual jurisdiction (ETEJ Order).

The rights not to suffer detriment or be dismissed for seeking to enforce rights to holiday pay flow from s45A, 101A and 104 ERA 1996 (see *Detriment* and *Unfair dismissal*).

Remedy: Reg 16(1) WTR 1998 provides that '*A worker is entitled to be paid in respect of any period of annual leave to which he is entitled under regulation 13, at the rate of a week's pay in respect of each week of leave*'. A week's pay is calculated according to s221 to 224 ERA 1996 subject to slight technical modifications and the removal of the limit on a week's pay (see *Week's pay*).

Note: the operation of ss221 to 224 has been the subject of extensive litigation in the last few years. The legislation often fails to take into account pay a worker would in fact receive during a pay period. The Working Time Regulations implement the Working Time Directive and ss221 to 224 in many respects fail to provide workers with the full entitlement to pay required by EU law (see *British Airways plc v Williams* [2012] IRLR 1014 and *Z.J.R. Lock v British Gas Trading Ltd and Others* [2014] ICR

813 (CJEU)). The Working Time Directive only provides for 4 weeks' leave, so the existing ERA 1996 provisions continue to apply unmodified to the additional statutory 1.6 weeks' leave available to employees unmodified.

It is now clear that the calculation of a week's pay in the ERA 1996 should not be followed blindly, but where possible should be interpreted in accordance with the Working Time Directive. The precise consequences of this have yet to be fully determined. Two key cases are:

- *Bear Scotland & Ors v Fulton & Ors* UKEATS/0047/13/BI; [2015] ICR 221: the EAT held that sums paid for non-guaranteed overtime (i.e. overtime that was offered at the employer's discretion, but not guaranteed, but which the employees were obliged to perform) should be included in the calculation of holiday pay. It modified regulation 16(3)(d) of the WTRs to read:

"as if the references to sections 227 and 228 did not apply and, in the case of the entitlement under regulation 13, sections 223(3) and 234 do not apply".

- *Lock v British* Gas: On 22 May 2014, the Court of Justice of the European Union (CJEU) handed down their decision in this case. The claimant successfully argued that his paid annual leave should include commission payments if these were part of his normal pay. On remission of the case to the Leicester Employment Tribunal in February 2015, the tribunal interpreted the WTR to achieve this result by inserting new words into regulation 16(3) of the Working Time Regulations 1998 as follows:

"(e) as if, in the case of the entitlement under regulation 13, a worker with normal working hours whose remuneration includes commission or similar payment shall be deemed to have remuneration which varies with the amount of work done for the purpose of section 221."

On 22 February 2016, the EAT dismissed the employer's appeal against this decision. The EAT saw no reason to depart from its earlier decision in *Bear Scotland*. The Court of Appeal (*British Gas Trading Ltd v Lock & Anor* [2016] EWCA Civ 983; [2016] IRLR 946) also dismissed the appeal. The WTRs have to be interpreted in conformity with the Directive, and holiday pay should be calculated by reference to an employee's normal remuneration.

The proposed wording above, however, was amended by the Court of Appeal because it was considered too wide insofar as it applied to all types of commission rather than just contractual 'results-based' commission. The judgment did not, however, state what form this amendment took.

In light of these authorities, the President has released a Direction saying that 'a claimant or group of claimants who have previously presented a claim or claims in respect of a complaint of alleged non-payment of holiday pay may, if so advised, apply to amend the claim or claims so presented in order to add a further complaint or complaints of alleged non-payment of holiday pay that have accrued or arisen after the presentation of the original claim and which could not have been included in the original claim or claims.'

Where the worker relies not upon the statutory minimum entitlement to holiday, but a contractual term, the calculation of holiday pay will be in accordance with the provisions of the contract.

Gross or net: Any order for the payment of accrued holiday pay should use gross figures, and the sum will be taxed by the employer.

Adjustments: Accrued holiday pay may be claimed as an unlawful deduction from wages, in which case the ACAS uplift could apply where there has been a failure in any grievance process.

Cap: Accrued holiday pay is not included in the award for financial losses arising from an unfair dismissal, so it falls outside the statutory cap.

Mitigation: N/A

Tax: Tax should be paid either by the employer through payroll or by the employee under Self-Assessment where this has not been done.

Recoupment: Recoupment will not apply to accrued holiday pay if the employee has been dismissed.

Statutory authorities: ERA 1996 s13; WTR 1998 Regs 13, 14, 16 and 30

Relevant case law: *Bear Scotland & Ors v Fulton & Ors* UKEATS/0047/13/BI; *British Airways plc v Williams* [2012] IRLR 1014; *Z.J.R. Lock v British Gas Trading Ltd and Others* [2014] ICR 813 (CJEU)

Housing benefit

**(see also Recoupment*)*

In the case of *Savage v Saxena* [1998] UKEAT/605/97 the EAT held that housing benefit the claimant had received since her dismissal should not be deducted from the compensatory award, as

it would not be just or equitable to allow a defaulting employer to retain the benefits and to place an unfairly dismissed employee at the disadvantage of possibly having to pay the benefit back once her situation had been reassessed. Housing benefit is not a recoupable benefit so the employer would not have to pay its value to the Secretary of State if it were deducted from the claimant's award. If a claimant's entitlement was reassessed and the benefit did not have to be paid back, the claimant would appear to recover from the employer a greater sum than his losses.

This view was confirmed in by the EAT in *Olayemi v Athena Medical Centre & Anor* UKEAT/0140/15, and applies to both unfair dismissal and discrimination awards.

Immediate loss of earnings

(see also Compensatory award; Future loss of earnings)

Immediate (sometimes called 'past') loss of earnings is the phrase used to describe the loss of earnings up until the tribunal hearing where remedy is determined. It is to be contrasted with future loss of earnings which are those losses suffered after the hearing. Immediate loss of earnings will often be simpler to assess than future loss, as the requirement to predict what will happen in the future is absent.

The tribunal will compare the financial circumstances of the claimant, had the unlawful act not occurred, with the circumstances in which they now find themselves. Both require the tribunal to assess uncertain scenarios: would the claimant have remained employed or would they have been dismissed in any event, if so would they have found equivalent employment or would they have suffered the same difficulties as they have experienced, or might they have been promoted and received higher pay; when did the claimant obtain equivalent remuneration, or when ought they to have done so? The tribunal will take into account the personal characteristics of the employee such as age and health.

The tribunal's assessment will be based on findings of fact, and then 'to assess the loss flowing from the dismissal, using its common sense, experience and sense of justice' (see *Software 2000 Ltd v Andrews* [2007] IRLR 568, per Elias P).

Incapacity benefit: see Employment and Support Allowance (ESA)

Income support

(see also Job seekers allowance; Recoupment)

Income Support is paid to those on a low income or none at all, who are working less than 16 hours a week and have not signed on as unemployed.

Income support is not deducted from an award of compensation but instead is subject to the recoupment regulations (see *Savage v Saxena* [1998] ICR 357).

If the tribunal is satisfied that in respect of each day falling within the period to which the prescribed element relates the employee has neither received nor claimed jobseeker's allowance or income support the recoupment regulations will not apply.

Statutory cap: If the statutory cap has been applied the prescribed element should be adjusted by the same proportion (see also *Recoupment*).

Statutory authorities: The Employment Protection (Recoupment of jobseekers allowance and income support) Regulations 1996

Relevant case law: *Savage v Saxena* [1998] ICR 357

Indirect discrimination: see Discrimination

Individual respondents

(see also Discrimination)

An individual employee may be a respondent to a discrimination claim, and it is often the case that claims will be brought against an employer and one or more individual employees responsible for the acts complained of (see s110 EA 2010).

Where a claim against an individual is upheld by the tribunal the tribunal may make individual awards against any particular respondent or make all respondents jointly and severally liable for the award. It is not possible to apportion an award between contributing respondents under the Civil Liability (Contribution) Act 1978 (see *London Borough of Hackney v Sivanandan* [2013] EWCA Civ 22).

Industrial action

Sections 237 to 239 TULR(C)A 1992 make specific provision governing the availability of the right to claim unfair dismissal under s111 ERA 1996 where the dismissal is related to having taken industrial action. Industrial action may take the form of strikes or action less than a strike. Dismissals related to official industrial action, where the action has the support of a trade union's ballot of its members, are treated differently from dismissals related to unofficial industrial action. In general terms, the right to claim unfair dismissal is restricted in some circumstances and a dismissal will be automatically unfair if other conditions are satisfied. The qualifying period and the time limit for bringing certain industrial action unfair dismissal claims are also altered.

Remedy: The unfair dismissal jurisdiction, and the principles that apply to the remedy available, are those for unfair dismissal generally (see *Unfair dismissal*).

Adjustments: The House of Lords in *Crosville Wales Ltd v Tracey* [1997] IRLR 691 held that tribunals should not reduce an award for contributory fault where an employee has been unfairly dismissed for taking industrial action under s238 TULR(C)A 1992. It is likely that where an employee is dismissed for threatening to take such industrial action a reduction for contributory fault will also be denied (see *Adapters and Eliminators v Paterson* EAT 21 April 1983 unreported). It may be possible to reduce an award for contributory fault where the actions of the employee have gone beyond mere participation in industrial action, for example if the individual has acted in an inflammatory or intimidatory manner (see also *Courtaulds Northern Spinning Ltd v Moosa* [1984] IRLR 43).

Statutory authorities: TULR(C)A 1992 ss237 to 239

Relevant case law: *Adapters and Eliminators v Paterson* EAT 21 April 1983 unreported; *Courtaulds Northern Spinning Ltd v Moosa* [1984] IRLR 43; *Crosville Wales Ltd v Tracey* [1997] IRLR 691

Injury to feelings

(see also Discrimination)

Injury to feelings awards compensate for non-pecuniary loss. Injury to feelings awards are available where a tribunal has upheld a complaint of discrimination (see s119(4) EA 2010) or unlawful detriment, but are not available for unfair dismissal (see *Dunnachie v Kingston upon Hull City Council*

[2004] IRLR 727), nor under the Working Time Regulations reg 30(4) (see *Gomes v Higher Level Care Ltd* UKEAT/0017/16/RN).

Subject to the following caveat, such an award is also not available where a worker has suffered the detriment of termination of his or her contract for making a protected disclosure or for reasons related to working time protections (see s49(5A) and (6) ERA 1996), since compensation is limited to that available for unfair dismissal. The caveat is that since both injury to feelings and a basic award compensate for non-pecuniary loss, it would appear that an injury to feelings award may be made, up to the level of an appropriate basic award had in fact the claim been brought as unfair dismissal. This approach would ensure that the availability of an injury to feelings award is not unnecessarily limited where a basic award for equivalent unfair dismissal is not available.

There are other heads of non-economic loss that may be compensated for by a tribunal (see *Aggravated damages; Exemplary damages; Physical and psychiatric injury*).

Remedy: The award of injury to feelings is intended to compensate the claimant for the anger, distress and upset caused by the unlawful treatment they have received. It is compensatory, not punitive. Tribunals have a broad discretion about what level of award to make, which can only be overturned on appeal if the figure chosen is obviously wrong. This will only occur very rarely.

General principles
The general principles that apply to assessing an appropriate injury to feelings award have been set out by the EAT in *Prison Service v Johnson* [1997] IRLR 162, para 27:

- Injury to feelings awards are compensatory and should be just to both parties. They should compensate fully without punishing the discriminator. Feelings of indignation at the discriminator's conduct should not be allowed to inflate the award;

- Awards should not be too low, as that would diminish respect for the policy of the anti-discrimination legislation. Society has condemned discrimination and awards must ensure that it is seen to be wrong. On the other hand, awards should be restrained, as excessive awards could be seen as the way to untaxed riches;

- Awards should bear some broad general similarity to the range of awards in personal injury cases – not to any particular type of

personal injury but to the whole range of such awards;

- Tribunals should take into account the value in everyday life of the sum they have in mind, by reference to purchasing power or by reference to earnings;

- Tribunals should bear in mind the need for public respect for the level of awards made.

The matters compensated for by an injury to feelings award encompass subjective feelings of upset, frustration, worry, anxiety, mental distress, fear, grief, anguish, humiliation, unhappiness, stress and depression (see *Vento v Chief Constable of West Yorkshire Police (No2)* [2003] IRLR 102).

Bands of compensation
In *Vento* the Court of Appeal identified three broad bands of compensation for injury to feelings and gave the following guidance (however, see below for revised figures):

1) The top band should normally be between £15,000 and £25,000. Sums in this range should be awarded in the most serious cases, such as where there has been a lengthy campaign of discriminatory harassment on the ground of sex or race. Only in the most exceptional case should an award of compensation for injury to feelings exceed £25,000;

2) The middle band of between £5,000 and £15,000 should be used for serious cases, which do not merit an award in the highest band;

3) Awards of between £500 and £5,000 are appropriate for less serious cases, such as where the act of discrimination is an isolated or one-off occurrence. In general, awards of less than £500 are to be avoided altogether, as they risk being regarded as so low as not to be a proper recognition of injury to feelings.

Within each band there is considerable flexibility, allowing tribunals to fix what is considered to be fair, reasonable and just compensation in the particular circumstances of the case.

The EAT revisited the exact boundaries of the three bands in *Da'Bell v NSPCC* [2010] IRLR 19 and accepted the arguments of both sides before it that the EAT should uprate the *Vento* guidelines in line with the RPI as follows:

1) The upper band should be £18,000 to £30,000;

2) The middle band should be £6,000 to £18,000;

3) The lower band should be £600 to £6,000.

Although it had been thought that the guideline figures would be updated from time to time by the EAT rather than Employment Tribunals themselves, *AA Solicitors Ltd (t/a AA Solicitors) & Anor v Majid* UKEAT/0217/15 holds that band ranges and awards for injury to feelings can be adjusted by individual Employment Tribunals where '*there is cogent evidence before [it] of the rate of change in the value of money (which could, in principle, go down as well as up).*'

In *Simmons v Castle* [2012] EWCA Civ 1288 the Court of Appeal announced that with effect from 1 April 2013, general damages in tort cases would be increased by 10% on existing levels, and the boundaries updated on that basis would be as follows:

1) The upper band would be £19,800 to £33,000;

2) The middle band would be £6,600 to £19,800;

3) The lower band would be £660 to £6,600.

Whether such an uplift should apply in employment cases has been the subject of debate at the EAT level. In *Sash Window Workshop Ltd & Anor v King* UKEAT/0057/14/MC; UKEAT/0058/14/MC and *The Cadogan Hotel Partners Ltd v Ozog* UKEAT/0001/14/DM applied the 10% increase; however, in *Chawla v Hewlett Packard Ltd (Disability Discrimination: Reasonable adjustments)* [2015] UKEAT/427/13/2502 addressed a broader range of arguments including that the reasons for the *Simmons v Castle* uplift did not apply in employment tribunals, and held that the 10% uplift to general damages which applies in the civil court does not apply to ET awards. The EAT in *De Souza v Vinci Construction UK Limited* UKEAT/0328/14/DXA agreed that the uplift did not apply, but this reasoning was rejected by Langstaff P in *Beckford v London Borough of Southwark* [2016] IRLR 178, where he held that the uplift applies '*across the board*' and to employment litigation in particular.

The Court of Appeal has now confirmed that the 10% *Simmons v Castle* uplift should be applied to both injury to feelings and psychiatric injury (see *De Souza v Vinci Construction (UK) Ltd* [2017] EWCA Civ 879).

Other relevant factors

Proof of injury: It is not inevitable that a tribunal will award an injury to feelings award where it is

permitted to, though it is very unusual for no such award to be made. It is necessary for the individual to prove the nature of the injury to feelings and its extent, though this could be at its simplest the fact that a claimant has stated he was upset by his dismissal (see *Murray v Powertech (Scotland) Ltd* [1992] IRLR 257 and *Ministry of Defence v Cannock* [1994] ICR 918). The evidence a claimant will want to produce is the material which shows the impact of the discrimination on any subjective feelings of upset, frustration, worry, anxiety, mental distress, fear, grief, anguish, humiliation, unhappiness, stress and depression. For example, this might include evidence about the impact the discrimination has had on relationships with colleagues, friends and family and any particular difficulties caused by the discrimination. Such evidence might include medical evidence, but where the injury to feelings amounts to a mental illness such as depression, the claimant might well consider seeking an award for personal injury in addition to injury to feelings.

Double recovery: Where an individual is awarded sums both for injury to feelings and personal injury (e.g. depression) caused by the discrimination, the injury to feelings and personal injury awards must compensate for different injuries and not overlap. The consequence is that for example where discrimination has caused a period of depression, either the injury to feelings award or the personal injuries award will be less than would be appropriate if only one of the awards had been made.

Claimant's knowledge: It is not necessary for an injury to feelings award to be made that the claimant's injured feelings are caused by his knowledge that he has been discriminated against, contrary to the interpretation given to *Skyrail Oceanic Ltd v Coleman* [1981] IRLR 398. The EAT in *Taylor v XLN Telecom Ltd* [2010] IRLR 49 held that the calculation of the remedy for discrimination is the same as in other torts, and that knowledge of the discriminator's motives was not necessary for recovery of injury to feelings. The EAT nevertheless observed that the distress and humiliation suffered by a claimant will generally be greater where the discrimination has been overt or the claimant appreciates at the time that the motivation was discriminatory.

Separate awards for separate grounds of discrimination: Where an individual has suffered a number of acts of discrimination, some caused by one protected ground, e.g. race, others by another protected ground, e.g. disability, the tribunal should make separate awards for each protected ground, as each is a separate wrong giving a right to damages (see *Al Jumard v Clywd Leisure Ltd* [2008] IRLR 345). However, where the discriminatory acts overlap as they arise from the same set of facts, such as where a dismissal is on grounds of both race and disability, a tribunal will not be expected to separate the injury to feelings and attribute parts to each form of discrimination. This may not necessarily result in an increased award compared to the situation where all the acts of discrimination are caused by one protected characteristic, as the tribunal must always have regard to the proportionality of the overall figure awarded for injury to feelings.

Future contingencies: Where the discriminatory act, such as a dismissal, would have occurred at some point in the future for legitimate reasons in any event, it is not appropriate to reduce the injury to feelings award to reflect that future possibility. The award reflects the injury to feelings caused by the knowledge that the reason for the act was discrimination, which cannot be offset by the fact that a lawful dismissal may have been carried out in any event (see *O'Donoghue v Redcar and Cleveland Borough Council* 2001 IRLR 615).

Adjustments: Interest can be awarded on the sum for injury to feelings (see *Interest*). Reg 6(1)(a) IT(IADC) Regs 1996 provides that the period over which interest accrues begins with the date of the discrimination and ends on the date the tribunal calculates compensation.

A percentage increase or reduction up to a maximum of 25% can be applied to reflect a failure by the employer or employee to comply with the ACAS disciplinary code of practice (see *ACAS*).

A 10% *Simmons v Castle* uplift should be applied (see *De Souza v Vinci Construction (UK) Ltd* [2017] EWCA Civ 879 paragraph 26).

A *Polkey*-type deduction should not be applied to the award, even if the claimant would have been fairly dismissed at a date soon afterwards (*O'Donoghue v Redcar and Cleveland Borough Council* [2001] IRLR 615).

Tax: It is widely understood that an award for injury to feelings in a discrimination case is not taxable and so therefore should not be grossed up (see *Walker v Adams* [2001] STC 101, *Orthet Ltd v Vince-Cain (2)* [2004] UKEAT/0801/03 and *Oti-Obihara v Commissioners for HM Revenue & Customs* [2011] IRLR 386). However, the issue is not clear cut as HMRC's Employment Income Manual states that awards for discrimination arising out of termination, including injury to feelings, should be taxed under s401 ITEPA. Also, in *Moorthy v The Commissioners for Her Majesty's Revenue & Customs* [2014] UKFTT

834 (TC) (where the claimant accepted £200,000 in compromise of his claim of age discrimination and argued that none of it was taxable), the tax tribunal ruled that the payment of £200,000 in its entirety was made *'directly or indirectly in consideration or in consequence of, or otherwise in connection with'* the termination of Mr Moorthy's employment, and therefore fell within ITEPA s401. Whether or not the payment was also to compensate Mr Moorthy for discrimination, unfair dismissal, injury to feelings, redundancy and/or financial loss was immaterial.

But the EAT in *Timothy James Consulting Ltd v Wilton* UKEAT/0082/14/DXA followed *Orthet Ltd v Vince-Cain* and *Oti-Obihara v Commissioners for HM Revenue & Customs*, not *Moorthy*, and ruled that the injury to feelings figure should not be taxed and therefore should not be grossed up.

In January 2016, Mr Moorthy appealed to the UKUT (see *Moorthy v Revenue & Customs* [2016] UKUT 13 (TCC)) but lost, the tribunal saying that *Orthet* and *Timothy James* were wrongly decided in so far as they held that 'injury' in section 406 ITEPA includes injury to feelings. The upper tribunal held that 'injury' in section 406 refers to a medical condition and does not include injury to feelings.

It should be remembered that awards for injury to feelings arising from discrimination that is **not** connected to dismissal will not be subject to tax.

From April 2018
The Government proposed that from April 2018, any compensation for injury to feelings in a termination payment will be taxable to the extent that the £30,000 'allowance' has been exceeded, except where the compensation is for a psychiatric injury or a recognised medical condition. However, the calling of the snap election meant that this measure was removed from the Finance Act 2017 in the wash-up period. The view of the Chartered Institute of Taxation is that a significant amount of the Bill would be re-enacted irrespective of who wins the election.

Recoupment: N/A

Relevant case law: *A v HM Revenue & Customs [2009]; AA Solicitors Ltd (t/a AA Solicitors) & Anor v Majid* UKEAT/0217/15; *Al Jumard v Clywd Leisure Ltd* [2008] IRLR 345; *Beckford v London Borough of Southwark* UKEAT/0210/14/JOJ; *Chawla v Hewlett Packard Ltd (Disability Discrimination: Reasonable adjustments)* [2015] UKEAT/427/13/2502; *Da'Bell v NSPCC* [2009] UKEAT/0227/09; *De Souza v Vinci Construction UK Limited* UKEAT/0328/14/DXA; *De Souza v Vinci Construction (UK) Ltd* [2017] EWCA Civ 879; *Dunnachie v Kingston upon Hull City Council* [2004] IRLR 727; *Gomes v Higher Level Care Ltd*

UKEAT/0017/16/RN; *Ministry of Defence v Cannock* [1994] ICR 918; *Moorthy v The Commissioners for Her Majesty's Revenue & Customs* [2014] UKFTT 834 (TC); *Moorthy v Revenue & Customs* [2016] UKUT 13 (TCC); *Murray v Powertech (Scotland) Ltd* [1992] IRLR 257; *O'Donoghue v Redcar and Cleveland Borough Council* [2001] IRLR 615; *Orthet Ltd v Vince-Cain (2)* [2004] UKEAT/0801/03; *Oti-Obihara v Commissioners for HM Revenue & Customs* [2011] IRLR 386; *Prison Service v Johnson* [1997] IRLR 162; *Sash Window Workshop Ltd & Anor v King* UKEAT/0057/14/MC; *Skyrail Oceanic Ltd v Coleman* [1981] IRLR 398; *Taylor v XLN Telecom Ltd* [2010] IRLR 49; *The Cadogan Hotel Partners Ltd v Ozog* UKEAT/0001/14/DM; *Vento v Chief Constable of West Yorkshire Police* [2002] EWCA Civ 1871; *Voith Turbo Ltd v Stowe* [2005] IRLR 228; *Walker v Adams* (SpC344)

Insolvency

The Redundancy Payments Service ("RPS") operates a scheme whereby the National Insurance Fund ("NIF") will make certain payments to ex-employees of an insolvent employer where certain conditions are satisfied (see ss182 to 190 ERA 1996). The ex-employee must make a claim to the RPS, who may make payments for a limited amount of the debts of the employer to the ex-employee. The debts covered are (s184):

- any arrears of pay in respect of one or more weeks, capped at 8 weeks;

- statutory notice pay;

- up to 6 weeks holiday pay accruing over the 12 months before 'the appropriate date';

- any basic award for unfair dismissal; and

- any reasonable sum by way of reimbursement of the whole or part of any fee or premium paid by an apprentice or articled clerk.

Unpaid maternity pay, paternity pay or sick pay cannot be claimed from the RPS under the insolvency rules. Maternity pay should be claimed from HMRC and sick pay from the DWP.

Sections 184(2) to 184(6) define what may amount to arrears of pay (which includes amongst other matters a guarantee payment and a protective award), what amounts to holiday pay and what may amount to 'a reasonable sum'.

The debts must have been due on 'the appropriate date' which is defined in s185, and depending on the nature of the debt may be the date of the formal insolvency of the employer, the date of termination of employment or the date on which the award was made (for example if the debt is the basic award or an unpaid protective award).

Where an individual has applied to the Redundancy Payments Service for payment, but it has not been made, or payment has not been made in full he can make a claim to the employment tribunal (s188 ERA 1996).

Under s124 Pension Schemes Act 1993 there is a comparable scheme for requesting (and enforcing) payment from the NIF for unpaid pension contributions.

Remedy: Where a tribunal upholds a claim for payment, the tribunal will make a declaration to that effect stating the amount that ought to be paid to the ex-employee from the NIF.

Calculation of remedy

Various limits apply to the entitlement of the ex-employee to be paid certain debts:

- Arrears of pay are limited to 8 weeks, with each week capped at a £489 (or an appropriate proportion of that if the debt arises from part of a week) (ss184 and 186);

- Statutory notice pay is anyway capped at 12 weeks, and each week is capped at £489 (or an appropriate proportion of that if the debt arises from part of a week) (ss184 and 186);

- Holiday pay is limited to 6 weeks, with each week capped at £489 (or an appropriate proportion of that if the debt arises from part of a week) (ss184 and s186).

Gross or net: Gross. A week's pay as defined in ss220 to 229 ERA 1996 applies (see *Week's pay*).

Limit on a week's pay: £489 (see Table 1 for historical rates).

Limit on number of weeks: See individual limits above.

Any maximum or minimum: Maximum = £3,912 (arrears) + £5,868 (notice pay) + £14,670 (basic award/redundancy) + £2,934 (holiday pay) = £27,384; No minimum

Adjustments: None

Mitigation: The nature of the underlying debt will determine whether the duty to mitigate applies. For example, the ex-employee is under a duty to mitigate their loss for failure to pay wages for the length of the statutory notice period, but there is no duty to mitigate loss in relation to a protective award or a basic award (see *Mitigation* and *Protective award*).

Any state benefits that have been received, or could have been claimed, will be deducted (see *'Redundancy & Insolvency: A Guide for Employees'* published by The Insolvency Service, paragraph 19).

Tax: Any arrears of pay/protective award and accrued holiday pay will have income tax and national insurance deducted at the basic rate. 'Notional' tax, equivalent to the basic rate, will be deducted from compensation for failure to give statutory notice (this tax is not actually paid to HMRC but may be claimed back by the employee if their total income for the year is less than their personal allowance). The basic award will not be taxed at all unless it exceeds £30,000, which will in practice never happen because of the statutory limit (see paragraphs 19 and 20 of *'Redundancy & Insolvency: A Guide for Employees'*).

Recoupment: Recoupment does not apply. Any state benefits received will be deducted from the award.

Statutory authorities: ERA 1996 ss182 to 190; Pension Schemes Act 1993 s124; TULR(C)A 1992 s188

Interest

(see also Discrimination; Injury to feelings; Interest on discrimination awards; Interest on unpaid compensation; Table 24)

There are two different situations in which interest is available on a tribunal award. First, where a tribunal award has not been paid interest accrues on the unpaid sum (see *Interest on unpaid compensation*). Secondly, a tribunal is able to award interest in discrimination claims brought under the EA 2010 as part of its award of compensation, to compensate for the fact that compensation has been awarded after the loss compensated for has been suffered (see *Interest on discrimination awards*).

Interest on discrimination awards

(see also Discrimination; Injury to feelings; Interest on unpaid compensation; Table 24)

A tribunal is able to award interest on awards of compensation made in discrimination claims brought under s124(2)(b) EA 2010, to compensate for the fact that compensation has been awarded after the relevant loss has been suffered (see s139

EA 2010, EA 2010 Commencement No 4 etc Order 2010/2317 and IT(IADC) Regs 1996).

The tribunal may award interest to the following types of discrimination award:

- Past financial loss;
- Injury to feelings;
- Aggravated and exemplary damages; and
- Physical and psychiatric injury.

Since a tribunal cannot award interest on past loss within a compensatory award for unfair dismissal, where an unfair dismissal is also a discriminatory dismissal, tribunals will often compensate such losses under the discrimination legislation.

Calculation of interest

Interest is calculated as simple interest accruing from day to day (Reg 3(1)).

Interest rate: Until 29 July 2013 the interest rate to be applied in England and Wales was that prescribed for the special investment account under rule 27(1) of the Court Funds Rules 1987. The interest rate until 29 July 2013 was 0.5%. For claims presented on or after 29 July 2013 the relevant interest rate is that specified in s17 of the Judgments Act 1838 (see The Employment Tribunals (Interest on Awards in Discrimination Cases) (Amendment) Regulations 2013). The interest rate now to be applied is 8% which is in line with Scotland (see Table 24 for a list of interest rates).

If the rate of interest changes during the period over which interest is calculated, the tribunal may use such median or average of those rates as seems to it appropriate, in the interests of simplicity (see The Industrial Tribunals (Interest on Awards in Discrimination Cases) Regulations 1996 Reg 3(3)).

Period of calculation, injury to feelings: interest is awarded on injury to feelings awards from the date of the act of discrimination complained of until the date on which the tribunal calculates the compensation (see Reg 6(1)(a)).

Period of calculation, all other sums: interest is awarded on all sums other than injury to feelings awards from the mid-point of the date of the act of discrimination complained of and the date the tribunal calculates the award (Reg 6(1)(b)). The mid-point date is the date half way through the period between the date of the discrimination complained of and the date the tribunal calculates the award (Reg 4).

Period of calculation, early payment: where payment of any of the sums attracting interest has already been made by the respondent, the date of payment is taken as the date of calculation of the award for those particular sums (Reg 6(2)).

Period of calculation, serious injustice discretion: where a tribunal considers that serious injustice would be caused if interest were to be calculated according to the approaches above, it can calculate interest on such different periods as it considers appropriate (Reg 6(3)). See *Ministry of Defence v Cannock* [1994] IRLR 509, where interest was awarded over a longer period than provided for by the regulations due to the long period since the loss was incurred.

Interest cannot be awarded in respect of future loss or loss arising before the discrimination complained of (Reg 5). This reflects the broad principle behind the award of interest which is that it is compensation to the successful claimant for the loss they have suffered by virtue of not having received payment of the award at the date of the loss suffered.

Calculation
Interest on past loss
Interest runs from the 'mid-point' date to the date of calculation. The mid-point is calculated as the date halfway between the date of the discriminatory act and ending on the calculation date (usually the judgment date). Interest accrues from day to day and is simple rather than compound.

Interest = (number of days from discriminatory act date to calculation date x 1/2 x interest rate x 1/100 x 1/365 x compensatory award (after all adjustments have been made - see *Adjustments*)

Example 1
Compensation award = £20,000

Discriminatory date = 01/04/2013

Calculation date = 05/02/2015

Interest rate = 8% (Note: the date of the discriminatory act is before 29 July 2013 when the interest rate changed, so the ET could apply some kind of average instead).

Number of days between discriminatory date and calculation date = 676 inclusive

Interest = 676 ÷ 2 x 0.08 x 1/365 x 20,000 = £1,481.64 (the number of days have been divided by 2 because of the mid-point rule)

Interest on Injury to feelings
Interest runs from the date of the discriminatory act to the date of calculation. Interest accrues from day to day and is simple rather than compound.

Example 2
Injury to feelings award = £5,000

Discriminatory date = 01/04/2014

Calculation date = 05/02/2016

Interest rate = 8%

Number of days = 676 inclusive

Interest = 676 x 0.08 x 1/365 x 5,000 = £740.82

Interest on Physical and psychiatric injury and Aggravated damages
Interest on physical and psychiatric injury runs from the 'mid-point' date to the date of calculation. The mid-point date is calculated as the date half way between the discriminatory act and the calculation date (usually the judgment date). Interest accrues from day to day and is simple rather than compound.

The calculation works in exactly the same way as that for interest on past loss.

Any maximum or minimum: There is no minimum, and interest does not have to be awarded if the tribunal considers it would be unjust to do so (Reg 2). The maximum would be determined by the interest rate in force during the relevant period.

Adjustments: Interest is calculated after the final adjustments have been made to the award and after enhanced redundancy has been deducted (see *Adjustments and order of adjustments*).

Tax: Interest is awarded on the net loss suffered by the individual, see *Bentwood Bros (Manchester) Ltd v Shepherd* [2003] IRLR 364. Any grossing up, if required, will apply after interest has been calculated (see *Grossing up*).

Recoupment: The recoupment regulations do not apply to discrimination claims and hence they will not apply to any interest awarded.

Statutory authorities: Court Funds Rules 1987 r27(1); Judgments Act 1838 s17; The Employment Tribunals (Interest on Awards in Discrimination Cases)(Amendment) Regulations 2013; The Employment Tribunals (Interest on Awards in Discrimination Cases) Regulations 1996 s3(3)

Interest on unpaid compensation

(See also Financial penalties on employers)

If the employer fails to pay the compensation that has been awarded to the claimant within a certain prescribed time period, interest will accrue to the award.

Until 29 July 2013, interest on unpaid compensation awards in cases other than discrimination did not start to accrue until 42 days after judgment had been given. However, for any claims received by the ET from 29 July 2013, interest will start accruing from the date of the judgment but no interest will be payable if the award is paid within 14 days of the judgment. This brings interest in non-discriminatory cases in line with interest in discrimination cases (see Employment Tribunals (Interest) Order (Amendment) Order 2013 Art 3).

Interest will accrue on unpaid sums but any sums withheld on account of the recoupment regulations will not accrue interest.

Interim relief

Where a claim for unfair dismissal is brought, and where it is alleged that the reason or principal reason for the dismissal was for one of a number of protected reasons, the claimant may claim interim relief. Specific procedural rules apply, including that the claim must be brought within 7 days of the effective date of termination (see s161 to 163 TULR(C)A 1992 and s128 to 129 ERA 1996). The protected reasons are:

- Relating to enforcement of rights given to shop and betting shop workers, s100(1)(a) and (b) (see s128(1)(a)(i));

- Relating to acting as a representative under the WTR 1998, s101A(d) (see s128(1)(a)(i));

- Relating to performing the functions of a pensions trustee, s102(1) (see s128(1)(a)(i));

- Performing the functions of an employee representative, s103 (see s128(1)(a)(i));

- Making a protected disclosure, s103A (see s128(1)(a)(i));

- Relating to action over trade union recognition, para 161(2) Sch 1A TULR(C)A 1992 (see s128(1)(a)(ii));

- Relating to blacklisting, s104F(1) (see s128(1)(b));

- Membership of a trade union, participating in its activities, or making use of trade union services, s152(1)(a), (b) and (c) TULR(C)A 1992 (see s161(1) TULR(C)A 1992);

- Refusing to accept an offer to give up membership or collective bargaining rights,

s152(bb) TULR(C)A 1992 (see s161(1) TULR(C)A 1992).

Remedy: If at the hearing of an application for interim relief it appears to the tribunal that the claim for unfair dismissal is likely to succeed, the tribunal will announce its findings and explain to the parties its powers and how it can exercise them. If the employer is willing, pending the final determination of the unfair dismissal complaint, the tribunal can order that the employee be reinstated or re-engaged. Otherwise, the tribunal will make an order that the contract of employment is continued. Such an order has the effect that, until the unfair dismissal complaint is determined, the contract of employment continues for the purposes of pay, seniority, pension rights and similar matters, and for continuity of employment.

Either party may apply to the tribunal for the revocation or variation of such an order on the grounds that there has been a relevant change in circumstances (see s165 TULR(C)A 1992 and s131 ERA 1992).

If a claimant makes a complaint, and the tribunal finds, that the employer has failed to comply with an order for reinstatement or re-engagement, the tribunal will make an order for the continuation of the contract of employment and such compensation as it considers just and equitable in all the circumstances having regard to the infringement of the order and the loss suffered as a consequence.

If a claimant makes a complaint, and the tribunal finds, that the employer has failed to comply with an order for the continuation of the contract of employment, it will make an order for such compensation as it considers just and equitable in all the circumstances having regard to the infringement of the order and the loss suffered as a consequence (see s166 TULR(C)A or s132 ERA 1996).

If an ET makes an order for the continuation of the contract of employment at an interim relief hearing, and subsequently at the full hearing the claimant loses and the respondent is successful, it is unlikely that the claimant will have to repay the interim relief payments (see *Initial Textile Services v Rendell* [1991] UKEAT 383/91/230).

Gross or net: The award of any unpaid salary will be made gross under the continuing contract of employment and subject to PAYE (but see *Tax below*).

Tax: Payments under an interim relief order are taxable as payments in connection with termination of employment under s401 **not** in full as earnings under s62 ITEPA (see also *Tax and termination* payments). See *Turullols v HMRC* where the First Tier Tribunal held that the claimant, who was found to have been unfairly dismissed, could claim back the tax that had been paid on the salary payments made under the interim relief order because they were payments in connection with the termination of her employment and therefore should have been tax-free up to £30,000. This would also have been the case even if the ET had ruled that the dismissal was fair.

Cap: There is no statutory cap, and this award falls outside the compensatory award (see s166 TULR(C)A 1992 and s132 ERA 196).

Statutory authorities: ERA 1996 ss128 to 132; TULR(C)A 1992 ss161 to 166

Relevant case law: *Initial Textile Services v Rendell* [1991] UKEAT 383/91/230; *Turullols v Revenue & Customs* [2014] UKFTT 672 (TC)

Itemised pay statement

An employee has the right to be given by his employer, at or before the time at which any payment of wages or salary is made to him, a written itemised pay statement (s8 ERA 1996).

Calculation: Where the tribunal finds that an itemised pay statement has not been given to the employee and further that any un-notified deductions have been made from the pay of the employee during the period of 13 weeks immediately preceding the date of the application for the reference (whether or not the deductions were made in breach of the contract of employment), the tribunal may order the employer to pay the employee a sum not exceeding the aggregate of the un-notified deductions so made (s12(4) ERA 1996).

Gross or net: Gross

Limit on a week's pay: None

Limit on number of weeks: 13

Any maximum or minimum: None

Adjustments: N/A

Tax: The employer will deduct tax and national insurance as normal if the employee is still employed. However, if the employee is no longer in employment, the employee will be responsible for declaring this income on their self-assessment.

Statutory authorities: ERA 1996 ss8 and 12(4)

Job seekers allowance

(see also Recoupment)

There are 2 types of job seekers allowance:

- Contribution based, where the claimant has paid enough national insurance contributions during their employment

- Income based, where the claimant has not paid enough national contributions as an employee but was on a low wage

Receipt of job seeker's allowance should be treated in 2 different ways, depending on whether the claim is for damages for wrongful dismissal or compensation for unfair dismissal.

Damages
Credit should be given for any job seekers allowance received during the damages period and during the statutory notice period. However, as with other state benefits, it could be argued that full credit should not be given if the employee did not receive their statutory notice period or payment in lieu, because they would exhaust their entitlement to state benefits sooner than they would have done if they had received their statutory notice.

Compensatory award
Job seekers allowance is not deducted from the compensatory award but is instead subject to the recoupment regulations (see *Recoupment*).

Adjustments: See *Recoupment* (Prescribed element)

Cap: See *Recoupment* (Prescribed element)

Recoupment: Only for compensation for unfair dismissal. Recoupment does not apply to wrongful dismissal.

Statutory authorities: The Employment Protection (Recoupment of Jobseeker's Allowance and Income Support) Regulations 1996

Judicial assessment/mediation

These two forms of Alternative Dispute Resolution are offered by tribunals in appropriate cases, and expressly considered at case management Preliminary Hearings.

Judicial Assessment
The principles and protocol are set out in the *Presidential Guidance – Rule 3 – Protocol on Judicial Assessment*.

Assessment is to take place at the first case management preliminary hearing, only after the identification of the issues and the making of case management orders. It is considered suitable for most cases and parties are encouraged to inform the tribunal in advance of their wish to undergo this procedure. Both parties must consent, and the process is strictly confidential. It is also free.

The assessment consists of a provisional Early Neutral Evaluation of the merits of liability and/or remedy by an Employment Judge.

The system is in its early days and it is too early to tell how it will work in practice. It is also unclear where the dividing line will fall between Judicial Assessment and the broad steer on merits common to case management Preliminary Hearings. [It is hoped that the former will not eliminate the latter].

From a remedy perspective, Judicial Assessment may be suitable where one party has unrealistic views of the quantum of their case that are easily identifiable without the need to resolve complex questions of fact or significant conflicts of evidence.

Judicial Mediation

This is mediation conducted by an Employment Judge over the course of a single day at the Employment Tribunal. Following an initial opening session, the parties sit in separate rooms and a Judge conducts 'shuttle diplomacy' between them.

Judicial Mediators tend to be facilitative rather than evaluative, focusing on relaying each party's position to the other side, and testing the realism of each party's position. The aim is to help each side understand the other's position, identify common ground and seek agreement.

The mediation is conducted on a Without Prejudice basis with the Judicial Mediator having no further involvement in the case following the mediation.

Although there are no formal criteria for Judicial Mediation, it tends to be offered in cases lasting more than 3 days and/or where there is a continuing employment relationship between the parties. The tribunal has to be satisfied that the mediation has a real prospect of success, and the respondent has to pay a £600 fee for the mediation to take place.

Leave for family and domestic reasons, maternity, paternity, adoption, shared parental: see Detriment; Parental leave; Time off

Limitation period

This is the maximum period allowed between the act complained of and when the claim should be lodged at the ET (see Table 30).

Loss of chance

Once a tribunal has upheld a complaint of unlawful treatment such as discrimination or unfair dismissal, it is necessary for it to assess the remedy available to the claimant. Where the remedy includes an award to compensate for financial loss, it will be necessary to identify the sums the claimant would have received had the unlawful conduct not taken place. For a dismissal, in a straightforward case this will be the salary that would have been earned by the claimant.

In assessing the loss suffered by the claimant, the tribunal will take into account the chance of events having occurred following the unlawful act, and determine the award on the basis of the loss of that chance. For example, if there was a 25% chance that an individual would have been dismissed fairly in any event 6 months after their unlawful dismissal, the tribunal will calculate the losses suffered after that date as 75% of salary etc that would have been earned had the individual remained in employment after that event.

Another example would be an individual who had, say, a 50% chance of being promoted shortly after their unlawful dismissal, where the tribunal could award future losses based on 50% of the increased salary to reflect the chance of it having been obtained (see *O'Donoghue v Redcar and Cleveland Borough Council* [2001] IRLR 615 and *Ministry of Defence v Wheeler* [1998] IRLR 23).

Where the chance of a future event is very high, or very low, the tribunal may well treat the chance as 100% or 0% as appropriate (see *Timothy James Consulting Ltd v Wilton* UKEAT/0082/14/DXA). There is no guideline cut off for such marginal chances.

The *Polkey* reduction is an example of this approach in the unfair dismissal context (see *Polkey*), but in considering the future actions of the employer the tribunal will take account of the actions of a reasonable employer (see *Abbey National v Formso* [1999] ICR 222). In discrimination cases the tribunal will seek to determine the future conduct of the actual employer. It will require evidence to demonstrate the chances of future events occurring (see *Wardle v Credit Agricole Corporate & Investment Bank* [2011] IRLR 604 and *Chagger v*

Abbey National plc & Anor [2010] IRLR 47). Statistical evidence may well be relevant and admissible (see *Vento v Chief Constable of West Yorkshire Police* [2003] ICR 318).

Marginal tax rate

(see also Grossing up)

The marginal tax rate is the rate that should be applied to a claimant's award when grossing up (see *Grossing up*). When deciding on the marginal tax rate, account should be taken of the claimant's personal tax free allowance (which can be found from their tax code at the date of dismissal), earnings already earned in that tax year (including since dismissal), the relevant tax thresholds (see Tax tables 16 and 17) and any other income the claimant may earn in the remainder of that tax year.

Different marginal tax rates may apply to different elements of the award (see *Yorkshire Housing Ltd v Cuerden* [2010] UKEAT/0397/09).

For example, if the employee had earned £15,000 gross and their tax code was 1000L at the date of dismissal, the first £10,000 would be tax free, leaving them having to pay tax (@20%) on the balance (£5,000). If in addition, their fully taxable tribunal award (i.e. the amount exceeding the £30,000 tax free limit) is £50,000, they would have to pay tax at the rate of 20% on the first £27,000 (£32,000, which is the 20% threshold for the year 2016-2017, minus £5,000) and 40% on the balance of £23,000. So the first element would need to be grossed up by 20% and the second element by 40%.

Maternity Equality Clause

Women on maternity leave must receive any increases in pay due to them at the time they would have received them, had they not been on maternity leave and their pay, when they return, must reflect the increases they would have had, had they not been absent. The Maternity Equality Clause (s73 EA 2010) modifies the woman's contract so that her maternity related pay is increased in line with any actual increase in pay, or any increase that she would have been paid had she not been on maternity leave.

The tribunal has jurisdiction to determine a complaint relating to breach of an equality clause under s127 EA 2010.

Remedy: Arrears of up to 6 years' actual pay may be ordered (s132 EA 2010).

Gross or net: Gross

Limit on a week's pay: None

Limit on number of years: 6

Any maximum or minimum: None

Tax: Taxable under s62 ITEPA 2003.

Statutory authorities: EA 2010 ss73, 127 and 132

Maternity: see Detriment; Maternity Equality Clause; Unfair dismissal; Table 28

Maximum compensatory award: see Statutory cap

Minimum wage: see National Minimum Wage

Misconduct: see Contributory conduct

Mitigation

It is a fundamental principle that any claimant will be expected to mitigate the losses they suffer as a result of an unlawful act by giving credit, for example for earnings in a new job (mitigation in fact), and that the tribunal will not make an award to cover losses that could reasonably have been avoided (mitigation in law). For example, an unfairly dismissed employee is expected to search for other work, and will not recover losses beyond a date by which the tribunal concludes the individual ought reasonably to have been able to find new employment at a similar rate of pay. Such an individual may be awarded the difference between the salary of a lower paid new job, and their previous salary, for a period until the tribunal concludes they could reasonably have found similarly well paid work.

The claimant is expected to take reasonable steps to minimise the losses suffered as a consequence of the unlawful act. The burden of proving a failure to mitigate is on the respondent (*Fyfe v Scientific Furnishing Ltd* [1989] IRLR 331). It is insufficient for a respondent merely to show that the claimant failed to take a step that it was reasonable for them to take: rather, they have to show that any such failure was *unreasonable* (*Wright v Silverline Car Caledonia Ltd* UKEATS/0008/16). The tribunal will consider:

1) what steps the claimant should have taken to mitigate his or her losses;

2) whether it was *un*reasonable for the claimant to have failed to take any such steps; and

3) if so, the date from which an alternative income would have been obtained.

The duty arises only after dismissal, so a failure to take up an alternative job offer made before that date will not constitute a failure to mitigate. It may be reasonable to attempt to mitigate loss by setting up a new business or becoming self-employed (see *Cooper Contracting Ltd v Lindsey* UKEAT/0184/15/JOJ and *Gardiner-Hill v Roland Berger Technics Ltd* [1982] IRLR 498) or by retraining (see *Sealy v Avon Aluminium Co Ltd* UKEAT/515/78, *Holroyd v Gravure Cylinders Ltd* [1984] IRLR 259 and *Orthet Ltd v Vince-Cain* [2004] IRLR 857).

Mitigation and 'good industrial relations practice': an unfairly dismissed employee will not need to give credit for earnings received from a new job during the notice period where good industrial relations practice would have required payment in lieu of notice to the employee (see *Norton Tool Co Ltd v Tewson* [1973] All ER 183 and *Voith Turbo Ltd v Stowe* [2005] IRLR 228). However, the principle does not apply to constructive dismissal (*Stuart Peters Ltd v Bell* [2009] IRLR 941).

Mitigation and receipt of pension: In *Knapton v ECC Card Clothing Ltd* [2006] IRLR 756 the EAT held that credit does not need to be given for the early receipt of pension following dismissal, as it is deferred wages not a sum analogous to incapacity benefit which would be brought into account. However, if an individual is dismissed after the date when the pension can be drawn and there is no reduction in the value of the pension by being drawn at dismissal, it may be that a failure to draw the pension would be seen as a failure to mitigate a loss, and a sum for which the ex-employer should receive credit.

Money purchase: see Pension loss

National Insurance Contributions

An unemployed person may receive Class 1 National Insurance credits to fill any gaps in their national insurance contributions (these contributions are automatically made if the person claims JSA). However, s7(1) of The Social Security (Unemployment, Sickness and Invalidity Benefit) Regulations 1983 SI 1983/1598 states that if the person has received compensation for unfair dismissal, they are not entitled to receive national insurance contributions for the same period. If the person is unemployed for a long time, this could affect their entitlement to a state pension and other state benefits. The loss of NI contributions can therefore be claimed from the employer as a head of loss. The amount of compensation is fixed by reference to the weekly Class 3 NIC rate (see Table 21).

Remedy: Compensation per week = weekly Class 3 NIC rate (see Table 21).

Limit on a week's pay: The class 3 rate

Limit on number of weeks: None

Any maximum or minimum: None

Adjustments: Loss of NIC will form part of the compensatory award or damages and thus will be adjusted along with these awards.

Recoupment: Recoupment does not apply to this head of loss.

Statutory authorities: Social Security (Unemployment, Sickness and Invalidity Benefit) Regulations 1983 (SI 1983/1598) Reg 7(1)

National Living Wage: see National Minimum Wage

National Minimum Wage

(see also Unlawful deductions from wages; Table 27)

A broad range of workers are entitled to receive the national minimum wage. The rate depends upon the age of the worker and whether they qualify for an apprentice rate or, if an agricultural worker, the agricultural minimum wage (see Table 27). Calculating the pay received for the purposes of assessing whether the national minimum wage has been paid may in some cases be complex. An employer must keep sufficient records to show that workers who qualify have been paid the national minimum wage (Reg 38(1) NMWR and s9 and s31 NMWA), and a worker is entitled to inspect those records (s10 NMWA 1998).

There are four main routes by which an individual may enforce NMW rights:

1) A worker may bring a claim to the ET for unlawful deductions from wages (s17 NMWR 1998) (see *Unlawful deductions from wages*);

2) It is automatically unfair to dismiss a worker because he has asserted his right to the NMW or might qualify for the NMW (s104A ERA 1996) (see *Unfair dismissal*);

3) Under section 23(1) NMWA 1998, a worker has the right not to be subjected to any detriment by any act or failure to act for specified reasons relating to the NMW (see *Detriment*);

4) A worker may bring a claim to the ET that his or her employer has refused access to records in accordance with s10 NMWA 1998 (s11 NMWA 1998).

Living accommodation

When an employer charges a worker for living accommodation the charge must be taken into account by comparing it to the worker's accommodation offset calculated using the accommodation offset rate (currently £6.40 per day or £44.80 per week). If the charge is higher than the accommodation offset, then any excess amount above the accommodation offset will reduce the worker's national minimum wage pay.

If the accommodation charge is at or below the offset rate, it does not have an effect on the worker's pay.

If the accommodation is free, the offset rate is added to the worker's pay.

No other kind of company benefit (eg food, a car, childcare vouchers) count towards the National Minimum Wage.

Penalty for not paying NMW

HMRC can impose a penalty on employers if they are found not to have paid the NMW. Penalties for non-payment were doubled from 1 April 2016, from 100% of arrears owed to 200%, although these will be halved if paid within 14 days. The maximum penalty will remain £20,000 per worker.

Remedy for failing to pay the NMW

If a worker who is entitled to be paid the NMW is paid less than the NMW, the worker is entitled to be paid the difference between the relevant remuneration received by the worker for the pay reference period; and the relevant remuneration which the worker would have received for that period had he been remunerated by the employer at a rate equal to the NMW (s17 National Minimum Wage Act 1998).

Living accommodation provided by the employer should be taken into account when assessing the employer's liability (see ss30(d) and 36(1) National Minimum Wage Regulations 1999 and *Eastern Eye (Plymouth) Ltd v Hassan & Anor* UKEAT/0383/14/DA).

Remedy for refusal to permit access to records

Where a tribunal finds a complaint under s11 well founded, it will make a declaration to that effect and will make an award of 80 times the hourly minimum wage in force at the date when the award is made (s11(2) NMWA 1998).

Gross or net: Gross

Tax: It is likely that this award will not be subject to tax, and should be characterised as a punishment or fine, not earnings or a payment connected to termination.

Statutory authorities: NMWA 1998 ss10 and 11

Net weekly pay

(see also *Gourley* principle; Gross weekly pay; Week's pay)

This is the figure used to calculate the actual net loss to the claimant in a number of awards. This will often be the gross weekly pay less tax and NI, and may also be less employer's pension contributions and other benefits if the value of the loss of those benefits is calculated separately, which is often the approach used. Some awards are calculated on gross weekly pay, for example where an employer is ordered to pay unpaid remuneration (where tax will be deducted at source upon payment in the usual way). The following awards use net weekly pay as the basis of the loss:

- Compensatory award;

- Damages for wrongful dismissal;

- Financial losses suffered as a result of unlawful discrimination.

Non-recoupable state benefits

(see also Recoupment)

The state benefits of job seekers allowance and income support, income-related employment support allowance and universal credit are subject to recoupment under the Employment Protection (Recoupment of Jobseeker's Allowance and Income Support) Regulations 1996 (SI 1996/2349). The Regulations provide that, where a monetary award is made by the tribunal, it must identify any part of that award that constitutes the prescribed element (past loss of earnings) and the period to which it relates.

Other benefits, benefits awarded outside of the 'prescribed period', or benefits received in relation to awards that do not fall within the recoupment provisions are non-recoupable benefits.

Normal retirement date

(see also Pension loss; Tables 32 and 33)

There is no longer a normal retirement age as between employers and their employees (see Employment Equality (Repeal of Retirement Age Provisions) Regulations 2011/1069). Any dismissal on grounds of age will be discriminatory, subject to any justification defence, and so far as unfair dismissal is concerned the usual protections, regardless of age, will apply. However, pension scheme rules may specify a normal age at which employees are able to begin to receive a pension, and some schemes may make provision for earlier receipt of benefits.

Normal working hours: see Week's pay

Notice pay

(see also Breach of contract; Contractual notice period; Effective date of termination; Garden leave; Statutory notice period; Table 26)

If an employee gives or is given notice of termination of their employment, they will usually be entitled to their normal pay during this period of notice. Four general approaches can be taken to whether the individual works their notice period and how they are paid:

1) The employee works their notice and gets paid their normal wage;

2) The employee is placed on garden leave, in which case they do not actually work during their notice but the employment contract is still in force and they get paid as normal;

3) The employee does not work their notice period, the contract is terminated earlier, and instead receives a payment equivalent to what would have been earned during this period (payment in lieu of notice or PILON);

4) The employee does not work during the notice period, and does not get paid all or some of their normal wage for the notice period.

In the fourth example, the employee may be entitled to compensation for breach of the obligation to be paid under the contract.

Occupational pension scheme: see Pension loss

Order of adjustments: see Adjustments and order of adjustments

Overtime: see Compensatory award; Holiday pay; Week's pay; Appendix 3: Calculating holiday entitlement

Parental leave

(see also Detriment)

Prior to 5 April 2015, parents with at least one year's service were permitted to take up to 18 weeks' unpaid leave before a child's 5th birthday (or before the child's 18th birthday if the child is disabled). From 5 April 2015, the period during which the entitlement may be taken was extended to allow 18 weeks' unpaid leave to be taken by qualifying employees before a child's 18th birthday in all cases and not just those where the child is disabled.

A system of Shared Parental Leave applies to births and adoptions from 5 April 2015 onwards and replaces the pre-existing additional paternity leave regime.

An employee may present a complaint to an employment tribunal that his employer:

a) has unreasonably postponed a period of parental leave requested by the employee; or

b) has prevented or attempted to prevent the employee from taking parental leave (s80 ERA 1996).

Remedy: By s80(4) ERA 1996 the amount of compensation shall be such as the tribunal considers just and equitable in all the circumstances having regard to:

a) the employer's behaviour; and

b) any loss sustained by the employee which is attributable to the matters complained of.

Gross or net: Whether this is paid gross or net will depend on whether payment amounts to earnings or some other loss.

Limit on a week's pay: None

Limit on number of weeks: No, except in relation to the amount of leave the employee is entitled to by statute.

Any maximum or minimum: None

Adjustments: None

Tax: The tax treatment of any award is unclear. To the extent that the sum awarded is compensation for lost earnings, it is likely to be taxed under s62 ITEPA 2003 (see *Tax and termination payments*).

Recoupment: N/A

Statutory authorities: ERA 1996 s80

Part-time worker protection

A worker working part time has the right not to be treated by his employer less favourably than the employer treats a comparable permanent employee, on the ground that the worker is a part time worker, either as regards the terms of his contract; or by being subjected to any other detriment by any act, or deliberate failure to act, of his employer. Less favourable treatment will be permitted where it can be objectively justified. In assessing whether a part time worker has been less favourably treated, the tribunal will apply the pro rata principle unless that is inappropriate (Reg 5 PTW(PLFT) Regs 2000).

A worker has the right to request written reasons for any treatment which he or she considers might infringe the Reg 5 right, and is entitled to be provided with such a statement within 21 days of the request (Reg 6(1)).

Reg 7 establishes automatic unfair dismissal and detriment protections for the actions of individuals related to exercising and enforcing their Reg 5 and 6 rights (see *Unfair dismissal* and *Detriment*).

A worker may present a complaint to the tribunal that a right conferred on him or her by Reg 5 has been infringed (Reg 8(1)).

Remedy: Where a tribunal upholds a complaint that a worker has been subject to less favourable treatment, the tribunal may take any of the following steps as it considers just and equitable (Reg 8(7)):

- make a declaration as to the rights of the complainant and the employer in relation to the complaint;

- order the employer to pay compensation to the complainant;

- make a recommendation that the employer take certain steps to obviate or reduce any relevant adverse effect.

Where compensation is awarded the amount will be that which the tribunal considers just and equitable in all the circumstances (this phrase is used in the assessment of the compensatory award for unfair dismissal and similar principles will apply). The tribunal will have regard to the infringement and any loss which is attributable to it. Losses suffered by the complainant will be taken to include any expenses reasonably incurred as a consequence of the infringement and the loss of any benefit he would have had but for the infringement (see Regs 8(9) and (10)). The common law principles of mitigation apply and the tribunal may reduce any award for contributory fault (Reg 8(13)).

There is no right to compensation for injury to feelings where there has been infringement of the right not to be less favourably treated under Reg 5 (however, an award for detriment under Reg 7 may include such an award (see *Detriment* and *Injury to feelings*).

If an employer fails, without reasonable justification, to comply with a recommendation (see above), the tribunal may make an award of compensation if it has not already done so, or increase an award of compensation it has already made (Reg 8(14)).

Gross or net: This will depend on whether the sums paid are treated as suppressed wages, an award for discrimination or injury to feelings (see *Tax* below within this entry). Where a sum is paid to represent a net loss it will be calculated on the net figure and grossed up where appropriate to make the final award. Where the sum is viewed as suppressed wages the award will be calculated on gross earnings, with the employer deducting tax and NI.

Any maximum or minimum: No, there is no statutory cap.

Adjustments: A percentage deduction for contributory conduct can be applied (Reg 8(13)). Also, if the employer fails to comply with a tribunal's recommendation, any award may be increased (Reg 8(14)).

Mitigation: The usual principles of mitigation apply.

Tax: Any payment to compensate for an employee's reduced wages or benefits would probably be classed as arrears of pay and taxed under s62 ITEPA 2003 in the normal way (see EIM02550 and EIM02530, HMRC). The tax to be paid should be calculated according to the tax year in which the pay was withheld, not the tax year in which the repayment is made.

However, EIM12965 of the Employment Income Manual states that payments of compensation for discrimination which occurs before termination is not employment income for the purposes of s401 and that they are therefore not taxable. It is arguable that the award for infringement of Reg 5 would not be subject to tax as it would be compensation for discrimination (in its broadest sense).

Statutory authorities: PTW(PLFT) Regs 2000 Regs 5 to 8

Paternity leave: see Detriment; SPP table; Unfair dismissal

Payment in lieu of notice (PILON)

(See also Effective date of termination; Tax and termination payments)

Where an employee's employment contract is terminated and the employee does not work a notice period, but instead receives a payment equivalent to what would have been earned during that period, this is often described as a payment in lieu of notice or a 'PILON'. It is not the same as payment during 'gardening leave', where the employee is still in employment during the notice period, even though he or she is not present at work.

There are four types of PILON:

- Contractual PILON, where the payment is made under an express contractual term (or occasionally an implied term);

- Automatic PILON, where payment is made as an automatic response by the employer to termination;

- Discretionary PILON, where payment is made under a discretionary power provided by a contractual term; and

- PILONs paid as compensation for breach of contractual entitlement to notice.

If the contract provides that termination can be achieved by making a payment in lieu of notice, the amount to be paid is a matter of the interpretation of the contract.

The employment contract is terminated when the terms of the PILON clause have been satisfied (such as payment being received by the employee), with the EDT being the date of termination of the contract (see *Société Générale, London Branch v Geys* [2013] IRLR 122).

If there is no contractual provision for PILON, a termination of employment with PILON is likely to be a breach of the employment contract. The value of the PILON sufficient to cover an employee's right to damages will be determined by what the terms of the contract establish the employee would have been entitled to receive had they been given their proper notice.

PILON is taxable as earnings if it has been provided for in a contract, or its payment is automatic (but see below). If the payment is made as damages, it will be taxable under s401 ITEPA 2003 (which is subject to a £30,000 exemption – see *Tax and termination payments*).

From April 2018
The Government proposed that, from April 2018, all payments in lieu of notice (PILONs) would be taxable as earnings, whether or not there is a right to make the payment in a contract of employment However, the calling of the snap election meant that this measure was removed from the Finance Act 2017 in the wash-up period. The view of the Chartered Institute of Taxation is that a significant amount of the Bill would be re-enacted irrespective of who wins the election.

Penalty for leaving pension scheme early: see Pension loss

Pension loss

(see also Ogden Tables 15 to 27)

Following the withdrawal of the 2003 edition of 'Compensation for Loss of Pension Rights: Employment Tribunals', a working party of Employment Judges was set up to provide guidelines for the calculation of pension loss. At the time of writing these guidelines have not yet been published although they are expected in July or August 2017. They will be called "Principles" for calculating pension loss. This entry will explain how it is proposed that the loss of pension under a defined contribution scheme and under a defined benefit scheme could be calculated.

Loss of State Pension

The starting position is that the retirement date will be the earlier of (a) state pension age or (b) the age at which a claimant would be entitled to significant benefits from an occupational pension scheme. In most cases it is assumed that there will be no loss of state pension rights. This includes additional state pension rights (S2P), which have now been withdrawn. If a tribunal decides it is appropriate to award a sum for loss of state pension rights, the Ogden Tables will be used.

Defined Contribution (DC or money purchase) schemes
Method of calculation
Where the claimant has lost benefits from a DC scheme, pension loss will be calculated on the basis of lost employer contributions as follows:

- obtain details of the claimant's pay and employer contributions (the tribunal may assume auto-enrolment levels if there is no evidence);

- identify the date at which the period of loss ends;

- calculate the employer contributions to the remedy hearing (no recoupment);

- calculate the future loss of employer contributions (taking account of future pay rises);

- credit any employer contributions made by a new employer against the award (again the tribunal may assume auto-enrolment with new employer, rebuttable by evidence).

There is no loss by reason of lost facility to make Additional Voluntary Contributions.

Defined Benefit (DB or final salary) schemes
There are two methods of calculation depending on the complexity of the case.

Simple cases
These could include cases where a *Polkey* type terminal date for loss of benefits is appropriate, or where the value of the loss is academic because the compensation cap will apply.

Method of calculation
There will usually be no award for loss of enhancement of accrued pension rights. The pension loss in simple cases should be calculated according to loss of contributions as for DC schemes as follows:

- obtain details of the employer's contribution rate (which could be an average for scheme members);

- identify the date at which the period of loss ends;

- calculate the employer contributions to the remedy hearing (no recoupment) by applying the average employer contribution rate to the claimant's gross salary at EDT;

- calculate the future loss of employer contributions in the same way (taking account of future pay rises);

- credit any employer contributions made by a new employer against the award (again the tribunal may assume auto-enrolment with the new employer, rebuttable by evidence).

Complex cases
These cases are typically career long loss cases, or where the losses are significant and the compensation cap does not apply.

Case management
Cases which could be described as complex should be identified at an early stage and parties should include a pension loss element on the schedule of loss at the start of the process i.e. before any liability is found. Use of expressions such as "to be confirmed" will be discouraged.

For complex cases, there will be a split liability and remedy hearing, the remedy hearing being in two stages:

1) The first stage will make findings of fact and identify the non-pension losses.

2) The second stage will identify the pension loss, either by using Ogden tables or expert actuarial evidence.

Calculation
There could be two types of loss to be considered: loss of annual pension and loss of a lump sum. The

Ogden Tables provide multipliers which are applied to the multiplicand for calculating loss of earnings and pension loss for different categories of people.

Essentially, the **multiplier** is the number of years for which the loss will be incurred and will depend on the sex, age at EDT, retirement age of the claimant, and the current rate of return. The multipliers have been calculated with reference to 2008 mortality rates for the population at large – these rates are not the same as for the population in DB schemes. A two-year mortality adjustment to both age and date of retirement will therefore need to be applied (see below).

The **multiplicand** is the present-day value of the future loss of annual pension.

For the purposes of pension loss in employment we are concerned only with tables 15 to 26 (for annual pension loss) and table 27 (for pension lump sums).

Method of calculation loss of annual pension using Ogden tables
The calculation of pension loss is as follows:

- Identify the multiplicand. This is:

   the annual pension that would have been paid at retirement if the claimant had not been dismissed

   minus

   the annual pension they will now receive, taking account of withdrawal factors.

- Identify the multiplier according to tables 15 to 26 (depending on retirement age and gender).

- Identify the age of the claimant at the date of the remedy hearing (the numbers down the side) and the claimant's retirement age with a two-year mortality adjustment both to age and the date of retirement. For example, if the claimant is 45 with a retirement age of 67, the adjusted age is 43 and the adjusted retirement age is 65. Interpolation methods should be used where necessary if the retirement age falls between the five-year intervals (see below).

- Choose the rate of return (the percentages across the top). The -0.75% column should be used.

- Multiply the multiplicand by the multiplier to obtain the capitalised value of the lost pension, subject to any further adjustment the tribunal considers appropriate.

Lump sums
At retirement, claimants could receive either (i) a commuted lump sum (i.e. a lump sum in return for

giving up some of their annual pension) or (ii) a non-commuted lump sum (i.e. one where the annual pension is not reduced). It may be appropriate to apply a discount factor, using Ogden Table 27, to any lost non-commuted lump sum to reflect the fact that it is being received early (any lost commuted lump sum will be ignored as this will already have been factored in when calculating annual pension loss).

Calculation method
The calculation of loss of lump sum is as follows:

- Identify the multiplicand. This is:

   the lump sum that would have been paid at retirement if the claimant had not been dismissed

   minus

   the lump sum they will now receive, taking account of withdrawal factors.

- Identify the number of years between dismissal and retirement date. This is the number down the side of Table 27.

- Identify the discount rate (along the top, which is currently -0.75%).

- Find the appropriate multiplier.

- Multiply the multiplicand by the multiplier to find the present capital value of that loss.

For example, if the lump sum loss is £5,000 and the number of years to retirement is 25, the capital value of that loss will be:

£5,000 x 1.2071 = £6,035.50

Interpolating between pension ages
The Ogden Tables only list multiplying factors for retirement ages of 50, 55, 60, 65, 70 and 75. However, in a particular case it may be appropriate to use a retirement age of, for example, 62 and it will be necessary to interpolate between 2 values. Using the guidance from the Ogden Tables the following calculations could be used – in this worked example the male claimant is age 47 at dismissal and his retirement age is 62 (assuming the two-year mortality adjustment has been applied and a rate of -0.75% is being used):

1) A retirement age of 62 falls between 60 and 65. In our case the person is 15 years from retirement so, assuming the same number of years to retirement, work out the ages of people who would retire at 60 and 65. They would be 45 and 50 respectively.

2) Look up from Ogden Table 19 the factors for retirement for men at age 60 (age at dismissal being 45) and from Ogden Table 21 the factors for retirement for men at age 65 (age at dismissal being 50). They are 32.85 and 26.15 respectively.

3) Work out the difference between the retirement age of the claimant and age 60 (which is 2) and between 65 (which is 3).

4) Multiply the factor applying to the younger retirement age (32.85) by 3 and the factor applying to the older retirement age (26.15) by 2 and add them together to get $32.85 \times 3 + 26.15 \times 2 = 150.85$

5) Finally, divide by the difference between 65 and 60 to get $150.85 \div 5 = 30.17$

30.17 is the factor to be applied.

Perks: see Financial losses

Permanent employment: see Damages for wrongful dismissal

Physical and psychiatric injury

(see also Discrimination; Interest)

Claimants can claim damages for personal injury caused by unlawful discriminatory acts including detriment for whistleblowing (see *Sheriff v Klyne Tugs (Lowestoft) Ltd* [1999] IRLR 481 and *Virgo Fidelis Senior School v Boyle* [2004] IRLR 268). However, it is not always easy to identify where injury to feelings ends and physical and psychiatric injury starts and there is a risk of double counting.

Although there is no absolute requirement for medical evidence to establish a claim for personal injury in employment tribunals, obtaining such evidence is advisable where possible, especially where claims are complex and there are issues over causation or divisibility (*Hampshire County Council v Wyatt* UKEAT/0013/16).

Divisible and Indivisible Harm

In some cases, issues may arise where a claimant has suffered an injury through multiple causes. In such cases, the tribunal will need to consider whether the harm is 'divisible' or 'indivisible'.

Divisible Harm is where different acts cause *different* damage, or *quantifiable parts* of the damage. In these cases, the tribunal must establish

and award compensation only for that part of the harm for which the respondent is truly responsible.

Indivisible Harm is where multiple acts result in the *same* damage, either:

> *Monocausally:* where all of the acts operate in the same way to cause the damage, only one act could have actually caused the damage, but it is impossible to tell which of them was the actual cause; or

> *Multicausally:* where a single condition or harm is caused by a combination of separate acts or factors. For example, where the cumulative effect of their separate acts crosses a threshold that gives rise to that damage, or distinct acts combine to produce a single form of damage.

If the harm is indivisible, any respondent whose act has been the proximate cause of the injury must compensate for the *whole* of it. That others had a part to play in the injury is a matter for *contribution*, not apportionment.

Whether an injury is divisible or indivisible will depend on evidence, but it is '*more likely that an injury will be held to be indivisible if the competing causes are closely related to the injury and it is difficult to separate out the consequences*' (*Olayemi v Athena Medical Centre & Anor* UKEAT/0140/15, paragraph. 25).

Remedy: When it comes to the assessment of damages in relation to a proven psychiatric injury, tribunals are '*obliged to approach the assessment of damages for psychiatric injury on the same basis as a common law court in an ordinary action for personal injuries*' (*HM Prison Service v Salmon* [2001] IRLR 425).

The Judicial College has published guidelines for the assessment of general damages in personal injury cases. According to the College, the following factors need to be taken into account when valuing claims of psychiatric injury:

a) the injured person's ability to cope with life and work;

b) the effect on the injured person's relationships with family, friends and those with whom he comes into contact;

c) the extent to which treatment would be successful;

d) future vulnerability;

e) prognosis;

f) whether medical help has been sought;

g) whether the injury results from sexual

and/or physical abuse and/or breach of trust; and if so, the nature of the relationship between victim and abuser, the nature of the abuse, its duration and the symptoms caused by it.

There are 4 categories of award:

a) Less Severe: between £1,170 and £4,450 (£1,290 and £4,900 including *Simmons v Castle* uplift). Where the claimant has suffered temporary symptoms that have adversely affected daily activities;

b) Moderate: between £4,450 and £14,500 (£4,900 and £15,950 including uplift). Where, while the claimant has suffered problems as a result of the discrimination, marked improvement has been made by the date of the hearing and the prognosis is good;

c) Moderately Severe: between £14,500 and £41,675 (£15,950 and £45,840 including uplift). Moderately severe cases include those where there is work-related stress resulting in a permanent or long-standing disability preventing a return to comparable employment. These are cases where there are problems with factors a) to d) above, but there is a much more optimistic prognosis than Severe;

d) Severe: between £41,675 and £88,000 (£45,840 and £96,800 including uplift). Where the claimant has serious problems in relation to the factors at a) to d) above, and the prognosis is poor.

Separate criteria apply for cases of Post-Traumatic Stress Disorder, and the Guidelines should be consulted accordingly in an appropriate case.

Any maximum or minimum: Only so far as the guidelines have suggested.

Adjustments:

Causation: The award can be adjusted to allow for the extent to which the act of discrimination caused the illness. So, if it is found that the discriminatory act caused the illness to the extent of 30%, the award will be reduced by 70%.

Double counting: Injury to feelings and physical and psychiatric injury are distinct heads of loss, but care should be taken that no double counting has taken place. Either one could be reduced if this is the case.

Discount rate: Where an employee suffers a life-changing personal injury resulting in long-term loss of earnings, the discount rate is applied to reflect early receipt. As of 2017, that rate is now -0.75% (see also ***Accelerated/decelerated receipt***).

Interest: Interest could also be awarded (see *Interest*).

Simmons v Castle uplift: The award should be increased by 10% (see *De Souza v Vinci Construction (UK) Ltd* [2017] EWCA Civ 879 paragraph 26) .

Mitigation: N/A

Tax: Awards for injury are exempted from tax under s406 ITEPA 2003 (see *Tax and termination payments*).

Recoupment: N/A

Relevant case law: *De Souza v Vinci Construction (UK) Ltd* [2017] EWCA Civ 879; *HM Prison Service v Salmon* [2001] IRLR 425; *Sheriff v Klyne Tugs (Lowestoft) Ltd* [1999] IRLR 481; *Virgo Fidelis Senior School v Boyle* [2004] IRLR 268

Polkey

(see also Adjustments)

A '*Polkey*' deduction is the phrase used in unfair dismissal cases to describe the reduction in any award for future loss to reflect the chance that the individual would have been dismissed fairly in any event (*Polkey v AE Dayton Services Ltd* [1987] IRLR 50 (HL)).

This may take the form of a percentage reduction, or it may take the form of a tribunal making a finding that the individual would have been dismissed fairly after a further period of employment (for example a period in which a fair procedure would have been completed). Alternatively a combination of the two approaches could be used, but not in the same period of loss (as confirmed in *Zebrowski v Concentric Birmingham Ltd* UKEAT/0245/16/DA)). The question for the tribunal is whether the *particular employer* (as opposed to a hypothetical reasonable employer) would have dismissed the claimant in any event had the unfairness not occurred.

There are useful reviews of the case law (which is not without its difficulties) in *V v Hertfordshire County Council and another* UKEAT/0427/14/LA and *Contract Bottling Ltd v Cave & Anor* UKEAT/0100/14/DM).

The *Polkey* adjustment is only applicable to the compensatory award, not the basic award (apart from in very limited circumstances where such a (fair) dismissal might have taken place virtually contemporaneously with the unfair dismissal which actually occurred, presumably applying s122(2) ERA 1996 - see *Granchester Construction (Eastern) Ltd v Attrill* UKEAT/0327/12/LA, paragraph 19). A similar approach to a *Polkey* deduction is taken in discrimination cases where the tribunal will assess the chance that a particular future loss has been suffered (see *Loss of chance*).

The tribunal must assess any *Polkey* deduction in two respects:

1) If a fair process had occurred, would it have affected when the claimant would have been dismissed? and

2) What is the percentage chance that a fair process would still have resulted in the claimant's dismissal?

Where there is a significant overlap between the factors taken into account in making a *Polkey* deduction and when making a deduction for contributory conduct, the ET should consider expressly, whether in the light of that overlap, it is just and equitable to make a finding of contributory conduct, and, if so, what its amount should be. This is to avoid the risk of penalizing the claimant twice for the same conduct (see *Lenlyn UK Ltd v Kular* UKEAT/0108/16/DM)).

Relevant case law: Contract Bottling Ltd v Cave & Anor UKEAT/0100/14/DM; *Granchester Construction (Eastern) Ltd v Attrill* UKEAT/0327/12/LA; *Lenlyn UK Ltd v Kular* UKEAT/0108/16/DM; *Polkey v AE Dayton Services Ltd* [1987] IRLR 50 (HL); *V v Hertfordshire County Council and another* UKEAT/0427/14/LA; *Zebrowski v Concentric Birmingham Ltd* UKEAT/0245/16/DA

Pregnancy: see Discrimination; Time off for ante-natal care

Prescribed element: see Recoupment

Prescribed period: see Recoupment

Presidential guidance on remedy

Appendix 1 reproduces paragraphs 1 to 25 of the Presidential Guidance on Remedy issued on 14 March 2014. This sets out in easily readable form the tribunal's procedure and expectations for dealing with remedy. The tribunal will expect parties to comply with the guidance.

Profit related bonus: see Financial losses; Bonuses

Protected act: see Discrimination

Protected disclosure

**(see also Detriment; Unfair dismissal*)*

Where an employee has suffered a detriment, or has been dismissed, for making a protected disclosure, the tribunal may award financial compensation.

The right to bring a claim for detriment is established by s47B ERA 1996, and the right to not be unfairly dismissed for the sole or principal reason of making a protected disclosure is established by s103A ERA 1996.

For detriment (not dismissal) the tribunal must award such an amount as it considers is just and equitable having regard to:

1) the infringement to which the complaint relates;

2) any loss which is attributable to the act, or failure to act, which infringed the claimant's right (s49(2) ERA 1996).

If the employee has been dismissed, awards can be made for unfair dismissal (see *Additional award; Basic award; Compensatory award; Unfair dismissal*)

Remedy: For detriment (not dismissal) the loss to be compensated shall be taken to include: any expenses reasonably incurred by the claimant in consequence of the act, or failure to act, to which the complaint relates; and loss of any benefit which the claimant might reasonably be expected to have had but for the act or failure to act (s49(3) ERA 1996).

Such a detriment award may also include compensation for injury to feelings. Where a worker has brought the claim under s47B and the detriment is termination of the contract, which is akin to a claim for unfair dismissal of an employee, it is arguable that injury to feelings may be awarded, but only up to the amount of a basic award (see *Injury to feelings*). Compensation for injury to feelings is not available in an award for unfair dismissal.

Gross or net: If the claimant has been dismissed, see the individual awards for unfair dismissal. Otherwise, it will be a figure that the tribunal considers just and equitable (see *Detriment*).

Any maximum or minimum: The award is unlimited unless the detriment is termination of the contract of a worker when any compensation must not exceed the compensation that would be payable if the worker had been an employee and had been dismissed for making a protected disclosure (there is currently no limit to such financial losses) (s49(6) ERA 1996).

Adjustments: If the tribunal considers that the act or failure to act was caused or contributed to by action of the claimant, it may reduce the award if it thinks that it would be just and equitable to do so (ss49(4) and (5) ERA 1996).

The tribunal can also reduce the award of compensation by up to 25% if they find that any disclosure occurring after 25 June 2013 was not made in good faith.

Cap: The statutory cap on unfair dismissal does not apply if the employee has been dismissed as a result of making the protected disclosure, and there is no statutory cap if the claim is for detriment.

Mitigation: The tribunal may reduce the amount if it considers that the claimant has failed to mitigate his/her loss.

Tax: The award will be taxable under s401 ITEPA 2003 if the employee has been dismissed, although the tax treatment is unclear in the case of an employee who receives a payment because of suffering detriment but is still employed (see *Detriment; Tax and termination payments*).

Recoupment: Recoupment will only apply to unfair dismissal awards.

Statutory authorities: ERA 1996 ss49 and 103A

Protective award

Where an employer is proposing to dismiss as redundant 20 or more employees at one establishment within a period of 90 days or less, the employer shall consult about the dismissals all the persons who are appropriate representatives of any of the employees who may be affected by the proposed dismissals or may be affected by measures taken in connection with those dismissals (s188 and s188A TULR(C)A 1992).

The consultation shall begin in good time and in any event:

a) where the employer is proposing to dismiss 100 or more employees, at least 45 days; and

b) otherwise, at least 30 days,

before the first of the dismissals takes effect.

Note that, for dismissals before 6 April 2013, the number of days referred to in a) above was 90, not 45.

Where it is alleged that an employer has failed to comply with the consultation requirements the appropriate representatives, or in some limited situations an affected employee, may bring a complaint to a tribunal who, if the complaint is well founded, shall make a declaration to that effect and may make a 'protective award' covering the employees affected by the failure.

The protective award is remuneration for the 'protected period', of up to 90 days.

If the employer is insolvent, the employees may make a claim to the National Insurance Fund for payment of some (or in some cases all) of this award (see *Insolvency*).

Remedy (1): Under TULR(C)A 1992 s189(3), (4) and s190 the tribunal may make an award of up to 90 days' pay, with the length of the period determined by what is just and equitable in all the circumstances having regard to the seriousness of the employer's failure to comply with TULR(C)A 1992 s188. The award is calculated as starting on the day the first dismissals took effect. The award will identify the description of employees to whom it applies, who will be those employees whose representative has not been consulted properly.

The rate of remuneration payable is a week's pay for each week of the protected period; and remuneration in respect of a period less than one week shall be calculated by reducing proportionally the amount of a week's pay (s190(2)).

A day's pay is found by dividing the employee's actual gross weekly pay by 7.

The principles for determining the size of a protective award are set out in *Susie Radin Ltd v GMB & Ors* [2004] ICR 893. The award is designed to be punitive, not to compensate the employee for losses suffered, with the calculation starting at 90 days where there has been no consultation and being reduced to reflect the seriousness of the breach and any mitigating factors. It is important to remember that, even if the consultation period is only 30 days, the starting point and maximum protected period is still 90 days.

Remedy (2): If the employer fails to comply with s190 by not paying an employee within the description the amount due under the award, the employee may bring a complaint to the tribunal who may order the employer to pay the amount of remuneration due (s192(1) and (3)).

Gross or net: Gross. A week's pay is as defined in ss220 to 229 ERA 1996 (see *Week's pay*). Part weeks are to be calculated pro rata. Only the basic pay should be taken into account and not any discretionary bonus (see *Canadian Imperial Bank of Commerce v Beck* UKEAT/0141/10/RN).

Limit on a week's pay: None. The limit on a week's pay does not apply.

Limit on number of days: 90.

An employee will be entitled to payment of the protective award from the date the protected period begins but will cease being entitled at the date he is fairly dismissed, unreasonably terminates his contract of employment or unreasonably refuses an offer of employment during the protected period (see s191 TULR(C)A 1992).

Any maximum or minimum: None

Adjustments: None

Cap: There is no cap on the award.

Mitigation: N/A, as the award is a sanction for breach, not compensation for losses suffered.

Tax: The award will be taxable under s401 ITEPA 2003 if the employee is no longer in employment (EIM02550, HMRC). Also, see *Mimtec Ltd v Inland Revenue* [2001] UKSC SPC00277 (see *Tax and termination payments*).

Recoupment: Yes, the prescribed element being any amount ordered to be paid to the employee in respect of so much of the relevant protected period as falls before the date of the conclusion of the tribunal proceedings (see Table 31).

Statutory authorities: ITEPA 2003 s401; The Employment Protection (Recoupment of Jobseeker's Allowance and Income Support) Regulations 1996; TULR(C)A 1992 ss189 and 190

Relevant case law: *Canadian Imperial Bank of Commerce v Beck* UKEAT/0141/10/RN; *Mimtec Ltd v Inland Revenue* [2001] UKSC SPC00277; *Susie Radin Ltd v GMB & Ors* [2004] ICR 893

Example

The claimant's gross weekly pay is £500 (which has been calculated in accordance with ss220 to 229 ERA as above) and is awarded 80 days' protective award.

A day's pay = 500/7 = £71.43 (note: the weekly pay must be divided by 7, not the number of days per week actually worked)

Thus, the protective award = £71.43 x 80 = £5,714.40

Qualifying period

(see also Effective date of termination)

This is the length of continuous employment (see s211 ERA 1996) that must have been worked by the claimant before a tribunal will consider any particular complaint. Different qualifying periods apply for different types of claim (see Table 30).

The employee's continuous employment begins with the day on which the employee starts work, and ends with the day by reference to which the length of the employee's period of continuous employment is to be ascertained for the purposes of the provision.

But, if an employee's period of continuous employment includes one or more periods which (by virtue of section 215, 216 or 217) while not counting in computing the length of the period do not break continuity of employment, the beginning of the period shall be treated as postponed by the number of days falling within that intervening period, or the aggregate number of days falling within those periods, calculated in accordance with the section in question.

Rate of pay: see Week's pay

Recoupment

(see also Non-recoupable state benefits)

A number of awards made by tribunals are subject to recoupment, whereby the state recovers from the respondent the value of certain state benefits paid to the claimant. This involves the tribunal identifying a part of the award that corresponds to a period of loss during which the claimant was in receipt of job seeker's allowance, income-related employment support allowance, income support or universal credit. The respondent is required to not pay the claimant the sum the tribunal identifies, but to wait until the DWP recoups from them any benefits paid, with the remainder then being paid to the claimant by the respondent. The principles to be applied are contained in the Employment Protection (Recoupment of Jobseeker's Allowance and Income Support) Regulations 1996 (SI 1996/2349).

The types of award which may be covered by the prescribed element (see below) are listed in Table 31, the most common awards being for unfair dismissal, failure to make a guarantee payment, failure to pay during a period of maternity or medical suspension and protective awards (see Column 1 of the Schedule to the regulations, and Reg 3(1)(a)).

The recoupment regulations do not apply if the claimant has not claimed the relevant benefits, or if the award is compensation for discrimination statutes or for dismissal by reason of redundancy.

The recoupment regulations do not apply to settlements – this may create an incentive to settle where, because the Secretary of State will not recoup the benefits paid, a smaller sum paid by the respondent than that which would be awarded by the tribunal may well result in a higher sum being received by the claimant.

Required information

The tribunal must in its judgment identify four items of information that will then be provided to the DWP: the amount of any 'prescribed element', the prescribed period, the total amount of the award and the balance. In essence, this will define the sum within any award from which the state may seek recoupment. No greater sum will be recouped, and the respondent will be ordered by the tribunal to pay the remainder to the claimant.

Prescribed element

The prescribed element is that part of the award which is held back from the claimant until the value of any state benefits subject to the recoupment procedures is known. It is defined in Reg 3(1)(a) and Column 3 of Schedule 1, and is that part of the monetary award attributable to loss of wages or arrears of pay or losses due to the claimant (including a protective award) for the period before the conclusion of the tribunal proceedings, or if it covers a protective award or award for failure to inform or consult under TUPE, up to the final day of the period covered by that protective award. The prescribed element does not include the figure that may have been awarded for loss of statutory rights, right to written particulars or the loss of benefits or pension.

The prescribed element will be reduced in line with any deduction for contributory fault that may have been made to the compensatory award. Further, the prescribed element will be reduced by the same proportion as the compensatory award when applying the statutory cap. For example, if the compensatory award has been reduced from £89,490 to the cap of £80,541 (that is, by 10%), the

prescribed element will also be reduced by 10% (see Reg 4(2)).

Prescribed period

The prescribed period is identified in column 3 of the Schedule to the regulations. For straightforward unfair dismissal claims the prescribed period is the period between the EDT and the date of the remedy hearing (or the date at which the tribunal sent the remedy judgment to the parties). For concurrent wrongful and unfair dismissal claims, since recoupment does not apply to the award for breach of contract, the prescribed period is the period between the end of the period over which damages have been awarded and the date of the hearing (or the date at which the parties were sent the remedy judgment).

Total award

This is the total of all the awards that have been made by the tribunal.

Balance

This is the difference between the total and the prescribed element and must be paid to the claimant.

Once the actual state benefits that are subject to recoupment are known, the DWP will claim this figure from the prescribed element retained by the respondent and any remaining monies must be paid by the employer to the employee.

Statutory authorities: Employment Protection (Recoupment of Jobseeker's Allowance and Income Support) Regulations 1996

Example 1 (where the statutory cap is not applicable)

Basic award = £500

Immediate loss of earnings = £2,000

Future loss of earnings = £700

Loss of statutory rights = £200

Contributory conduct of 20% applies to compensatory award only

Calculation

Prescribed element applies only to the immediate loss of earnings, i.e. £2,000

But this amount has been reduced by 20% and is now 2,000 x 0.8 = £1,600

Total award = 500 + 1,600 + 700 + 200 = £3,000

Prescribed element is therefore £1,600 which should be held back from the claimant. Balance payable immediately to claimant = 500 + 700 + 200 = £1,400, the other £1,600 being payable if the DWP does not serve a recoupment notice on the employer. If the DWP does serve a recoupment notice, and the value of the state benefits received by the claimant is, say, £500, the employer must pay £500 to the DWP and the remaining £1,100 to the claimant.

Example 2 (where adjustments have to be made for the statutory cap)

Basic award = £11,000

Compensatory award = £100,000, of which immediate loss = £30,000 and future loss is £70,000

Loss of statutory rights = £200

Contributory conduct of 20% applies to compensatory award only

Calculation

First, the basic award remains intact.

Secondly, the compensatory award AND the loss of statutory rights should be reduced for contributory conduct = (£100,000 + £200) x 0.8 = £80,160

Thirdly, a grossing up calculation needs to be performed:

Gross up £11,000 + £80,160 - £30,000 = £61,160

Grossing up £61,160 at, say, 20% = 61,160 ÷ 0.8 = £76,450

The compensatory award is now the remainder of £30,000 - £11,000 = £19,000 plus the grossed up figure of £76,450 which comes to £95,450. This will be capped at £80,541.

Before the contributory conduct and the cap, the compensatory award was £100,200, and after these adjustments the award was £80,541, so we need to calculate the proportion by which the compensatory award has been reduced as a result. The calculation is (100,200 − 80,541) x 100/100,200 = 19.6% approximately.

So, the prescribed element of £30,000 (i.e. the immediate loss) should be reduced by 19.6%. Therefore, the prescribed element = 30,000 (immediate loss) x 0.804 = £24,120.

Redundancy

An employee with 2 years' service is entitled to be paid a redundancy payment if he or she is dismissed by reason of redundancy, or eligible by reason of being laid off or kept on short-time (see s135 ERA 1996). An employee may also be entitled to an enhanced redundancy payment by virtue of an express, incorporated or implied term of their contract of employment.

Statutory redundancy pay (see also *Basic award*)

If an employee has been dismissed by reason of redundancy and has not been paid the statutory redundancy pay to which they are entitled, s163 ERA 1996 permits the employee to bring a claim to the tribunal, which may order the employer to pay such amount as it thinks appropriate to compensate the worker for any financial loss arising from this non-payment (s163(5)). However, the claimant is not entitled to receive both a redundancy payment and a basic award, and any redundancy pay already paid will reduce the basic award accordingly. If redundancy was not the real reason for dismissal, the redundancy payment will not be set off against any basic award (*Boorman v Allmakes Ltd* [1995] IRLR 553).

Calculation: The redundancy payment is calculated according to the employee's length of service, age and gross weekly pay (up to the specified limit) (s162 ERA 1996). The calculation is identical to that for working out the basic award.

The employee will receive 1 ½ weeks' gross pay for each year of employment in which they were not below the age of 41, 1 week's gross pay for each year of employment in which they were at some point below the age of 41 but not below the age of 22 and ½ a week's gross pay for each year of employment in which they were at any point below the age of 22. The maximum number of reckonable years is 20.

Limit on a week's pay: £489. A week's pay as defined in ss220 to 229 ERA 1996 applies (see *Week's pay* and Table 1 for historical rates).

Limit on the number of weeks: 30

Adjustments: The ACAS uplift does not apply. The 2015 ACAS Code of Practice states that it does not apply to redundancy dismissals, and therefore nor does the ACAS adjustment. *Holmes v Qinetiq Ltd* UKEAT/0206/15 confirms that the Code only applies to dismissals involving some form of '*culpable conduct*'.

The redundancy payment can be reduced or in certain circumstances withheld completely, for example if the employee commits an act of misconduct, leaves before the redundancy notice period has expired or the employee had taken part in a strike and refused to comply with a notice of extension served by the employer (see ss140 to 143 ERA 1996).

Mitigation: N/A

Tax: Any redundancy pay will be taxed under s401 ITEPA 2003 and therefore be counted towards the £30,000 tax free allowance.

Recoupment: N/A

Enhanced redundancy payment (awarded at tribunal)

An employee entitled to an enhanced redundancy payment may claim this from the tribunal.

Remedy: Any amount that the employee would have been entitled to over and above the statutory redundancy payment can be claimed.

Adjustments: Any enhanced redundancy payment will be part of the compensatory award and adjusted accordingly.

Cap: The statutory cap will apply to the whole of the compensatory award which includes any enhanced redundancy payment.

Tax: The enhanced redundancy payment, if awarded, will form part of the compensatory award and will be taxed under s401 ITEPA 2003 and therefore be counted towards the £30,000, tax free allowance.

Recoupment: Recoupment does not apply to any enhanced redundancy pay awarded.

Statutory authorities: ERA 1996 ss155, 162 and 163

Enhanced redundancy payment (paid on termination of employment)

The employee is not permitted to receive both a statutory redundancy payment and a basic award. The basic award will be reduced by the equivalent of the statutory redundancy payment made (s122(4) ERA 1996), and any enhanced redundancy payment that has been paid in excess of the statutory redundancy figure will go towards reducing the compensatory award (s123(7) ERA 1996). Note that the employer will enjoy the full benefit of any enhanced redundancy paid. In other words, any adjustments, such as contributory conduct, are made before the enhanced redundancy payment is taken off the compensatory award but interest will apply after the enhanced redundancy payment. The statutory cap is applied after the enhanced redundancy payment has been taken into account. It is important that the order is complied with, as in the following example:

Example 1

Compensatory award before adjustments = £50,000

After contributory conduct @ 10% has been applied, compensatory award = £45,000

Enhanced redundancy payment of £25,000 reduces the compensatory award to £20,000

Example 2 (where the redundancy pay received reduces the tax free sum available for other awards)

Redundancy payment received (tax free) = £5,000

The tax free sum available after the redundancy payment has been made is £30,000 - £5,000 = £25,000

Basic award = £11,000

Compensatory award = £40,000

The amount that should be grossed up = £11,000 + £40,000 - £25,000 = £26,000.

Statutory authorities: ERA 1996 ss122(4) and 123(7)

Re-engagement and reinstatement

(see also Additional award; Unfair dismissal)

When a claimant succeeds in an unfair dismissal claim the three remedies available are reinstatement, re-engagement and compensation (ss112-126 Employment Rights Act 1996)).

The tribunal is obliged to explain to a successful claimant the availability of these three orders (s112(2) ERA 1996) and ask them whether they wish the tribunal to make such an order. Although reinstatement and re-engagement are stated as the primary remedies for unfair dismissal, such orders are rarely granted in practice, with most cases resulting in an award of compensation only.

If the claimant has expressed a wish to be reinstated or re-engaged, and communicated that to the respondent not fewer than 7 days before the final hearing, the respondent is obliged to adduce reasonable evidence about the availability of the job from which the claimant was dismissed, or of comparable or suitable employment. If the respondent fails to do so without special reason, and this results in the postponement or adjournment of the final hearing, the tribunal is obliged to order that the respondent pay the costs incurred as a result of that postponement or adjournment (Employment Tribunals (Constitution and Rules of Procedure) Regulations 2013, r76(3)).

Reinstatement

This is an order that the employer shall treat the claimant in all respects as if they had not been dismissed (s114(1) ERA 1996).

The claimant is to be reinstated to the same contractual rights, terms and conditions as they had before they were dismissed, and the tribunal has no right to order reinstatement that alters the terms of the claimant's employment (although there is a limited right to change job duties insofar as this is not a change to the contract of employment) (*McBride v Scottish Police Authority* [2016] UKSC 27).

In making such an order the tribunal shall:

• Specify an amount payable in respect of any benefit the claimant might reasonably have expected to have had between the Effective Date of Termination and his reinstatement, including back pay.

In calculating this figure, the tribunal must reduce the respondent's liability by the amount of any payment in lieu of notice or ex gratia payments by the employer, and any remuneration by another employer in the period between the EDT and the date of reinstatement, as well as any such other benefits as the tribunal thinks appropriate in the circumstances;

• State any rights and privileges to be restored to the employee;

• Specify the date by which the order must be complied with; and

• Require that the claimant be treated as if they had benefited from any improvement to their terms and conditions of employment that they would have obtained had they not been dismissed.

Re-engagement

This is an order that the claimant be engaged by the employer, a successor or associated employer, 'in employment comparable to that from which he was dismissed or other suitable employment' (s115(1) ERA 1996)). There is an exception where the employee caused or contributed to their dismissal, in which case the tribunal can order re-engagement on less favourable terms.

Any such order must specify: the identity of the employer; the nature of the employment; remuneration; back pay (as with reinstatement above); any rights and privileges to be restored to the employee; and the date to comply with the order. There are identical provisions for reducing back pay liability for re-engaged employees as there are for reinstatement.

The terms of an order for re-engagement 'must be specified with a degree of precision'. It is not sufficient to simply order that the employer employ the claimant in a comparable role (*Lincolnshire County Council v Lupton* UKEAT/0328/15/DM).

Procedure

The tribunal must first consider reinstatement and, if it decides against it, then move on to consider re-engagement.

In assessing the suitability of each order, the tribunal must consider:

• the claimant's wishes;

• the practicability of compliance by the employer;

• if the claimant caused or contributed to his dismissal, whether it is just to order reinstatement or re-engagement.

Practicability

This is considered in two stages: first on a provisional basis at the time of making the order; second on a conclusive basis if the employer fails to comply with the order. At this second stage the burden is on the employer to prove impracticability.

Practicability is a question of fact for the tribunal, not a matter of whether the employer's views fall within a band of reasonable responses. However, where the barrier to practicability is said to be a lack of trust and confidence in an employee, the tribunal must look at whether the employer's loss of trust (for example because of the employee's dishonesty) is genuinely believed and based on rational grounds.

The matter is to be judged in a broad common-sense fashion and is to be assessed at the time an order would take effect. It is a question of possibility bearing in mind the circumstances of the employer's business and industrial relations realities. Relevant factors include matters such as:

• whether the parties are able to trust each other;

• whether the nature of the allegations makes it impossible for the employee and the subjects of those allegations to work together;

• whether the industrial atmosphere has been poisoned against the employee or their reinstatement or re-engagement is otherwise likely to lead to strife.

In reaching such a decision, however, the tribunal is not to take into account the fact that an employer has engaged a permanent replacement for the employee unless the employer shows that it is not practicable to arrange for the work to be done without engaging a permanent replacement.

Non-Compliance

If an employer fails to comply with an order for reinstatement or re-engagement the tribunal will, as noted above, consider practicability on a conclusive basis with the burden of proof on the employer. If the employer fails to establish impracticability, the tribunal will make an Additional Award (see *Additional award*).

Retirement: see Normal retirement date; Pension loss; Tables 32 and 33

Schedule of loss

The schedule of loss is an integral part of the claim and needs to be devised with care. The sum being claimed must reflect the claimant's reasonable losses, and several versions of the schedule of loss might need to be designed to illustrate the effect of any adjustments that could be made for contributory fault for example.

In particular, future loss is notoriously difficult to calculate due the high degree of speculation involved, but the period needs to be justified, for example by taking into account the health and age of the claimant, their particular expertise and the state of the job market. Any representative should ask very direct questions of their client and check carefully all the information that has been given to them before serving a schedule of loss on the other parties and the tribunal.

See Appendix 2 for an example schedule of loss.

SERPS: see State Second Pension (S2P)

Settlement agreements

(see also Tax and termination payments)

Employment may be terminated by mutual agreement, as may tribunal proceedings. Tribunal claims may be settled through early conciliation through ACAS, after the proceedings have begun through a COT3 by ACAS, by agreement between the parties or in the form of a tribunal order dismissing the proceedings upon agreement having been reached between the parties. Agreement between the parties may be reached by a number of routes both informal and formal including mediation, with some cases being mediated by tribunal judges under the official judicial mediation schemes.

Formalities
Where the agreement between the parties is reached other than by use of the COT3 procedure,

any agreement by an individual that they will not bring any of a number of employment rights will be ineffective unless certain formalities have been undertaken (see for example s203 ERA 1996 and s144 and 147 EA 2010). For the compromise of a claim to be valid:

- The contract must be in writing;

- The contract must relate to a particular complaint;

- The individual must, before entering into the contract, have received advice from a relevant independent legal advisor about its terms and effect;

- On the date of giving the advice there must have been in force insurance or an indemnity against losses arising from giving the advice;

- The contract must identify the advisor;

- The contract must state that bullet points 3 and 4 above have been complied with.

Contractual entitlements
Where a settlement agreement makes payment for contractual payments that have already crystallised, it may well be that such sums would be taxable as earnings rather than under s401 ITEPA 2003 (see EIM12856).

Legal expenses
The employer may agree to pay legal costs incurred by the employee. Such a payment may be within s401 ITEPA 2003 since it is made in connection with the termination (see EIM13010), but there is a potential tax exemption where the fees are paid directly to the employee's lawyers (see *Tax and termination payments*).

What tax rate should be used when deducting tax?
PAYE74015 explains the different rules when deducting tax.

Termination payment made on or before date of P45
If the termination payment is paid on or before the P45 is issued, tax and NI will be deducted from any taxable termination payment through the normal payroll using the employee's tax code at that date.

Termination payment made after the date of P45
Prior to 6 April 2011, any taxable termination payment made after the P45 was issued was taxed by the employer at the basic rate. For employees who paid tax at a higher rate this regime gave them a cash flow advantage in that any further tax to be paid via their self-assessment would not be due for several months. This changed from 6 April 2011 such that any taxable termination payments made

after the P45 was issued should have tax deducted using the tax code 0T (effectively ignoring any personal tax allowance) and on a non-cumulative basis (which treats each pay period as a separate tax period). This can mean that the employee pays too much tax initially and would have to claim it back from HMRC on their self-assessment.

Sometimes payments paid in instalments may benefit the cash flow for both parties. Each tranche of the termination payment will be taxable independently on the above 0T basis, on the date of entitlement.

For monthly paid employees (using 2017/2018 tax bands)
Only the first £2,792 (i.e. 1/12 x £33,500) of the settlement payment will be charged at the basic rate of 20%;

The next £9,708 (i.e. 1/12 x (£150,000 - £33,500) = 1/12 x £118,000) will be charged to tax at the higher rate of 40%; and

Any remaining balance of the termination payment will be taxed at 45%.

Example
A termination payment of £75,000 is paid to an employee on 01/05/2017 after his P45 has been issued. £55,000 of this payment is taxable. He will pay:

20% of £2,792 = £558.40, plus

40% of £9,708 = £3,883.20, plus

45% of (£55,000 – £2,792 – £9,708) = 45% of £42,500 = £19,125.00

So his total tax liability, which is payable immediately by the employer, is £23,566.60.

If the employee had received his payment prior to 6 April 2011, his immediate tax liability would have been 20% of £55,000 = £11,000.

Sex discrimination: see Discrimination

Sex Equality Clause

A 'sex equality clause' is implied into every contract of employment, if one is not already present (s66 EA 2010). The effect of a sex equality clause is that any term of an individual's contract of employment, if it is less favourable to him or her than the same term is to a comparable employee of the opposite sex, will be modified so as to not be less favourable. A comparable employee will be of the opposite sex, and the work they are employed to do will be equal

(s64 and 65 EA 2010).

This applies to all the parts of the contract including:

- wages and salaries;
- non-discretionary bonuses;
- holiday pay;
- sick pay;
- overtime;
- shift payments;
- occupational pension benefits; and
- non-monetary terms such as holiday or other leave entitlements or access to sports and social benefits.

An employee may bring a claim to the tribunal for breach of his/her sex equality clause under s132 EA 2010.

Remedy: If a tribunal finds that there has been a breach of the sex equality clause it may make a declaration as to the rights of the parties (for example, stating what pay or rate of pay the individual is entitled to). The tribunal may also order an award of arrears of pay or damages (s132 EA 2010).

A limit is imposed on the period over which arrears of pay may be claimed (see s132(4)). In the standard case arrears over the preceding 6 years may be awarded, but where the breach of the clause has been concealed or the individual had an incapacity at the date of the breach, and the claim was presented within 6 years of the date the claimant knew of the claim or was capable of bringing the claim, arrears may be claimed from the date the arrears first occurred (s132(3) EA 2010).

Gross or net: Gross (but then taxed by the employer in the normal way through the payroll).

Limit on a week's pay: None

Limit on number of years: Normally 6

Adjustments: Interest can be awarded for arrears of pay and will be calculated according to the mid-point rule (see *Interest*).

Any maximum or minimum: None

Tax: Awards (or settlements) in respect of claims under the Equal Pay Act 1970 (now EA 2010 Part V, Ch 3) are arrears of pay and therefore should be taxed under s62 ITEPA 2003 (see EIM02530 HMRC). The tax liability arises in the year of entitlement not in the year of eventual payment. It is unclear whether any interest would also be taxed.

Statutory authorities: EA 2010 ss66 and 132; The Employment Tribunals (Interest on Awards in Discrimination Cases) Regulations 1996

Share options: see Financial losses

Shared parental leave (SPL): see Parental leave

Short time working: see Guarantee payment; Week's pay

Sickness: see Holiday pay

Simplified approach: see Pension loss

Social security benefits: see Income support; Job seekers allowance; Non-recoupable state benefits; Recoupment

State pension

This is the pension based on previous NI contributions paid (see Tables 32 and 33 for state pension ages for men and women). Claimants are not expected to give credit for any state pension benefits received when a tribunal assesses losses suffered by a claimant.

State Second Pension (S2P)

The State Second Pension was replaced with a new State Pension as of 6 April 2016. This entry is retained for historic purposes and will be removed from next year's edition.

The State Second Pension, or S2P, (formerly SERPS) is additional to the basic State Pension and is based on the level of National Insurance contributions paid. To lift the burden of paying additional state pension to every worker, the government previously allowed pension savers to 'contract out' of the state second pension. This meant that people who contracted out paid less National Insurance and therefore didn't get the additional state pension, the money saved in National Insurance being put into a workplace or private pension instead.

For any employee who is not a member of an occupational scheme or is a member of an occupational pension scheme which was not contracted out of S2P (circumstances which applied to about three-quarters of the private sector working population in 2003, but to only a small proportion of public sector workers) there is a potential future loss of rights in relation to S2P if an employee is dismissed and does not obtain another job immediately.

Until 2004, this loss of S2P was calculated with reference to a table of factors which was produced when the third edition of *'Compensation for Loss of Pension Rights - Employment Tribunals'* was published in 2003. However, this guidance has now been withdrawn. Thus, for dismissals after 2004, there is no approved method for calculating the loss of S2P unless actuarial advice is sought. For this reason, the table of factors has not been reproduced.

Contracting out of money purchase pension schemes was abolished in 2012. Both the state second pension and contracting out of defined benefit pension schemes ended when the new flat-rate pension came into force in 2016.

Statutory cap

(see also Additional award; Arrears; Compensatory award; Discrimination; Recoupment; Table 1)

A statutory cap applies to a compensatory award under s117(1) and (2) ERA and s123. For dismissals with an EDT before 29 July 2013 the statutory cap is as detailed in Table 1. For dismissals with an EDT on or after 29 July 2013 the applicable statutory cap is the lower of the current figure of £80,541 or 52 weeks' gross pay (as defined in ss220 to 229 ERA 1996) (see s124 ERA 1996). Because the definition of a week's pay does not cover all pay or valuable benefits received, an employee may not be compensated for an entire year's losses. However, the cap applies to 52 weeks' gross pay, which effectively means that a claimant could be awarded up to 15 to 16 months' net pay, assuming a combined tax/NI rate of 30%.

There are three situations in which the cap does not apply:

- If the reason for dismissal was discriminatory, the financial losses will be awarded under the discrimination legislation where there is no cap;

- If the employee is regarded as unfairly dismissed by virtue of section 100 or 105(3)

(Health and Safety cases), 103A or 105(6A) (Whistleblowing);

• If an award under s117 would otherwise not fully reflect the amount of arrears payable to the employee (see also *Arrears of pay*).

The cap is applied after all the adjustments such as contributory conduct and *Polkey* have been applied. It is also applied after any grossing up calculation has been done. Table 1 lists the historical statutory caps.

Example

Basic award = £11,000

Compensatory award after all adjustments (see *Adjustments*) = £90,000

Grossing up calculation (assuming marginal tax rate of 25%)

Gross up £11,000 + £90,000 - £30,000 = £71,000

Grossed up compensatory award of £71,000 = 71,000 ÷ 0.75 = £94,666.67

Compensatory award now = £19,000 + £94,666.67 = £113,666.67

Statutory cap = £80,541

Total award = £11,000 + £80,541 = £91,541

Note: the grossing up should be done **before** the cap is applied.

Statutory authorities: ERA 1996 ss117(1) & (2), 100, 103A, 105(3), 105(6A), 123 and 124

Statutory notice period

(see also Contractual notice period; Effective date of termination; Table 26)

Section 86 ERA 1996) provides for minimum notice of termination to be given by the parties to the contract of employment. Under normal circumstances, an employee with more than 1 month's continuous service is entitled to 1 week's notice, and having completed 2 years' service is entitled to 2 weeks, with the number of weeks increasing by one each year until a maximum of 12 weeks' notice. The notice an employee must give an employer, having completed 1 month's service, is 1 week (see Table 38).

By s86(6) no notice need be given by either party where the other has so seriously breached the contract as to be regarded as having repudiated the contract, in which case the other party may accept the breach and terminate the contract without notice, for example where an employee has committed gross misconduct.

The parties to an employment contract may agree to a longer, contractual notice period. The parties may also waive their right to notice on any occasion or accept payment in lieu of notice (see s86(3)).

Statutory redundancy: see Redundancy; Table 25

Statutory rights

One of the heads of loss for which a tribunal may award compensation is the value of accrued statutory rights that have been lost: where an employee begins a new job following the termination of their employment, they will need to accrue 2 years' continuous service before they will have acquired the right to claim unfair dismissal or a statutory redundancy payment, and may have lost the right to a lengthy statutory notice period if they have been employed for several years. The sum awarded is usually between £250 and £350, and is not generally governed by the personal circumstances of the employee such as would increase or decrease the actual value of the loss.

Remedy: There is no particular figure that should be awarded, but it is usually around £250 to £350. In *Countrywide Estate Agents & Ors v Turner* UKEAT/0208/13/LA, the EAT held that the ET was entitled to award 2 weeks' gross pay (limited to the weekly pay in force) for loss of statutory rights, as the claimant would take another 2 years to accrue those rights.

No award should be made where there is a finding that the claimant would have been fairly dismissed in any event (*Puglia v C James and Sons* [1996] IRLR 70).

Any maximum or minimum: None

Adjustments: The award is part of the compensatory award and will be adjusted accordingly (see *Hope v Jordan Engineering Ltd* [2008] UKEAT/0545/07).

Cap: The award is part of the compensatory award (see *Statutory cap*).

Tax: The award is part of the compensatory award and will be subject to the grossing up calculation, if appropriate, in the normal way.

Recoupment: Recoupment will not apply to this head of loss.

Relevant case law: Countrywide Estate Agents &

Ors v Turner UKEAT/0208/13/LA; Hope v Jordan Engineering Ltd [2008] UKEAT/0545/07; *Puglia v C James and Sons* [1996] IRLR 70

Substantial loss approach: see Pension loss

Summary dismissal: see Effective date of termination; Notice pay

Suspension

Part VII ERA 1996 provides the express right for an employee to be paid whilst suspended for particular reasons:

1) An employee who is suspended from work by his employer on medical grounds is entitled to be paid by his employer remuneration while he is so suspended for a period not exceeding 26 weeks (s64(1) ERA 1996);

2) An employee who is suspended from work on maternity grounds is entitled to be paid remuneration by her employer while she is so suspended (s68(1) ERA 1996). Suspension on maternity grounds in effect means suspension on grounds that a woman is pregnant, has recently given birth or is breastfeeding;

3) However, the employee has a right to be offered suitable alternative work, where it exists, before being suspended from work on maternity grounds (s67(1) ERA 1996);

4) Related rights to remuneration or alternative work apply to agency workers, see s68A to 68D ERA 1996.

A common thread between these rights is that the suspension must be required by other legislative provisions, generally regarding the health and safety of workers (see s64(2) to (4) and s66).

An employee may bring a claim that his or her employer has not paid them the remuneration to which they are entitled (see s70 ERA 1996). A similar right exists for agency workers, regarding their maternity suspension rights (see s70A ERA 1996).

Remedy: Where the tribunal finds that the employee or agency worker has not been paid the remuneration to which he or she was entitled, the tribunal will order the employer (or agency) to pay the individual the amount of remuneration which it finds is due to him or her (ss70(3 and 70A(3) ERA

1996). Remuneration is calculated according to the definition of a week's pay (see *Week's pay*) in s220 to s229 (see s69), save that the limit on a week's pay does not apply.

Where a tribunal finds that suitable alternative work has not been provided to an employee or agency worker, the tribunal may make an award of compensation (see s70(6) and (7) and s70A(6) and (7) ERA 1996). The amount of the compensation is that which the tribunal considers just and equitable in all the circumstances having regard to:

a) the infringement of the employee's right under section 67 by the failure on the part of the employer to which the complaint relates; and

b) any loss sustained by the employee which is attributable to that failure.

It is likely that an award for injury to feelings can be made where there has been a failure to provide suitable alternative work, since the statutory wording for calculating the loss is that used in the detriment provisions (s49 ERA 1996) and the protection of a woman who may be suspended on maternity grounds may be seen to be akin to the protection provided by discrimination legislation.

Gross or net: The award for lost remuneration will be calculated gross, as the definition of a week's pay in ss220 to 229 ERA 1996 applies (see *Week's pay*).

The award for a failure to provide suitable alternative work will be based on net losses, and also any injury to feelings award.

Limit on a week's pay: None

Limit on number of weeks: 26 weeks' remuneration for suspension on medical grounds (see s64(1)); otherwise unlimited

Any maximum or minimum: None, other than the maximum award will be 26 weeks' actual gross pay where the award is for remuneration for suspension on medical grounds (see s64(1)).

Adjustments: None

Tax: To the extent that the sum awarded is compensation for lost earnings, it is likely to be taxed under s62 ITEPA 2003 (see *Tax and termination payments* and EIM02550).

Recoupment: Recoupment applies to awards made in respect of a failure to pay remuneration (see Schedule to The Employment Protection (Recoupment of Jobseeker's Allowance and Income Support) Regulations 1996).

Statutory authorities: ERA 1996 ss64(1), 67(1) and

s68(1); Schedule to The Employment Protection (Recoupment of Jobseeker's Allowance and Income Support) Regulations 1996

Tax and termination payments

(see also *Gourley* principle; Grossing up; Injury to feelings)

Specific tax regimes apply to income and benefits derived from employment (s62 ITEPA 2003), and to payments made in connection with employment (s401 to 416 ITEPA 2003). Where a tribunal makes a monetary award it will take into account how that sum will be treated for tax: the award may amount to an order that the employer pay salary; the award may be for a sum due in connection with employment; an award may fall outside the tax regimes or fall within an exception or allowance. Where tax will be paid by the claimant on the sum he receives, the tribunal will gross up the award to ensure that the sum received after tax is appropriate.

The tax regimes apply to a variety of sums including earnings, ex gratia payments, sums paid under settlement agreements and tribunal awards. The tax treatment of any sum will depend on the nature of the underlying sum, and the circumstances of its payment. Essentially, any sum will be taxed under the applicable employment provisions (see further below) - if none of them apply then the sum may be taxed as being paid in connection with termination. If none of the foregoing regimes apply, the payment will not be subject to tax.

By way of example:

- Earnings and benefits will be taxed (and have NIC deducted) by the employer under the applicable tax code;

- An award by a tribunal that an employer pay unlawfully deducted wages will be calculated gross, and the employer will pay the sum (and deduct tax on it) as he does wages;

- Sums paid under a termination agreement between employer and employee, providing for sums owing under the contract that are earnings, will be taxed by the employer under the applicable tax code;

- Sums paid under a termination agreement between employer and employee, which do not amount to sums owing under the contract that are earnings, such as an enhanced redundancy payment, may fall within the regime for payments made in connection with termination. A £30,000 allowance applies to such sums;

- An award by a tribunal for losses arising from unfair dismissal, including the failure to pay an enhanced redundancy payment, will be treated as a payment made in connection with termination, where the £30,000 allowance applies.

Some sums do not fall within easily identifiable categories, for example, punitive awards such as a protective award, injury to feelings, an award for discrimination occurring independently of termination, and payments in lieu of notice.

The applicable principles are dealt with below.

Identifying the applicable tax regime

The starting point is to ascertain whether the payment could be classed as earnings, in which case tax and employee and employer NI will be payable under s62 ITEPA 2003, or as a taxable benefit under Part 3 Chapters 2 to 11 ITEPA 2003.

If the payment does not fall under the category of earnings, the next consideration is whether it is a payment in consideration of a restrictive covenant, in which case it is fully taxable (s225 ITEPA 2003).

If neither of the first two conditions apply, the next question is whether the payment is in respect of an employer-financed retirement benefit, taxable under Part 6 Chapter 2 of ITEPA 2003.

If the answer to all the previous questions is in the negative, and the payment is '*received directly or indirectly in consideration of or in consequence of or otherwise in connection with the termination of employment*', it will be taxed under Part 6 Chapter 3 of ITEPA. A tax free allowance of £30,000 applies to such payments.

Any payments which fall under s401 ITEPA 2003 are also exempt from National Insurance completely, even if they exceed £30,000 (s401 and 403 ITEPA 2003). However, from 2018, employer National Insurance will become payable on any amount exceeding £30,000.

If none of the above apply, the compensation is unconnected with the employment or its termination and is therefore outside the scope of income tax and NIC. For example, payments or awards for damages for breach of contract prior to termination do not fall within the above provisions, neither do awards for injury to feelings from discrimination unconnected with termination.

Fully taxable and subject to NI deductions

- Earnings from employment;

- Arrears of pay (but see 'Reinstatement or re-engagement' later in this entry);

- Accrued holiday pay;

- Payments made in consideration of restrictive covenants (s225 ITEPA 2003), unless the specific consideration is attached to the restatement of existing covenants or an agreement to discontinue proceedings (see *Appellant v Inspector of Taxes* [2001] STC (SCD) 21);

- Payment in respect of a non-approved retirement benefit;

- Contractual PILONs;

- Implied contractual right to a PILON;

- Contractual termination payments;

- Contractual benefits in kind;

- Payments during garden leave;

- Payments to an employee suspended from work on medical grounds under Sections 64 and 70(3) ERA 1996 (EIM02550, HMRC);

- Maternity suspension payments under Sections 68 and 70(3) ERA 1996 (EIM02550, HMRC);

- Payments under Sections 51(3)(b) or 63(4) ERA 1996 for infringing the employee's rights to time off for public duties under Section 50 or Trade Union duties or activities under Sections 61 and 62 respectively (EIM02550, HMRC);

- Payments under the Sex Discrimination Acts, the Equal Pay Act 1970 (see EIM02530), the Wages Act 1986, the Trade Union and Labour Relations (Consolidation) Act 1992 and the National Minimum Wage Act 1998 for wrongfully depressing the employee's remuneration in the employment (EIM02550, HMRC).

Payments which are fully taxable by the employer before payment to the individual should not be grossed up by the tribunal.

Payments in lieu of notice (PILONS)
Payments made in exercise of contractual PILONs are fully taxable as earnings; they will not be taxed under, or qualify for any exemptions in, ss401-416 ITEPA 2003. Similarly, if there is an implied contractual right to a PILON, or where there is a discretion to make a PILON (see *EMI Group Electronics Ltd v Coldicott* [1999] IRLR 630), such a payment will be fully taxable. It is possible for an

employer to terminate an employment contract without notice, and not exercise a PILON, so that the sums are not taxed as earnings (see *Cerberus Software v Rowley* [2001] IRLR 160). The factors that HMRC will take into account in such a situation have been set out in Tax Bulletin 63 (February 2003), and include whether there has been a reduction for mitigation, whether all salary and benefits are compensated for, and that the payment takes into account appropriate tax treatments for termination payments.

Termination payments
Where a payment made on termination, in a settlement agreement or in the form of a tribunal award, falls within Part 6 Chapter 3 of ITEPA, that particular regime will apply. This includes a £30,000 allowance, so for example in a straightforward unfair dismissal award made by a tribunal the first £30,000 will be exempt from tax, and any award above this will be grossed up by the tribunal to ensure the individual retains the value of his net loss. However, note *Hill v Revenue & Customs* [2015] UKFTT 295 (TC) where the claimant was transferred under TUPE and the tribunal did not accept his argument that a payment of £30,000 in settlement of his grievance was not taxable because his employment was ongoing.

Payments and other benefits that fall within this regime include:

- Non-contractual benefits in kind;

- Statutory, non-contractual and contractual redundancy payments, provided that they are genuinely on account of redundancy (see *Mairs v Haughey* [1994] 1 AC 303);

- Basic award;

- Awards for financial loss whether for unfair dismissal or as a result of discrimination;

- Damages for wrongful dismissal;

- An additional award;

- An award for employer failing to provide a statement of written particulars (see EIM12960);

- Protective awards;

- Payment by the employer of the employee's legal expenses (but see 'Specific categories of award' below).

Any part of the total award in excess of the £30,000 tax free allowance and which has been calculated on a net basis should be grossed up to ensure the employee receives the sum that has been awarded. This means that any of the compensatory award or award of damages which forms part or all of the excess figure should be grossed up.

Exempt from taxation

Certain payments are exempted from taxation under s401 ITEPA 2003 and will therefore not be taxed at all. Payments include:

- Payment made by reason of the death of an employee or on account of an injury to, or disability of, the employee;

- Payment of legal expenses where the sum is either awarded by the tribunal or paid under a settlement agreement directly to the individual's lawyer (Enactment of Extra-Statutory Concessions Order 2011 SI 2011/1037, Article 10);

- Certain costs in connection with counselling, outplacement and retraining courses (ss310 and 311 ITEPA 2003);

- Foreign service exemption - full and partial exemptions apply to payments made in respect of foreign service, where an employee was both non-resident and non-ordinarily resident in the UK (s413 ITEPA 2003).

Payments which are exempt from tax should not be grossed up.

Specific categories of award
Unlawful deduction from wages

A tribunal ought to award payment for unlawful deduction from wages under s13 ERA 1996 gross, with the employer deducting tax and NIC at source, as such payments fall within s62 ITEPA 2003.

Reinstatement or re-engagement

Where a tribunal has made an award for lost salary between the date of dismissal and the reinstatement or re-engagement, that sum is not taxed as earnings under s62 ITEPA 2003 but will fall within s401 (*Wilson v Clayton* [2005] IRLR 108). Such sums will be calculated on a net basis and grossed up where appropriate (see EIM 12960).

Discrimination not involving termination

According to HMRC in EIM12965 and *Yorkshire Housing Ltd v Cuerden* UKEAT/0397/09, compensation payments made for discrimination that does not cause termination will not be subject to tax. See also *Mr A v Revenue & Customs (Income tax/Corporation tax: Employment income)* [2015] UKFTT 189 where the claimant accepted £600,000 in settlement of his threatened claim for discrimination. The first tier tribunal ruled that the reason the payment was made by the employer was (rightly or wrongly on their part) to settle a discrimination claim and not to pay back money which they thought the appellant was entitled to in respect of underpaid salary and bonus.

Compensation payments would include any financial and non-financial losses such as an award for injury to feelings. Such an award should be calculated on a net basis, and there will not be a need to gross up.

Discrimination involving termination

Awards made in connection with termination arising from discrimination will be taxable under s401 ITEPA 2003 (*Walker v Adams* [2001] STC 101, *Orthet v Vince Cain* [2004] IRLR 857 and *Oti-Obihara v Commissioners for HM Revenue & Customs* [2011] IRLR 386 and *Moorthy v The Commissioners for Her Majesty's Revenue & Customs* [2014] UKFTT 834 (TC), and *Moorthy v Revenue & Customs* [2016] UKUT 13 TCC).

Equality clauses

Where an award is made for breach of an equality clause, the award will be subject to tax on the basis of the tax due in the year the sum ought to have been paid (EIM02530). The award should be calculated on a gross basis, with the employer operating an appropriate special PAYE procedure.

Injury to feelings

An injury to feelings award made in relation to discrimination that does not amount to termination will not be subject to tax (EIM12965 and *Yorkshire Housing Ltd v Cuerden* UKEAT/0397/09). However, there is uncertainty regarding injury to feelings awards arising from a discriminatory termination and whether they fall within s401 ITEPA 2003. HMRC take the view that such injury to feelings awards are subject to tax (EIM12965), confirmed by the tax tribunal in *Moorthy v The Commissioners for Her Majesty's Revenue & Customs* [2014] UKFTT 834 (TC). The claimant had accepted £200,000 in compromise of his claim of age discrimination and argued that none of it was taxable. The tax tribunal held that the payment of £200,000 in its entirety was made "*directly or indirectly in consideration or in consequence of, or otherwise in connection with*" the termination of Mr Moorthy's employment, and therefore fell within ITEPA s 401. Whether or not the payment was also to compensate Mr Moorthy for discrimination, unfair dismissal, injury to feelings, redundancy and/or financial loss was immaterial.

A number of tribunals have applied the contrary approach (see *Walker v Adams* [2001] STC 101, *Orthet v Vince Cain* [2004] IRLR 857 and *Oti-Obihara v Commissioners for HM Revenue & Customs* [2011] IRLR 386). Most recently, the EAT in *Timothy James Consulting Ltd v Wilton* UKEAT/0082/14/DXA held that the injury to feelings award would not be taxed and therefore should not be grossed up.

There is also an argument that s406 ITEPA 2003 which applies to payments made on account of injury, which is not expressly restricted to actual personal injury, might therefore include mere injury to feelings. It is the experience of the authors that employment tribunals tend to regard all injury to feelings awards as not subject to tax and so do not gross up such awards. However, in January 2016, Mr Moorthy appealed to the UKUT (see *Moorthy v Revenue & Customs* [2016] UKUT 13 (TCC)) but lost, the tribunal saying that *Orthet* and *Timothy James* were wrongly decided in so far as they held that 'injury' in section 406 ITEPA includes injury to feelings. The upper tribunal held that 'injury' in section 406 refers to a medical condition and does not include injury to feelings.

Protective awards and TUPE consultation

Though protective awards are calculated by reference to pay over a protected period, such sums are not paid by reference to the individual acting as an employee, but under statute (and as punishment for breach of a statutory obligation) (see *Mimtec Ltd v Inland Revenue* [2001] UKSC SPC00277). They therefore fall under s401 rather than s62 ITEPA 2003.

The logic applied in *Mimtec* might suggest that where an award has been made for failure to inform and consult under TUPE, which is unconnected to any termination, the award would not be subject to tax at all. Where an individual in receipt of such an award has been subject to a transfer, it might be argued that the transfer, for the purposes of the tax regime, did amount to a termination (see *Kuehne & Nagel Drinks Logistics Ltd, Scott & Joyce v HMRC* [2009] UKFTT 379 (TC)). That argument would not however apply to an individual affected by the transfer, whose representatives were not appropriately consulted, but who did not themselves transfer.

Payments unrelated to termination

Where an award is made for breach of a statutory right, for example if the employer has not complied with the right of an employee to be accompanied at a disciplinary hearing, this is unrelated to the individual's termination and may well not be earnings. There is no official guidance on how such sums should be treated. However, the logic in *Mimtec Ltd v Inland Revenue* [2001] UKSC SPC00277, that such sums are not paid by reference to the individual acting as an employee but under statute (and as punishment for breach of a statutory obligation), could apply. Such payments may well not be subject to tax and should not be grossed up.

Payment of employee's legal expenses by the employer

An employer may agree to pay legal costs incurred by an employee in relation to a claim against the employer after the contract of employment has been terminated. Such a payment falls within Section 401 ITEPA 2003 since it is made in connection with the termination (see EIM13010), but as a concession the sum will not be charged where:

1) the dispute is settled without recourse to the courts and three conditions are met:

   a) the payment is made direct to the employee's solicitor rather than to the employee himself or herself; and

   b) the payment is applied to discharge the bill for solicitor's costs that the employee has incurred only in connection with the termination of the employment; and

   c) the payment is made under a specific term in the agreement that settles the dispute;

or

2) the payment of costs by the employer is made in accordance with a court order. This applies even if the payment is made directly to the employee.

Note that the concession:

• applies only to legal costs, not to any other professional costs (such as accountancy fees). However, it does include the expenses of expert professional witnesses incurred by the employee's legal advisor;

• does not allow an employee to claim a deduction for his or her own legal costs in any way.

Interim relief

Payments made under a continuation order are taxable as payments in connection with termination under s401, not in full as earnings under s62 ITEPA (see also *Interim relief*). See *Turullols v HMRC* [2014] UKFTT 672 (TC) where the First Tier Tribunal held that the claimant, who was found to have been unfairly dismissed, could claim back the tax that had been paid on the salary payments made under the interim relief order because they were payments in connection with the termination of her employment and therefore should have been tax-free up to £30,000. This would also have been the case even if the ET had not upheld the unfair dismissal claim.

April 2018

The Government proposed that from April 2018:

- All payments in lieu of notice (PILONs) will be taxable, whether or not there is a right to make the payment in a contract of employment;

- Employer National Insurance, but not employee NI, will be payable on any amount above £30,000;

- The foreign service relief exemptions will be removed for termination payments;

- Any compensation for injury to feelings in a termination payment will be taxable to the extent that the £30,000 'allowance' has been exceeded, except where the compensation is for a psychiatric injury or a recognised medical condition.

However, the calling of the snap election meant that these measures were removed from the Finance Act 2017 in the wash-up period. The view of the Chartered Institute of Taxation is that a significant amount of the Bill would be re-enacted irrespective of who wins the election.

Time off to accompany to ante-natal appointment

(see also Time off for ante-natal care)

From 1 October 2014 an expectant father, or the partner of a pregnant woman, and other employees who have a qualifying relationship with a pregnant woman or her expected child are entitled to be permitted by his or her employer to take time off during the employee's working hours in order that he or she may accompany the woman when she attends by appointment at any place for the purpose of receiving ante-natal care (s57ZE ERA 1996).

An employee may present a complaint to an employment tribunal that his or her employer has unreasonably refused to let him or her take time off as required by s57ZE.

Equivalent rights to time off and remuneration for the period of absence are given to agency workers, with the remuneration to be paid by the agency (see s57ZH).

Remedy: Where a tribunal finds a complaint well founded, it will make a declaration to that effect (s57ZF(4a)).

Further, if the tribunal has found that the employer has unreasonably refused to permit the employee to take time off, the tribunal will also order the employer to pay compensation to the employee according to the following formula (s57ZF(5)):

Amount to be paid = Appropriate hourly rate for the employee x Number of working hours for which the employee would have been entitled under section 57ZE to be absent if the time off had not been refused x 2

Unless the employee works a varying number of working hours, the appropriate hourly rate is one week's pay divided by the normal working hours in a week when the time off would have been taken. For employees whose hours of work vary over a week or longer period, the appropriate hourly rate is obtained by dividing one week's pay by the average number of hours worked over the previous 12 weeks, or where the employee has not been employed for 12 weeks, a number which fairly represents the number of normal working hours in a week (see s57ZF(7)).

A week's pay will be calculated in accordance with s220 to s229 ERA 1996 (see *Week's pay*).

Gross or net: The sum for unpaid earnings will be calculated gross and paid through payroll as with ordinary remuneration.

Any maximum or minimum: None

Adjustments: The claimant will have to give credit for any amount paid towards the entitlement under the contract.

Mitigation: N/A

Tax: The tax treatment is not clear. To the extent that the sum awarded is compensation for lost earnings for work done, it is likely to be taxed under s62 ITEPA 2003 (see *Tax and termination payments*).

Recoupment: N/A

Statutory authorities: ERA 1996 ss57ZE and 57ZF

Time off to attend adoption appointments

From 5 April 2015 employees proposing to adopt a child may take time off to attend up to 5 adoption appointments. The time off must be paid where the employee is adopting the child on their own (ss57ZJ-ZL ERA 1996).

If the employee is adopting jointly, then one of the parents may elect to receive the time off as paid and the other will be entitled to take unpaid leave for up to 2 appointments.

A maximum of 6 ½ hours is allowed for each appointment in all cases.

An employee may present a complaint to an employment tribunal that his or her employer has unreasonably refused to let him or her take time off as required by s57ZJ-L. Equivalent rights to time off and remuneration for the period of absence are given to agency workers, with the remuneration to be paid by the agency (see s57ZN).

Remedy: Where a tribunal finds a complaint well founded, it will make a declaration to that effect (s57ZM(4)).

If the complaint is that the employer has failed to pay the employee the whole or part of any amount to which the employee is entitled under section 57ZK (paid time off), the tribunal must order the employer to pay compensation to the employee the amount which it finds due to the employee

Further, if the tribunal has found that the employer has unreasonably refused to permit the employee to take time off, the tribunal will also order the employer to pay to the employee according to the following formula (s57ZM(7)):

Amount to be paid = Appropriate hourly rate for the employee x Number of working hours for which the employee would have been entitled under section 57Z to be absent if the time off had not been refused x 2

Unless the employee works a varying number of working hours, the appropriate hourly rate is one week's pay divided by the normal working hours in a week when the time off would have been taken. For employees whose hours of work vary over a week or longer period, the appropriate hourly rate is obtained by dividing one week's pay by the average number of hours worked over the previous 12 weeks, or where the employee has not been employed for 12 weeks, a number which fairly represents the number of normal working hours in a week (see s57ZK).

A week's pay will be calculated in accordance with s220 to s229 ERA 1996 (see *Week's pay*).

Gross or net: The sum for unpaid earnings will be calculated gross and paid through payroll as with ordinary remuneration.

Any maximum or minimum: None

Adjustments: The claimant will have to give credit for any amount paid towards the entitlement under the contract.

Mitigation: N/A

Tax: The tax treatment is not clear. To the extent that the sum awarded is compensation for lost earnings for work done, it is likely to be taxed under s62 ITEPA 2003 (see *Tax and termination payments*).

Recoupment: N/A

Statutory authorities: ERA 1996 ss57ZJ-N

Time off for ante-natal care

(see also Time off to accompany to ante-natal appointment)

An employee who has an appointment for the purpose of receiving ante-natal care is entitled to be permitted by her employer to take time off during the employee's working hours in order to enable her to keep the appointment (s55 ERA 1996).

The employee is entitled to be paid at their 'appropriate hourly rate' for their period of absence. Unless the employee works a varying number of working hours, the appropriate hourly rate is one week's pay divided by the normal working hours in a week when the time off was taken. For employees whose hours of work vary over a week or longer period, the appropriate hourly rate is obtained by dividing one week's pay by the average number of hours worked over the previous 12 weeks, or where the employee has not been employed for 12 weeks, a number which fairly represents the number of normal working hours in a week (see s56(2), (3) and (4)).

A week's pay will be calculated in accordance with s220 to s229 ERA 1996 (see *Week's pay*).

Any contractual remuneration paid to an employee in respect of such a period of time off goes towards discharging the liability under s56 (see s56(5) and (6)).

An employee may bring a complaint to a tribunal that her employer has unreasonably refused to permit her to take the time off under s55, or has failed to pay the sums due under s56 (see s57(1) ERA 1996).

Equivalent rights to time off and remuneration for the period of absence are given to agency workers, with the remuneration to be paid by the agency (see s57ZA to 57ZD).

Remedy: Where a tribunal finds a complaint well founded, it will make a declaration to that effect (s57(3)).

Further, if the tribunal has found that the employer has unreasonably refused to permit the employee to take time off, the tribunal will also order the employer to pay to the employee an amount equal to the remuneration to which she would have been entitled under s56 if the employer had not refused (s57(4)). Also, if the tribunal finds that the employer has failed to pay the employee the whole or part of any amount to which she is entitled under s56, the tribunal will also order the employer to pay to the employee the amount she is owed (s57(5)).

For employees working fixed number of hours per week

Sum to which the employee is entitled = (gross weekly pay) x 1/(number of normal working hours in a week) x (number of hours absent) (s56(2) ERA 1996)

For employees with varying number of hours worked per week

Sum to which the employee is entitled = gross weekly pay x 12/(number of normal hours worked in the last 12 weeks ending with the last complete week before the day on which the time off is taken) x (number of hours absent) (s56(3) ERA 1996)

For employees with varying number of hours worked per week and who have worked for less than 12 weeks

Sum to which the employee is entitled = (gross weekly pay) x 1/(number of normal hours which fairly represents the number of normal working hours in a week) x (number of hours absent) (s56(3) and (4) ERA 1996)

Gross or net: The sum for unpaid earnings will be calculated gross and paid through payroll as with ordinary remuneration.

Any maximum or minimum: None

Adjustments: The claimant will have to give credit for any amount paid towards the entitlement under the contract.

Mitigation: N/A

Tax: The tax treatment is not clear. To the extent that the sum awarded is compensation for lost earnings for work done, it is likely to be taxed under s62 ITEPA 2003 (see *Tax and termination payments*).

Recoupment: N/A

Statutory authorities: ERA 1996 ss55, 56 and s57ZA to 57ZD

Time off for dependants

An employee is entitled to be permitted by his employer to take a reasonable amount of time off during the employee's working hours in order to care for or sort out issues in relation to a dependant (s57A ERA 1996). The definition of a dependant includes amongst others a spouse, a civil partner, a child and a parent.

An employee may bring a complaint to a tribunal that his employer has unreasonably refused to permit him to take this time off (s57B ERA 1996).

Remedy: Where the tribunal finds such a complaint well founded it will make a declaration to that effect (s57B(3)(a)).

It may also make an award of compensation to be paid by the employer (s57B(3)(b) and (4)).

The amount of compensation will be that which it considers just and equitable in all the circumstances having regard to:

a) the employer's default in refusing to permit time off to be taken by the employee; and

b) any loss sustained by the employee as a result.

Any maximum or minimum: There is no statutory limit to the compensation.

Adjustments: N/A

Mitigation: It is likely that the principle of mitigation would be applied in an appropriate case. However, this would most likely operate to restrict the losses that would be compensated for where it would have been reasonable for the employee to have incurred a lower level of losses than were in fact incurred, for example where the alternative care was unreasonably expensive and reasonably avoidable.

Tax: The tax treatment is not clear. To the extent that the sum awarded is compensation for lost earnings for work done, it is likely to be taxed under s62 ITEPA 2003 (see *Tax and termination payments* and EIM02550).

Recoupment: N/A

Statutory authorities: ERA 1996 s57A and 57B

Time off for employee representatives

An employee representative for the purposes of collective consultation or TUPE consultation is entitled to take reasonable time off during the employee's working hours to perform his functions as such an employee representative, or candidate in an election for such a role, or in order to undergo training to perform such functions (s61 ERA 1996).

The employee is entitled to be paid at their 'appropriate hourly rate' for their period of absence. Unless the employee works a varying number of working hours, the appropriate hourly rate is one week's pay divided by the normal working hours in a week when the time off was taken.

For employees whose hours of work vary over a week or longer period, the appropriate hourly rate is obtained by dividing one week's pay by the average number of hours worked over the previous 12 weeks, or where the employee has not been employed for 12 weeks, a number which fairly represents the number of normal working hours in a week (s62 ERA 1996).

A week's pay will be calculated in accordance with s220 to s229 ERA 1996 (see *Week's pay*).

Any contractual remuneration paid to an employee in respect of such a period of time off goes towards discharging the liability under s62 (see s62(5) and (6)).

An employee may bring a complaint to a tribunal that his or her employer has unreasonably refused to permit him or her to take the time off under s61, or has failed to pay the sums due under s62 (see s63(1) ERA 1996).

Remedy: Where a tribunal finds a complaint well founded, it will make a declaration to that effect (s63(3) ERA 1996).

Further, if the tribunal has found that the employer has unreasonably refused to permit the employee to take time off, the tribunal will also order the employer to pay to the employee an amount equal to the remuneration to which he or she would have been entitled under s62 if the employer had not refused (s63(4) ERA 1996).

Also, if the tribunal finds that the employer has failed to pay the employee the whole or part of any amount to which he or she is entitled under s62, the tribunal will also order the employer to pay to the employee the amount he or she is owed (s63(5) ERA 1996).

For employees working fixed number of hours per week
Sum to which the employee is entitled = (gross weekly pay) x 1/(number of normal working hours in a week) x (number of hours absent) (s62(2) ERA 1996)

For employees with varying number of hours worked per week
Sum to which the employee is entitled = gross weekly pay x 12/(number of normal hours worked in the last 12 weeks ending with the last complete week before the day on which the time off is taken) x (number of hours absent) (s62(3)(a) ERA 1996)

For employees with varying number of hours worked per week and who have worked for less than 12 weeks
Sum to which the employee is entitled = (gross weekly pay) x 1/(number of normal hours which fairly represents the number of normal working hours in a week) x (number of hours absent) (s62(3) and (4) ERA 1996)

Gross or net: The sum will be calculated gross and paid through payroll as with ordinary remuneration.

Any maximum or minimum: None

Adjustments: The claimant will have to give credit for any amount paid towards the entitlement under the contract.

Mitigation: N/A

Tax: Taxable under s62 ITEPA 2003 (see EIM02550).

Recoupment: N/A

Statutory authorities: ERA 1996 ss61 to 63

Time off for employee representatives (ICE)

An employee representative who is a negotiating representative or an information and consultation representative within the Information and Consultation of Employees Regulations 2004 is entitled to take reasonable time off during the employee's working hours to perform his functions as such a representative (Reg 27 ICE Regs 2004).

The employee is entitled to be paid at their 'appropriate hourly rate' for their period of absence. Unless the employee works a varying number of working hours, the appropriate hourly rate is one week's pay divided by the normal working hours in a week when the time off was taken. For employees whose hours of work vary over a week or longer period, the appropriate hourly rate is obtained by dividing one week's pay by the average number of hours worked over the previous 12 weeks, or where the employee has not been employed for 12 weeks, a number which fairly represents the number of normal working hours in a week (see Reg 28(3), (4) and (5)).

A week's pay will be calculated in accordance with s220 to s229 ERA 1996 (see *Week's pay*) (Reg 28(2)).

Any contractual remuneration paid to an employee in respect of such a period of time off goes towards discharging the liability under Reg 28 (see Reg 28(6) and (7)).

An employee may bring a complaint to a tribunal that his or her employer has unreasonably refused to permit him or her to take the time off under Reg 27, or has failed to pay the sums due under Reg 28 (see Reg 29 ICE 2004).

Remedy: Where a tribunal finds a complaint well founded, it will make a declaration to that effect (Reg 29(3)).

Further, if the tribunal has found that the employer has unreasonably refused to permit the employee to take time off, the tribunal will also order the employer to pay to the employee an amount equal to the remuneration to which he or she would have been entitled under Reg 28 if the employer had not refused (Reg 29(4)).

Also, if the tribunal finds that the employer has failed to pay the employee the whole or part of any amount to which he or she is entitled under Reg 28, the tribunal will also order the employer to pay to the employee the amount he or she is owed (Reg 29(5).

For employees working fixed number of hours per week

Sum to which the employee is entitled = (gross weekly pay) x 1/(number of normal working hours in a week) x (number of hours absent) (Reg 28(3) ICE 2004))

For employees with varying number of hours worked per week

Sum to which the employee is entitled = gross weekly pay x 12/(number of normal hours worked in the last 12 weeks ending with the last complete week before the day on which the time off is taken) x (number of hours absent)

For employees with varying number of hours worked per week and who have worked for less than 12 weeks

Sum to which the employee is entitled = (gross weekly pay) x 1/(number of normal hours which fairly represents the number of normal working hours in a week) x (number of hours absent) (Reg 28(4) and (5) ICE 2004)

Gross or net: Gross. A week's pay as defined in ss220 to 229 ERA 1996 applies (see *Week's pay*) (Reg 28(2)).

Limit on a week's pay: None. The calculation is based on actual gross weekly pay.

Limit on number of weeks: None

Any maximum or minimum: None

Adjustments: None

Mitigation: N/A

Tax: The tax treatment is not clear. To the extent that the sum awarded is compensation for lost earnings for work done, it is likely to be taxed under s62 ITEPA 2003 (see *Tax and termination payments* and EIM02550).

Recoupment: N/A

Statutory authorities: ICE 2004 (SI 2004/3426) Regs 27 and 29

Time off for employee representatives (OPPS)

A 'consulted representative' within the Occupational and Personal Pension Schemes (Consultation by Employers and Miscellaneous Amendment) Regulations 2006 is entitled to take reasonable time off during the employee's working hours to perform his functions as such a representative (Sch para 2 OPPS 2006). A 'consulted representative' is an employee who is a trade union representative, appointed representative, elected representative or one identified in an appropriate agreement (Reg 12(2)(a) and (3) and Reg 13(2) of OPPS Regs 2006).

The employee is entitled to be paid at their 'appropriate hourly rate' for their period of absence. Unless the employee works a varying number of working hours, the appropriate hourly rate is one week's pay divided by the normal working hours in a week when the time off was taken. For employees whose hours of work vary over a week or longer period, the appropriate hourly rate is obtained by dividing one week's pay by the average number of hours worked over the previous 12 weeks, or where the employee has not been employed for 12 weeks, a number which fairly represents the number of normal working hours in a week (see Sch para 3 (3), (4) and (5)).

A week's pay will be calculated in accordance with s220 to s229 ERA 1996 (see *Week's pay*) (Sch para 3(2)).

Any contractual remuneration paid to an employee in respect of such a period of time off goes towards discharging the liability under Sch para 3 (see Sch para 3(6) and (7)).

An employee may bring a complaint to a tribunal that his or her employer has unreasonably refused to permit him or her to take the time off under Sch para 2, or has failed to pay the sums due under Sch para 3 (see Sch para 4 OPPS 2006).

Remedy: Where a tribunal finds a complaint well founded, it will make a declaration to that effect (Sch para 4(3) OPPS 2006).

Further, if the tribunal has found that the employer has unreasonably refused to permit the employee to take time off, the tribunal will also order the employer to pay to the employee an amount equal to the remuneration to which he or she would have been entitled under Sch para 3 if the employer had not refused (Sch para 4(4)).

Also, if the tribunal finds that the employer has failed to pay the employee the whole or part of any amount to which he or she is entitled under Reg 28, the tribunal will also order the employer to pay to the employee the amount he or she is owed (Sch para 4(5)).

For employees working fixed number of hours per week
Sum to which the employee is entitled = (gross weekly pay) x 1/(number of normal working hours in a week) x (number of hours absent) (Sch para 3(3) OPPS 2006)

For employees with varying number of hours worked per week
Sum to which the employee is entitled = gross weekly pay x 12/(number of normal hours worked in the last 12 weeks ending with the last complete week before the day on which the time off is taken) x (number of hours absent) (Sch para 3(4) OPPS 2006)

For employees with varying number of hours worked per week and who have worked for less than 12 weeks
Sum to which the employee is entitled = (gross weekly pay) x 1/(number of normal hours which fairly represents the number of normal working hours in a week) x (number of hours absent) (Sch para 3(4) and (5) OPPS 2006)

Gross or net: Gross. A week's pay as defined in ss220 to 229 ERA 1996 applies (see *Week's pay*).

Limit on a week's pay: None. The calculation is based on actual gross weekly pay.

Limit on number of weeks: None

Any maximum or minimum: None

Adjustments: None

Mitigation: N/A

Tax: The tax treatment is not clear. To the extent that the sum awarded is compensation for lost earnings for work done, it is likely to be taxed under

s62 ITEPA 2003 (see *Tax and termination payments* and EIM02550).

Recoupment: N/A

Statutory authorities: OPPS 2006 (SI 2006/349) Regs 12, 13 and Schedule paragraphs 2 to 4

Time off for members of a European Works Council

An employee who is:

a) a member of a special negotiating body;

b) a member of a European Works Council;

c) an information and consultation representative; or

d) a candidate in an election in which any person elected will, on being elected, be such a member or representative,

is entitled to take reasonable time off during the employee's working hours to perform his functions as such a representative (Reg 25 TICE 1999).

An employee who is:

a) a member of a special negotiating body;

b) a member of a European Works Council,

is entitled to take reasonable time off during the employee's working hours to undertake the training permitted by Reg 19B (Reg 25(1A) TICE Regs 1999).

The employee is entitled to be paid at their 'appropriate hourly rate' for their period of absence. Unless the employee works a varying number of working hours, the appropriate hourly rate is one week's pay divided by the normal working hours in a week when the time off was taken. For employees whose hours of work vary over a week or longer period, the appropriate hourly rate is obtained by dividing one week's pay by the average number of hours worked over the previous 12 weeks, or where the employee has not been employed for 12 weeks, a number which fairly represents the number of normal working hours in a week (see Reg 26 (3), (4) and (5)).

A week's pay will be calculated in accordance with s220 to s229 ERA 1996 (see *Week's pay*) (Reg 26(2)).

Any contractual remuneration paid to an employee in respect of such a period of time off goes towards discharging the liability under Reg 26 (see Reg 26(6) and (7)).

An employee may bring a complaint to a tribunal that his or her employer has unreasonably refused to permit him or her to take the time off under Reg 25, or has failed to pay the sums due under Reg 26 (see Reg 27 TICE 1999).

Remedy: Where a tribunal finds a complaint well founded, it will make a declaration to that effect (Reg 27(3)).

Further, if the tribunal has found that the employer has unreasonably refused to permit the employee to take time off, the tribunal will also order the employer to pay to the employee an amount equal to the remuneration to which he or she would have been entitled under Reg 26 if the employer had not refused (Reg 27(4)).

Also, if the tribunal finds that the employer has failed to pay the employee the whole or part of any amount to which he or she is entitled under Reg 26, the tribunal will also order the employer to pay to the employee the amount he or she is owed (Reg 27(5)).

For employees working a fixed number of hours per week
Sum to which the employee is entitled = (gross weekly pay) x 1/(number of normal working hours in a week) x (number of hours absent) (Reg 26(3) TICE 1999)

For employees with varying number of hours worked per week
Sum to which the employee is entitled = gross weekly pay x 12/(number of normal hours worked in the last 12 weeks ending with the last complete week before the day on which the time off is taken) x (number of hours absent) (Reg 26(4) TICE 1999)

For employees with varying number of hours worked per week and who have worked for less than 12 weeks
Sum to which the employee is entitled = (gross weekly pay) x 1/(number of normal hours which fairly represents the number of normal working hours in a week) x (number of hours absent) (Reg 26(4) and (5) TICE 1999)

Gross or net: Gross. A week's pay as defined in ss220 to 229 ERA 1996 applies (see *Week's pay*).

Limit on a week's pay: None. The calculation is based on actual gross weekly pay.

Limit on number of weeks: None

Any maximum or minimum: None

Adjustments: None

Mitigation: N/A

Tax: The tax treatment is not clear. To the extent that the sum awarded is compensation for lost earnings for work done, it is likely to be taxed under s62 ITEPA 2003 (see *Tax and termination payments* and EIM02550).

Recoupment: N/A

Statutory authorities: TICE 1999 (SI 1999/3323) Regs 19B, 25 to 27

Time off for pension scheme trustees

An employee who is the trustee of his employer's pension scheme is permitted to take time off to perform the duties of a trustee and undergo relevant training. The amount of time off is that which is reasonable in all the circumstances having regard to how much time is required to be taken off and the effect of the employee's absence on the running of the employer's business (s58 ERA 1996).

The employee must be paid by his or her employer for the time taken off under section 58 (s59). Where the employee's remuneration would not have varied with the amount of work done during the period of absence, the employee should be paid as if he or she had worked for the whole of that time (s59(2)). However, where the employee's remuneration would have varied with the amount of work done, he or she should be paid their average hourly earnings for the period (s59(3) and (4)).

Any contractual remuneration paid to an employee in respect of such a period of time off goes towards discharging the liability under Reg 26 (see s59(5) and (6)).

An employee may bring a complaint to a tribunal that his or her employer has unreasonably refused to permit him or her to take the time off under s58, or has failed to pay the sums due under s59 (see s60 ERA 1996).

Remedy: Where the tribunal finds such a complaint well founded it will make a declaration to that effect (s60(3)(a)). It may also make an award of compensation to be paid by the employer (s60(3)(b) and (4)).

The amount of compensation will be that which it considers just and equitable in all the circumstances having regard to:

a) the employer's default in refusing to permit the employee to take time off; and

b) any loss sustained by the employee as a result.

Gross or net: Payment under s60(5): gross but taxable as normal under PAYE; Payment under s60(4): N/A

Limit on a week's pay: None. For payment under s60(5) the calculation is based on actual weekly pay.

Any maximum or minimum: There is no statutory limit to the award.

Mitigation: It is likely that the principle of mitigation would be applied in an appropriate case. However, this would most likely operate to restrict the losses that would be compensated for where it would have been reasonable for the employee to have incurred a lower level of losses than were in fact incurred, for example where the expenses incurred in making alternative arrangements were unreasonably expensive and reasonably avoidable.

Tax: The tax treatment is not clear. To the extent that the sum awarded is compensation for lost earnings for work done, it is likely to be taxed under s62 ITEPA 2003 (see *Tax and termination payments* and EIM02550).

Statutory authorities: ERA 1996 ss58 to 60

Time off for public duties

An employee who holds any of a number of specified public offices is entitled to take time off during his or her working hours for the purpose of performing specified duties. The duties that fall within the right depend on the office held. Offices include Justices of the Peace, and members of statutory tribunals, independent monitoring boards and visiting committees of a prison, a relevant health or education body, the Environment Agency, the Scottish Environment Protection Agency and Scottish Water. Duties for which an individual is entitled to time off include meetings and discharging the functions of the body (see s50(1) to (3) and (5) to 9B ERA 1996).

The amount of time off permitted is that which is reasonable in all the circumstances having regard to how much time is required to be taken off, how much time off the individual has taken off for trade union duties and activities and the effect of the employee's absence on the running of the employer's business (s50(4) ERA 1996).

An employee may bring a complaint to a tribunal that his or her employer has unreasonably refused to permit him or her to take the time off under s50 (s51).

Remedy: Where the tribunal finds such a complaint well founded it will make a declaration to that effect (s51(3)(a)). It may also make an award of compensation to be paid by the employer (s51(3)(b) and (4)).

The amount of the compensation shall be such as the tribunal considers just and equitable in all the circumstances having regard to:

a) the employer's default in refusing to permit the employee to take time off; and

b) any loss sustained by the employee as a result.

Any maximum or minimum: There is no statutory limit to the compensation.

Mitigation: It is likely that the principle of mitigation would be applied in an appropriate case. However, this would most likely operate to restrict the losses that would be compensated for where it would have been reasonable for the employee to have incurred a lower level of losses than were in fact incurred, for example where the expenses incurred in making alternative arrangements were unreasonably expensive and reasonably avoidable.

Tax: See EIM02550. To the extent that the sum awarded is compensation for lost earnings for work done, it is likely to be taxed under s62 ITEPA 2003 (see *Tax and termination payments* and EIM02550).

Statutory authorities: ERA 1996 ss50 and 51

Time off for study or training

Section 63D ERA 1996 creates the right to make a request for time off in relation to study or training where the purpose of the study or training is to improve the employee's effectiveness or performance in the employer's business. The procedure for making the application and for the employer's consideration of it are set out at s63D to 63H ERA 1996.

An employee may bring a complaint to an employment tribunal that his or her employer has failed to follow the required procedure, reached its decision on impermissible basis or based its decision on incorrect facts (s63I(1) ERA 1996). There are various procedural hurdles to bringing such a claim (s63I(2) to (6) ERA 1996).

Remedy: If an employment tribunal finds the complaint well founded it must make a declaration to that effect and may make an order for:

a)   reconsideration of the application; and/or

b)   an award of compensation.

The amount of any compensation will be that which the tribunal considers just and equitable in all the circumstances, limited to 8 weeks' pay (see s63J ERA 1996 and EST(ECR) Regs 2010).

Gross or net: Gross. The definition of a week's pay as defined in ss220 to 229 ERA 1996 will apply (see *Week's pay*).

Limit on a week's pay: Currently £489 (see Table 1 for historical rates).

Limit on number of weeks: 8 (see the Employee Study and Training (Eligibility, Complaints and Remedies) Regulations 2010 SI No. 156)

Any maximum or minimum: Currently the maximum is £3,912

Adjustments: None

Mitigation: N/A

Tax: The tax treatment is not clear. To the extent that the sum awarded is compensation for lost earnings for work done, it is likely to be taxed under s62 ITEPA 2003 (see *Tax and termination payments* and EIM02550).

Statutory authorities: ERA 1996 s63D to K, The Employee Study and Training (Eligibility, Complaints and Remedies) Regulations 2010 (SI 2010/156)

Time off for union duties, activities and union learning reps

An employee who is an official of an independent trade union recognised by his or her employer is entitled to take time off during working hours to carry out various official union duties (s168 TULR(C)A 1992)

An employee who is a member of a recognised trade union and a learning representative of that trade union is entitled to take time off during his working hours for a number of training related activities (s168A).

An employee who is a member of a recognised trade union is entitled to take time off during his working hours to take part in activities of the union, and activities in relation to which the employee is acting as a representative of the union (s170).

The amount of time off which must be permitted is

that which is reasonable in all the circumstances having regard to any relevant provisions of a code of practice issued by ACAS (s168(3), s168A(8) and 170(3)).

The employee must be paid by his or her employer for the time taken off under section s168 or 168A, but not s170 (s169). Where the employee's remuneration would not have varied with the amount of work done during the period of absence, the employee should be paid as if he or she had worked for the whole of that time (s169(2)). However, where the employee's remuneration would have varied with the amount of work done, he or she should be paid their average hourly earnings for the period (s169(3) and (4)).

Any contractual remuneration paid to an employee in respect of such a period of time off goes towards discharging the liability under s169 (see s169(4)).

An employee may bring a complaint to a tribunal that his employer has unreasonably refused to permit him to take time off (s168(4), s168A(9) and s170(4)). An employee may bring a complaint to a tribunal that his or her employer has failed to pay them during their time off under s169 (s169(5)).

Remedy: Where the tribunal upholds a complaint for failure to permit time off it will make a declaration to that effect and may also make an award of compensation to be paid by the employer (172(1) and (2) TULR(C)A 1992).

The amount of compensation will be that which it considers just and equitable in all the circumstances having regard to:

a)   the employer's default in refusing to permit the employee to take time off; and

b)   any loss sustained by the employee as a result.

Where a tribunal finds that an employer has failed to pay the employee during their time off, the tribunal will order that the employer pay the amount found to be due (s172(3)).

Gross or net: Net loss, or gross where taxable under s62ITEPA 2003.

Adjustments: None

Mitigation: It is likely that the principle of mitigation would be applied in an appropriate case. However, this would most likely operate to restrict the losses that would be compensated for where it would have been reasonable for the employee to have incurred a lower level of losses than were in fact incurred, for example where the expenses incurred in making alternative arrangements were unreasonably expensive and reasonably avoidable.

Tax: The tax treatment is not clear. To the extent that the sum awarded is compensation for lost earnings for work done, it is likely to be taxed under s62 ITEPA 2003 (see *Tax and termination payments* and EIM02550).

Recoupment: N/A

Statutory authorities: TULR(C)A 1992 ss168 to 173

Time off for young person for study or training

An employee who is aged 16 or 17, is not receiving full-time secondary or further education, and has not attained such standard of achievement as is prescribed by regulations made by the Secretary of State, is entitled to take time off during his or her working hours to undertake study or training leading to a relevant qualification (s63A(1) and (2) ERA 1996). The right extends to such employees who are supplied by their employer to another 'principal' (s63A(3)). The right also extends to employees who have begun their study or training but have turned 18 (s63A(4)).

The amount of time off permitted is that which is reasonable in all the circumstances having regard to the requirements of the employee's study or training and the effect of the employee's absence on the running of the employer's business (s63A(5) ERA 1996).

The employee is entitled to be paid at their 'appropriate hourly rate' for their period of absence. Unless the employee works a varying number of working hours, the appropriate hourly rate is one week's pay divided by the normal working hours in a week when the time off was taken. For employees whose hours of work vary over a week or longer period, the appropriate hourly rate is obtained by dividing one week's pay by the average number of hours worked over the previous 12 weeks, or where the employee has not been employed for 12 weeks, a number which fairly represents the number of normal working hours in a week (see s63B(1) to (4)).

A week's pay will be calculated in accordance with s220 to s229 ERA 1996 (see *Week's pay*). Any contractual remuneration paid to an employee in respect of such a period of time off goes towards discharging the liability under S63B (see s63B(5) and (6)).

An employee may bring a complaint to a tribunal that his or her employer has unreasonably refused to permit him or her to take the time off under S63A, or has failed to pay the sums due under s63B (see s63C).

Remedy: Where a tribunal finds a complaint well founded, it will make a declaration to that effect (s65C(3)).

Further, if the tribunal has found that the employer has unreasonably refused to permit the employee to take time off, the tribunal will also order the employer to pay to the employee an amount equal to the remuneration to which he or she would have been entitled under s63B if the employer had not refused (s63C(4)).

Also, if the tribunal finds that the employer has failed to pay the employee the whole or part of any amount to which he or she is entitled under s63B, the tribunal will also order the employer to pay to the employee the amount he or she is owed (s63C(5)).

For employees working fixed number of hours per week
Sum to which the employee is entitled = (gross weekly pay) x 1/(number of normal working hours in a week) x (number of hours absent) (s63B(2) ERA 1996)

For employees with varying number of hours worked per week
Sum to which the employee is entitled = gross weekly pay x 12/(number of normal hours worked in the last 12 weeks ending with the last complete week before the day on which the time off is taken) x (number of hours absent) (s63B(3) ERA 1996)

For employees with varying number of hours worked per week and who have worked for less than 12 weeks
Sum to which the employee is entitled = (gross weekly pay) x 1/(number of normal hours which fairly represents the number of normal working hours in a week) x (number of hours absent) (s63B(3) and (4) ERA 1996)

Gross or net: Gross. The definition of a week's pay as defined in ss220 to 229 ERA 1996 will apply (see *Week's pay*).

Limit on a week's pay: None. The calculation is based on actual gross weekly pay.

Limit on number of weeks: None

Any maximum or minimum: None

Adjustments: None

Mitigation: N/A

Tax: The tax treatment is not clear. To the extent that the sum awarded is compensation for lost earnings for work done, it is likely to be taxed under s62 ITEPA 2003 (see *Tax and termination payments* and EIM02550).

Recoupment: N/A

Statutory authorities: ERA 1996 s63A to 63C

Time off to look for work or arrange training after being made redundant

An employee who is given notice of dismissal by reason of redundancy and who has sufficient continuity of service to receive a statutory redundancy payment, is entitled to take reasonable time off during his or her working hours before the end of his notice in order to look for new employment, or make arrangements for training for future employment (s52 ERA 1996).

The employee is entitled to be paid at their 'appropriate hourly rate' for their period of absence. Unless the employee works a varying number of working hours, the appropriate hourly rate is one week's pay divided by the normal working hours in a week when the time off was taken. For employees whose hours of work vary over a week or longer period, the appropriate hourly rate is obtained by dividing one week's pay by the average number of hours per week worked over the previous 12 weeks (s53(1) to (3)).

If an employer unreasonably refuses to permit an employee to take the time permitted by s52, the employee is entitled to be paid the amount of remuneration he would have been entitled to if he had been given the time off (s53(4)). A week's pay will be calculated in accordance with s220 to s229 ERA 1996 (see *Week's pay*). Any contractual remuneration paid to an employee in respect of such a period of time off goes towards discharging the liability under s53 (see s53(6) and (7)).

The total liability to pay remuneration for an employee's time off is limited to 40 per cent of a week's pay for that employee (s53(5) ERA 1996).

An employee may bring a complaint to a tribunal that his or her employer has unreasonably refused to permit him or her to take the time off under s52, or has failed to pay the sums due under s53 (see s54).

Remedy: Where a tribunal finds a complaint well founded, it will make a declaration to that effect (s54(3)(a)) and will order the employer to pay the employee the amount which it finds due to him (s54(3)(b)).

For employees working fixed number of hours per week
Sum to which the employee is entitled = (gross weekly pay) x 1/(number of normal working hours in a week) x (number of hours absent) (s53(2) ERA 1996)

For employees with varying number of hours worked per week
Sum to which the employee is entitled = gross weekly pay x 12/(number of normal hours worked in the last 12 weeks ending with the last complete week before the day on which the time off is taken) x (number of hours absent) (s53(3) ERA 1996)

Gross or net: Gross. The definition of a week's pay as defined in ss220 to 229 ERA 1996 will apply (see *Week's pay*).

Limit on a week's pay: None. The calculation is based on actual gross weekly pay.

Limit on number of weeks: None

Any maximum or minimum: Yes, the maximum payable is 40% of an actual week's gross pay (s53(5) ERA 1996).

Tax: The tax treatment is not clear. To the extent that the sum awarded is compensation for lost earnings for work done, it is likely to be taxed under s62 ITEPA 2003 (see EIM02550). The sum may also be paid in connection with termination and be taxable under s401 (see *Tax and termination payments*).

Statutory authorities: ERA 1996 ss52 to 54

Trade unions: see Union activities or collective bargaining (inducements); Union member (deduction of unauthorised or excessive subscriptions); Union member (deduction of contributions to political fund); Union member (unjustifiably disciplined); Union member (refusal of employment); Union member (expelled or excluded)

TUPE information and consultation

The employer of any employees affected by a TUPE transfer must inform and consult their appropriate representatives before the transfer to enable consultation with any affected employees. The information must include: the fact that the transfer is to take place, the date or proposed date of the transfer and the reasons for it; the legal, economic and social implications of the transfer for any affected employees; the measures which he envisages he will take in relation to any affected employees; and if the employer is the transferor, the measures, in connection with the transfer, which he envisages the transferee will take in relation to any affected employees who will become employees of the transferee after the transfer by virtue of regulation 4. The employer is under a duty to consult where they envisage that they will be taking measures in relation to any affected employee. Consultation must be with a view to seeking the agreement of the representatives to the intended measures (Reg 13 TUPE 2006).

Appropriate employee representatives will be the representatives of a recognised trade union, or if none exist, representatives appointed or elected with the authority to be informed and consulted (Regs 13(3) and 14). There is an exception for employers with fewer than 10 employees who, if certain conditions are met, may inform and consult the affected employees directly (Reg 13A (in force for transfers occurring on or after 31 July 2014)).

Generally speaking, it is the representatives who may bring a claim to a tribunal for failure to inform and/or consult (Reg 15(1)). Once a tribunal has made an award, any employee who falls within the description of employees covered by that award may bring a complaint to a tribunal that the particular award to which he is entitled has not been paid to him (Reg 15(10)).

Remedy: Where the tribunal finds a complaint under s15(1) well founded it will make a declaration to that effect and can award such compensation as the tribunal considers just and equitable having regard to the seriousness of the failure of the employer to comply with the duty, of up to 13 weeks' pay. The compensation will be ordered to be paid to '*such descriptions of affected employees as may be specified*', which will reflect the employees in respect of whom there has been a failure (Reg 15(7) and (8)).

The award is punitive, not compensatory. Its purpose is to provide a sanction for breach of the obligation to inform and consult. The tribunal has a wide discretion but it will focus on the seriousness of the default, which may vary from the merely technical to a complete failure to comply with the duties, and it may consider the deliberateness of the failure.

The proper approach where there has been no consultation is to start at the maximum and reduce it if there are mitigating circumstances justifying a reduction (see *Susie Radin Ltd v GMB & Ors* [2004] ICR 893).

However, the tribunal should not take this approach where there has been some information given and/or some consultation (see *Todd v Strain & Ors* [2011] IRLR 11 and *London Borough of Barnet v Unison & Ors* UKEAT/0191/13).

Gross or net: Gross. A week's pay as defined in ss220 to 229 ERA 1996 applies (see *Week's pay*).

Limit on a week's pay: None. The calculation is based on actual gross weekly pay (see *Zaman & Ors v Kozee Sleep Products Ltd t/a Dorlux Beds* UK UKEAT/0312/10/CEA).

Limit on number of weeks: 13

Adjustments: None

Mitigation: N/A

Tax: The tax treatment is unclear but it is likely that HMRC would regard any payment made under TUPE to fall under s401 ITEPA 2003 (see *Tax and termination payments*).

Recoupment: N/A

Statutory authorities: TUPE 2006 Regs 13 to 16

Relevant case law: *Cable Realisations Ltd v GMB Northern* [2010] IRLR 42; *London Borough of Barnet v Unison & Ors* UKEAT/0191/13; *Susie Radin Ltd v GMB & Ors* [2004] ICR 893; *Sweeting v Coral Racing* [2006] IRLR 252; *Todd v Strain & Ors* [2011] IRLR 11; *Zaman & Ors v Kozee Sleep Products Ltd t/a Dorlux Beds UK* UKEAT/0312/10/CEA

TUPE (failure to notify employee liability information)

The transferor is obliged to provide specified employee liability information to the transferee for any employees who will be transferred, at least 14 days before the relevant transfer (Reg 11 TUPE

2006). For any transfer occurring on or after 1 May 2014, the information must be provided at least 28 days before the relevant transfer (Reg 10 CRATU(PE) Regs 2014).

A transferee may present a complaint to a tribunal that the transferor has failed to comply with any provisions of Reg 11 (Reg 12(1)).

Remedy: Where a tribunal finds a complaint well founded it must make a declaration to that effect and may make an award of compensation to be paid by the transferor to the transferee (Reg 12(3)). The amount of compensation will be that which the tribunal considers just and equitable in all the circumstances having particular regard to the losses sustained by the transferee as a result of the failure to provide information, and any relevant terms of any contract between the transferor and transferee dealing with payment for such a failure (Reg 12(4)).

There are two further provisions that may influence the amount of any award:

- By Reg 12(5) the amount of compensation must be a minimum of £500 per employee whose liability information has not been provided, subject to the discretion of the tribunal to award a lesser sum if in all the circumstances it considers it just and equitable.

- By Reg 12(6) the tribunal must apply the common law rules as to mitigation in assessing the loss suffered by the transferee.

Gross or net: Loss will likely be calculated net of any tax that may be payable

Any maximum or minimum: Minimum is £500 per employee whose liability information has not been provided, unless the tribunal considers it is just and equitable to award a lesser sum.

Adjustments: N/A

Mitigation: The transferee is under a duty to mitigate their loss.

Tax: The tax treatment is unclear.

Statutory authorities: TUPE 2006 Regs 11 and 12; CRATU(PE) Regs 2014 Reg 10

Unauthorised deductions: see Unlawful deductions from wages

Unfair dismissal

(see also Additional award; Adjustments; Basic award; Compensatory award; Damages for wrongful dismissal; Mitigation)

The right not to be unfairly dismissed is established by s94 ERA 1996. The definition of a dismissal is set out at s95, and includes dismissal with or without notice, the termination of a fixed term contract and dismissal where the employer or employee has committed a repudiatory breach of contract entitling the other to terminate the contract immediately (constructive dismissal). Whether a dismissal is fair or unfair will be determined by a tribunal applying the tests set out in s98, which include that the employer's reason for the dismissal must be one of a number of specified reasons (including misconduct and redundancy), and require the tribunal to assess whether the employer acted reasonably or unreasonably in treating its reason as a sufficient reason for dismissing the employee. This second stage is itself the subject of extensive further guideline cases, which are outside the scope of this work.

Where the reason, or if more than one reason the principal reason for the dismissal is one of a number of protected reasons, the dismissal will be automatically unfair. The protected reasons are:

- Being summoned to attend for jury service or being absent for attending jury service (s98B ERA 1996);

- Exercising rights to family leave (s99 ERA 1996);

- Exercising various health and safety functions (s100 ERA 1996);

- Refusing to work on a Sunday (if a specified shop or betting worker) (s101 ERA 1996) or refusing to work additional hours on a Sunday (s101ZA ERA 1996);

- Taking various actions under the Working Time Regulations 1998 (s101A ERA 1996);

- Exercising various rights to participate in education or training (s101B ERA 1996);

- Performing various functions of the trustee of an occupational pension scheme (s102 ERA 1996);

- Performing various functions related to being an employee representative (s103 ERA 1996);

- Making a protected disclosure (whistleblowing) (s103A ERA 1996);

• Asserting one of a number of statutory rights (s104 ERA 1996);

• Reasons related to action taken under the National Minimum Wage Act 1998 (s104A ERA 1996);

• Reasons related to actions taken under the Tax Credits Act 2002 (s104B ERA 1996);

• Exercising various rights to flexible working (s104C ERA 1996);

• Reasons related to actions taken relating to pension enrolment (s104D ERA 1996);

• Exercising various rights to study and training (s104E ERA 1996);

• Reasons related to the existence of trade union blacklist (s104F ERA 1996);

• Refusing to accept an offer of employee shareholder status (s104G ERA 1996);

• Reasons relating to actions taken related to trade union recognition (para 161 Sch A1 TULR(C)A 1992);

• Reasons related to trade union membership or activities (s152 TULR(C)A 1992); and

• Redundancy, but the reason or principal reason for selection for redundancy was one of a long list of protected reasons (s105(3) to (7N), s153 TULR(C)A 1992 and paragraph 162 Sch 1A TULR(C)A 1992).

The right to not be dismissed unfairly generally accrues to an employee after the completion of 2 years' service (see s108(1) ERA 1996). However, where the dismissal relates to a number of protected reasons, the period of continuous service required is either reduced or removed entirely (s108(2) to (4)). Most of the automatically unfair dismissal provisions can be relied upon by a dismissed employee who has not completed 2 years' continuous service.

Where the reason for a dismissal is related to industrial action, specific provisions apply (see s237 to 239 TULR(C)A 1992).

An individual may bring a complaint to a tribunal that he or she has been unfairly dismissed (s111 ERA 1996).

An individual may also bring a complaint to a tribunal that he or she has been unfairly dismissed and seek an order for continuation of the contract of employment under the interim relief provisions (s128 to 132 ERA 1996 and s161 to 167 TULR(C)A 1992). This remedy is limited to allegations of unfair

dismissal where the alleged reason or principal reason for the dismissal falls within the automatically unfair dismissal provisions relating to representative roles, the existence of a blacklist, trade union membership and activities and making a protected disclosure.

Remedy: Where a tribunal has found a dismissal to be unfair the remedies available are reinstatement, re-engagement and compensation (s112 to 126 ERA 1996). See *Re-engagement and reinstatement*.

The tribunal must explain to a successful claimant the three orders available to it (s112(2) ERA 1996). Though the primary remedies are reinstatement or re-engagement, this is rarely granted in practice and it is most often the case that claimants seek only an award of compensation.

Where an order for reinstatement or re-engagement is not fully complied with (and the respondent fails to establish that such reinstatement or re-engagement was not practicable), the tribunal will award compensation under s117(2) (s117(1) ERA 1996).

Where the tribunal is not asked to order reinstatement or re-engagement, or where a claimant has not been reinstated or re-engaged, the tribunal will make an award of compensation under s118 to 126 ERA 1996 (s117(3) and (4) and s112(4) ERA 1996) (see also *Additional award*).

The award of compensation under s118 to 126 ERA 1996 consists of a basic award and compensatory award (see *Basic award, Compensatory award*).

The basic award is calculated on the basis of (capped) gross weekly pay and the number of years' continuous service (the longer the service the higher the award).

The compensatory award compensates the individual for the financial losses suffered as a result of the dismissal and is based on actual net weekly pay. Except where the dismissal is for one of a limited number of protected reasons, the compensatory award is capped at the lesser of one year's gross pay and currently £80,541 (see *Statutory cap* and Table 1). Compensation for non-pecuniary losses, such as injury to feelings, is not available within a compensatory award (see *Dunnachie v Kingston upon Hull City Council* [2005] 1 AC 226).

Awards of compensation for unfair dismissal may be adjusted for failure to comply with a relevant code of practice (see *Adjustments and order of adjustments*).

The specific interim remedy of a continuation order

is available in limited circumstances where a claimant has sought interim relief under s128 to s132 ERA 1996 and s161 to 167 TULR(C)A 1992 (see *Interim relief*).

Union activities or collective bargaining (inducements)

A worker has the right not to have an offer made to him by his employer to induce the worker: not to be or seek to become a member of a trade union; not to take part in the activities of a trade union; not to make use of trade union services; or to be or become a member of any trade union (s145A of TULR(C)A 1992).

A worker who is a member of a trade union which is recognised, or seeking to be recognised, by his employer has the right not to have an offer made to him by his employer if: acceptance of the offer, together with other workers' acceptance of offers which the employer also makes to them, would have 'the prohibited result', and the employer's sole or main purpose in making the offers is to achieve that result. The 'prohibited result' is that the workers' terms will not or will not continue to be determined by collective bargaining (s145B of TULR(C)A 1992).

A worker or former worker may bring a complaint to a tribunal that the employer has made an offer in contravention of s145A or 145B (s145A(5) and s145B(5)).

Remedy: Where a tribunal finds such a complaint well founded, it will make a declaration to that effect and will make an award of £3,907 (s145E(1) to (3) TULR(C)A 1992).

Section 145E prescribes certain other consequences where an unlawful offer has been made, which exist without a claim having been brought to a tribunal. By s145E(4) any agreement to vary the terms of employment between the worker and employer will not be enforceable by the employer, however if merely as a result of the acceptance (e.g. because collectively agreed terms would have been different in those circumstances) nothing in s145A or 145B makes the variation unenforceable by either party.

Adjustments: s38 EA 2002 adjustment for failure to give statement of employment particulars applies. ACAS uplift applies (Schedule A2 TULR(C)A).

Mitigation: N/A

Tax: The tax treatment of this award is unclear.

Recoupment: N/A

Statutory authorities: TULR(C)A 1992 ss145A, B & E

Union member (deduction of unauthorised or excessive subscriptions)

Where arrangements exist between an employer and a trade union for the deduction of membership subscriptions from an employee, the employer must ensure that no subscription deductions are made for any worker if he or she has not authorised the deduction or has withdrawn authorisation (see s68 TULR(C)A 1992).

A worker may bring a complaint to a tribunal that that his employer has made such a deduction (s68A(1) TULR(C)A 1992).

Remedy: Where a tribunal finds that the complaint is well founded, it will make a declaration to that effect and will order the employer to pay to the worker the amount of the deduction owing to the employee (s68A(3)). s68A(4) makes provision to ensure there is no double recovery where the sum deducted might also be claimed under another jurisdiction, such as s13 ERA 1996 (unlawful deductions from wages).

Gross or net: The actual amount of any deductions owing should be paid.

Any maximum or minimum: None

Statutory authorities: TULR(C)A 1992 ss68 and 68A

Union member (deduction of contributions to political fund)

Trade unions may maintain political funds, and seek contributions to that fund from members. A member may object to contributing to the political fund. If a member of a trade union which has a political fund informs his employer in writing that he is exempt from the obligation to contribute to the fund, or he has notified the union in writing of his objection to contributing to the fund, the employer is obliged to ensure that no amount representing a contribution to the political fund is deducted by him from emoluments payable to that individual (see s84 and s86 TULR(C)A 1992).

A member may bring a claim to the tribunal alleging that his employer has made a deduction contrary to s86 (s87(1) TULR(C)A 1992).

A member may bring a further complaint in circumstances where an order granted under the first complaint to prevent a repetition of the failure has not been complied with (s87(5) TULR(C)A 1992).

Remedy: Where a tribunal finds a complaint under s87(1) well founded, it will make a declaration to that effect and may order the employer to pay to the complainant the amount deducted less any part of that amount already paid to him by the employer (s87(4)(a) TULR(C)A) The tribunal may also order the employer to take steps to prevent a repetition of the failure (s87(4)(b)).

A complainant may bring a complaint alleging that his or her employer has not complied with the order under s87(4)(b) (s87(5)). If the tribunal finds that the employer has without reasonable excuse failed to comply with the order, it will order the employer to pay the complainant 2 weeks' pay (s87(7)).

Gross or net:

Deductions under s87(4)(a): the actual amount of the deducted owing must be paid.

Non-compliance with s87(4)(b): gross weekly pay according to s220 to s229 ERA 1996 (s87(8) TULR(C)A 1992).

Limit on a week's pay: None

Limit on number of weeks: For a complaint under s87(7) the limit is 2 weeks' pay.

Any maximum or minimum: None

Adjustments: None

Mitigation: N/A

Tax: The actual deductions should be repaid, and there should be no impact on tax calculations. It is unclear whether the 2 weeks' pay will be subject to tax.

Recoupment: N/A

Statutory authorities: TULR(C)A 1992 ss84 to 87

Union member (unjustifiably disciplined)

An individual who is or has been a member of a trade union has the right not to be unjustifiably disciplined by the union (s64(1) TULR(C)A 1992). Section 64(2) identifies what actions of the union amount to 'discipline', whilst s65 identifies those reasons for the discipline which render the discipline 'unjustified'.

This right gives rise to two circumstances in which a claim may be brought to a tribunal. First, a member may bring a claim alleging that he or she has been unjustifiably disciplined (s66(1)). Second, where such a claim has been declared well founded it is envisaged the parties may reach agreement to deal with the issue between them, but the individual may bring a claim under s67(1) to enforce such an agreement or seek compensation.

Remedy: The primary remedy, following a complaint under s66(1), is a declaration from the tribunal that the individual has been unjustifiably disciplined (s66(3)).

Where the individual has succeeded under a s66(1) claim, it is envisaged the parties may reach agreement to deal with the issue between them, but the individual may bring a claim under s67(1) to enforce such an agreement or seek compensation.

The amount of compensation awarded will be that which the employment tribunal considers just and equitable in all the circumstances (s67(3)). The tribunal will apply the common law principles of mitigation (s67(4)) and may reduce any award for contributory fault (s67(5)).

Gross or net: It is likely that this will be paid gross.

Any maximum or minimum:
Minimum: The amount of compensation will not be less than £9,118 where on the date the s67(1) application was made the union has not revoked the decision to discipline the member or taken all necessary steps to secure the reversal of anything done to give effect to the disciplinary sanction (TULR(C)A 1992 s67(8A) and s176(6A)).

Maximum: The total award will not exceed the aggregate of the maximum basic award (£14,670) and the maximum compensatory award (£80,541) i.e. £95,211 (TULR(C)A 1992 s67(7) and ERA 1996 s227(1)(a) and s124(1)).

Adjustments: Yes, for contributory conduct.

Cap: A cap applies (see above).

Mitigation: Yes, the member is under a duty to mitigate any losses.

Tax: It is likely that this will be treated as a punishment or fine, and not taxed.

Recoupment: N/A

Statutory authorities: ERA 1996 s227(1)(a) and s124(1); TULR(C)A 1992 ss64 to 67

Union member (refusal of employment)

It is unlawful to refuse a person employment because he is or is not a member of a trade union, or because he is unwilling to accept a requirement that he take steps to cease to be or to remain or to become a member of a trade union, or a requirement to make payments or suffer deductions in the event of him not being a member of a trade union (s137 TULR(C)A 1992).

An equivalent right applies where an employment agency refuses such a person any of its services (s138 TULR(C)A 1992).

An individual may bring a complaint to a tribunal that this right has been infringed (s137(2) and s138(2) TULR(C)A 1992).

Remedy: Where a tribunal finds such a complaint well founded, it will make a declaration to that effect and may make an order of compensation (s140(1)(a)) and/or a recommendation (s140(1)(b)).

Compensation will be assessed on the same basis as damages for breach of statutory duty (as are discrimination claims) and may include compensation for injury to feelings (s140(1)(a) and s140(2) TULR(C)A). The total compensation is limited to the maximum sum available under a compensatory award (s140(4)).

Any recommendation will require the respondent to take action to obviate or reduce the adverse effect on the complainant of the conduct that forms the basis of the complaint (s140(1)(b)).

Where the respondent fails without reasonable justification to comply with a recommendation, the tribunal may make an award of compensation, or increase it if it has already made an award (s140(3)).

Gross or net: The award of compensation will be made on the basis of net loss.

Limit on a week's pay: None

Limit on number of weeks: None

Any maximum or minimum: The maximum award is that of the statutory cap on unfair dismissal in force at the date of the breach under s124(1) ERA 1996, currently the lesser of £80,541 and 52 weeks' gross pay. There is no minimum.

Adjustments: None

Compensation cap: See maximum above.

Mitigation: The usual rules as to mitigation in discrimination claims will apply.

Tax: The tax treatment of this award is unclear.

Recoupment: N/A

Statutory authorities: ERA 1996 s124(1); TULR(C)A 1992 ss137 to 143

Union member (expelled or excluded)

An individual is protected from being excluded or expelled from a trade union unless the exclusion or expulsion is permitted by s174(2) TULR(C)A. The legitimate reasons for exclusion or expulsion include that the individual no longer satisfies enforceable membership criteria or has committed misconduct.

This right gives rise to two circumstances in which a claim may be brought to a tribunal. First, a member may bring a claim alleging that he or she has been excluded or expelled from a trade union (s174(5)). Second, where such a claim has been declared well founded it is envisaged the parties may reach agreement to deal with the issue between them, but the individual is may bring a claim under s176(2) to enforce such an agreement or seek compensation.

Remedy: The primary remedy, following a complaint under s174(5), is a declaration from the tribunal that the claim is well founded (s176(1)). The tribunal must also make a declaration, stating that effect, where the exclusion or expulsion was mainly attributable to a reason relating to the individual being a member of a political party (s176(1A)) and (if it applies) that the exclusion or expulsion was otherwise wholly or mainly attributable to conduct of the individual contrary to a rule of the union or an objective of the union (s176(1B)).

Where the individual has succeeded under a s176(1) claim, the individual may bring a claim under s176(2) to seek compensation. The amount of compensation awarded will be that which the employment tribunal considers just and equitable in all the circumstances (s176(4)). The tribunal may reduce any award for contributory fault (s176(5)).

Gross or net: It is likely that this will be paid gross.

Any maximum or minimum:
Minimum: The amount of compensation will not be less than £9,118 where on the date the s176(1) application was made the union has not admitted or readmitted the member (TULR(C)A 1992 s67(8A) and s176(6A)), unless the tribunal also made declarations under s176(1A) and (1B) (see s176(6B)).

Maximum: The total award will not exceed the aggregate of 30 times the limit on a week's pay under s227(1)(a) ERA 1996 (£14,670) and the maximum compensatory award (£80,541) i.e. £95,211 (TULR(C)A 1992 s176(7) and ERA 1996 s227(1)(a) and s124(1)).

Adjustments: Yes, for contributory conduct.

Cap: A cap applies (see above).

Mitigation: The member is likely to be under a duty to mitigate any losses for which he or she seeks compensation

Tax: It is likely that this will be treated as a punishment or fine, and not taxed.

Recoupment: N/A

Statutory authorities: ERA 1996 ss113, 124(1) and 227(1); TULR(C)A 1992 ss174 to 176

Union membership (blacklists, unfair dismissal/redundancy): see Basic award, minimum; Unfair dismissal

Union membership or activities (detriment): see Detriment

Unlawful deductions from wages

(see also Holiday pay; National Minimum Wage)

A worker has the right not to suffer deductions from wages except under prescribed circumstances, which are as follows:

- Deductions required or authorised by statute (such as PAYE) or by a provision in the worker's contract (s13(1)(a));

- Deductions previously agreed to and signified in writing by the worker (s13(1)(b));

- Deductions for reimbursement of an overpayment of wages or expenses (s14(1));

- Payment to third parties for which the individual has given written consent (s14(4));

- Deductions on account of the worker's participation in industrial action (s14(5));

- Deductions made in respect of an attachment of earnings order made by a court, where the individual has given written consent (s14(6));

- Deductions made to a public authority as required under statute (s14(3)).

Wages is broadly interpreted, including salaries, fees, bonuses, commissions and holiday pay (both contractual and under the WTR 1998 (see *HMRC v Stringer* [2009] IRLR 677). The definition of wages does not usually include pay in lieu of notice (see *Delaney v Staples* [1992] ICR 483). Also, where the sum claimed is dependent on the exercise of a discretion by the employer that has yet to be determined, such as a discretionary bonus, no identifiable sum exists and the claim must be brought as a breach of contract claim in the tribunal or the civil courts, rather than as an unlawful deduction claim (see *Adcock v Coors Brewers Ltd* [2007] IRLR 440).

Workers in the retail industry have special protection, whereby deductions to compensate for cash or stock shortages within a period may not exceed 10% of the worker's gross wages in that period (see ss17 to 22).

A worker may bring a claim to a tribunal that his employer has made unlawful deductions from his wages (s23(1) ERA 1996).

Remedy: Where a tribunal finds a complaint under s23 well founded, it will make a declaration to that effect and will order the employer to pay the worker the sum found to have been deducted unlawfully (s24(1)). The tribunal may also make such award as it considers appropriate in all the circumstances to compensate the worker for any financial loss sustained by him which is attributable to the unlawful deduction (s24(2)).

Gross or net: The sums awarded ought to be calculated on a gross basis, since they will be taxable under s62 ITEPA 2003.

Adjustments: The ACAS uplift applies (Schedule A2 TULR(C)A).

Cap: There is no statutory cap on the sums that may be awarded by the tribunal but sums can only be claimed for the previous 2 years before the claim was made (Deductions from Wages (Limitation)

Regulations 2014 SI 2014/322, effective 1 July 2015). This includes holiday pay as well as any other deduction.

Mitigation: The usual principles of mitigation will likely apply to any award under s24(2), but the award for repayment of deductions does not need to be mitigated.

Tax: Taxable under s62 ITEPA 2003

Recoupment: N/A

Statutory authorities: ERA 1996 ss13 to 26; Deductions from Wages (Limitation) Regulations 2014 SI 2014/322

Unreasonable refusal to be reinstated: see Additional award

Variable hours: see Holiday pay; Week's pay

Varying pay with output: see Holiday pay; Week's pay

Victimisation: see Discrimination

Week's pay

The concept of a week's pay is defined by ss220 to 229 and s234 ERA 1996. It is used for calculating a remedy in each of the following employment rights (see Table 5 for a list of claims, the relevant calculation date and whether a limit on a week's pay applies):

- Additional award (s117(1) ERA 1996);

- Basic award/Redundancy pay (ss119(2), 121 and 162(2) ERA 1996);

- Guarantee pay (s30(2) ERA 1996);

- Payments on the insolvency of an employer;

- Protective award (s190(2) TULR(C)A 1992);

- Remuneration whilst suspended on medical or maternity grounds (s69(1) ERA 1996);

- Right for union member not to be unjustifiably disciplined/expelled and blacklisting claims (ss67(8)(a) and 176(6)(a) TULR(C)A 1992);

- Failure to inform and consult union on training for workers (s70C(4) TULR(C)A 1992);

- Time off to look for work or arrange training after being made redundant (s54(4) ERA 1996);

- Time off for antenatal care (s56(2) ERA 1996);

- Absence during statutory notice period (ss88(1) to 89(1) ERA 1996);

- Time off for employee representatives (including ICE and OPPS) (s62(2) ERA 1996, Reg 28(2) ICE Regs 2004, Sch para 3(2) OPPS Regs 2006);

- Time off for study or training (s63J(3) ERA 1996);

- Time off for young person for study or training (s63B(2) ERA 1996);

- Time off for members of a European Works Council (Reg 26(2) TICE 1999);

- Failure to inform and consult under TUPE (Reg 16(3) TUPE Regs 2006);

- Right to be accompanied at a disciplinary or grievance meeting (s11(3) ERelA 1999);

- Infringement of right to be accompanied at flexible working meeting (Reg 15(3) FW(PRR) Regs 2002);

- Rejection of flexible working application (Reg 7 FW(ECR) Regs 2002);

- Written reasons for dismissal (s93(2) ERA 1996);

- Written statement of particulars (s38 EA 2002); and

- Paid annual leave under the Working Time Regulations (Reg 16(1) WTR 1998).

What is a week's pay?

In essence, a week's pay is the gross contractual remuneration an employee is entitled to be paid when working their normal hours each week. Difficulties emerge in the calculation where an individual typically receives pay in addition to their contractual salary (such as voluntary overtime), or where they do not have normal working hours each week, such as when working irregular shift patterns.

Since pay will vary over the period of employment of an individual, for each remedy that uses the definition of a week's pay, a calculation date is specified (see Table 5). For a number of remedies, a week's pay is capped, currently at £489 (see Table 5 for a full list).

Working hours

An employee's normal working hours will often be identified in their written particulars (s221(1)) or other contractual documentation. Failing this, it may be clear from the hours actually worked.

Matters are complicated where a contract specifies a minimum number of hours to be worked each week and also provides for an increased overtime wage to be paid beyond a certain number of hours. By s234, in that situation the normal working hours will be the minimum number of hours specified, even if overtime is paid for a smaller number of hours, and even if the minimum number of hours can be reduced in certain circumstances.

- Where overtime is obligatory for the employee, but is not guaranteed by the employer, the normal working hours will not include those additional hours - they will only amount to normal working hours if the obligation to work and provide work for that period is mutual (see *Tarmac Roadstone Holdings Ltd v Peacock* [1973] ICR 273). Further, where employees are paid on the basis of a pre-estimate of the number of hours a task will take, though the time taken may vary, the pre-estimate will not amount to normal working hours (see *Sanderson v Exel Management Services Ltd* [2006] ICR 1337).

- Remuneration where an employee has normal working hours is calculated as the contractual payments made to the employee for the work they have done.

- Contractual bonuses are usually included, such as a regular shift bonus (see *Mole Mining Ltd v Jenkins* [1972] ICR 282). It may be possible to infer a contractual term that a regular bonus, such as a site bonus in the construction industry, will be paid unless certain conditions are met, such that it falls within remuneration (see *Donelan v Kerrby Constructions* [1983] ICR 237).

- Discretionary bonuses will not form part of the remuneration, unless deemed a contractual payment (see *Canadian Imperial Bank of Commerce v Beck* EAT/0141/10/RN and *Hoyland v Asda Stores Ltd* [2006] IRLR 468).

- Tips paid by the employer (but not by customers to the employee in cash) will count as remuneration (see *Palmanor Ltd v Cedron* [1978] ICR 1008 and *Nerva v RL&G Ltd* [1997] ICR 11). However, it may be that non-cash tips distributed through a tronc system set up by the employer do not count as remuneration, as they do not count towards the minimum wage (see *Revenue and Customs Commissioners v Annabel's (Berkeley Square) Ltd* [2009] ICR 1123).

- Commission which is a regular part of an employee's earnings will amount to remuneration, and can be apportioned as the tribunal deems appropriate (see *Weevsmay Ltd v Kings* [1977] ICR 244 and *J and S Bickley Ltd v Washer* [1977] ICR 425).

- Benefits in kind, such as free lodging, will not count as remuneration.

- Where an individual has been paid less than the minimum wage, the calculation of a week's pay should be based on the pay the individual ought to have received, but at the rate applicable at the date of the hearing (see *Paggetti v Cobb* [2002] IRLR 861).

Where an employee has normal working hours
There are three alternative routes to calculating a week's pay:

- **'time workers'**, where the remuneration does not vary with the amount of work done, which includes work where commission is awarded for success achieved, as opposed to being awarded for the work actually done (see *Evans v Malley Organisation Ltd t/a First Business Support* [2003] ICR 432). A week's pay is the amount payable by the employer to the employee under the contract in force at the calculation date if the individual works the normal working hours in a week (s221(2));

- **'piece workers'**, where the remuneration varies according to the amount of work done during normal working hours but does not vary according to the times or days when the work is done. A week's pay is the average hourly rate for the normal working hours calculated over the previous 12 weeks (s221(3)). For these purposes remuneration will include commission which is awarded for success achieved, as opposed to being awarded for the work actually done (see *Evans v Malley Organisation Ltd t/a First Business Support* [2003] ICR 432);

- **'shift workers'**, where normal working hours are worked at times of the day or days of the week that vary from week to week and where remuneration also varies from week to week. A week's pay is calculated over a period of 12 weeks by reference to the average hourly rate multiplied by the average number of normal weekly hours (s222).

Where an employee has no normal working hours
A week's pay is calculated by reference to average weekly remuneration over a 12 week period (s224). In this situation, any overtime payments received will count towards remuneration, whether or not

there is a mutual obligation to work and provide overtime (see above re normal working hours).

The 12 week period is based on complete weeks worked (s221(3) and (4) and s235(1)). Any week in which the individual was not working or was not paid remuneration will not count, and an earlier week will be brought in to make up the 12 weeks (s223(2) and s224(3)).

Is the calculation of a week's pay in compliance with EU law?

The concept of a week's pay is used in the working time regulations to calculate holiday pay entitlement. However, the particular means to calculate a week's pay frequently leads to individuals receiving less money than they would have received had they not taken the holiday, for example where regular overtime is required but there is no obligation on the employer to offer it. Please see the section on *Holiday pay* for a more detailed discussion of this issue.

The following examples demonstrate the calculation of a week's pay.

Normal working hours

Straightforward number of hours and constant pay per hour/week/month

1. Weekly pay for hourly paid employees
Weekly pay for hourly paid employees = Number of normal hours worked per week x (hourly rate + hourly commission/bonus if they are constant).

If the commission is not constant, this calculation does not apply (see below). If the period of commission does not coincide with the period of payment, the weekly pay should be calculated in a manner which is just, over the whole period (s229(2)).

2. Weekly pay for monthly, annual or other period paid employees
The tribunal must apportion the payment in the manner that is considers just (ERA 1996 s229(2)).

One way in which this could be done is as follows:

> Weekly pay = Monthly salary ÷ 4.3 (or alternatively, monthly salary x 12 ÷ 365 x 7 which produces a slightly different answer because of rounding errors)

> Weekly pay = Annual salary ÷ 52

> Weekly pay = Other period salary ÷ number of days in which it was earned x 7

3. Weekly pay with differing commission
Weekly pay with differing commission = Number of hours worked in a week x hourly rate + (total commission earned ÷ number of weeks in which it was earned)

Straightforward but pay and/or commission/bonus varying with output (piece workers)

Weekly pay = Average hourly rate x hours in a normal working week = (Total remuneration, including overtime, in the previous 12 week period ÷ total hours worked in the 12 week period) x hours in a normal working week

However, note that overtime hours are rated as basic hours - overtime premiums are ignored.

Variable hours (shift workers)

Weekly pay = Average hourly rate x average hours in a normal working week = (Total remuneration in previous 12 weeks ÷ Total hours worked in previous 12 weeks, including overtime hours if they form part of the normal working hours) x (number of hours worked in the 12 week period ÷12)

Note: the 12 weeks needs to be taken prior to the pay date or the calculation date, whichever is the earlier.

Also, if in any week no remuneration or guaranteed pay was paid, those weeks are ignored and an earlier week is used in the calculation.

No normal working hours (casual workers)

Weekly pay = Total remuneration, including overtime and overtime rates, in 12 weeks immediately before calculation date (or the pay day immediately before the calculation date if calculation date is not the same as the pay date) ÷ 12

Statutory authorities: Chapter II ERA 1996

Relevant case law: *BA v Williams* [2011] IRLR 948; *Bear Scotland & Ors v Fulton & Ors* UKEATS/0047/13/BI; *Canadian Imperial Bank of Commerce v Beck* EAT 0141/10; *Donelan v Kerrby Constructions* [1983] ICR 237; *Evans v Malley Organisation Ltd t/a First Business Support* [2003] ICR 432; *Fox v C Wright (Farmers) Ltd* [1978] ICR 98; *Hoyland v Asda Stores Ltd* [2006] IRLR 468; *J and S Bickley Ltd v Washer* [1977] ICR 425; *Mole Mining Ltd v Jenkins* [1972] ICR 282; *Nerva v RL&G Ltd* [1997] ICR 11; *Paggetti v Cobb* [2002] IRLR 861; *Palmanor Ltd v Cedron* [1978] ICR 1008; *Revenue and Customs Commissioners v Annabel's (Berkeley Square) Ltd* [2009] ICR 1123; *Sanderson v Exel Management Services Ltd* [2006] ICR 1337; *Tarmac Roadstone Holdings Ltd v Peacock* [1973] ICR 273; *Toni & Guys (St Pauls) Ltd v Georgiou* UKEAT/0085/13/DM; *Weevsmay Ltd v Kings* [1977] ICR 244; *Z.J.R. Lock v British Gas Trading Ltd and Others* [2014] ICR 813 (CJEU)

Working Time Regulations

An adult worker is entitled to various periods of rest as detailed in the WTR 1998. A breach of these regulations could entitle the worker to bring a claim at the ET.

By Reg 30(1)(a) a worker may bring a claim to the tribunal that his employer has denied him the following rights:

- Sufficient daily rest under Reg 10(1) or (2);

- Sufficient weekly rest under Reg 11(1), (2) or (3);

- Sufficient rest breaks within a working day under Reg 12(1) or (4);

- Sufficient annual leave under Reg 13;

- Entitlement to additional annual leave under Reg 13A;

- Compensatory rest under Reg 24;

- Adequate rest (if a mobile worker) under Reg 24A;

- Compensatory rest (if a young worker in the armed forces) under Reg 25(3);

- Compensatory rest (during night work if a young worker) under Reg 27A(4)(b); or

- Compensatory rest (if a young worker and certain exceptional circumstances apply) under Reg 27(3).

By Reg 30(1)(b) a worker may bring a bring a claim to the tribunal that his employer has failed to pay him the whole or any part of his or her entitlement to paid leave or payment in lieu of leave untaken at termination (Reg 30(1)(b)). Such a claim may also be brought as a deduction from wages claim under s13 ERA 1996 (see *Stringer v HM Revenue and Customs* [2009] IRLR 677).

Remedy: Where a tribunal finds a complaint under Reg 30(1)(a) well founded, it will make a declaration to that effect and may make an award compensation.

Compensation will be determined as that which the tribunal considers to be just and equitable in all the circumstances having regard to the employer's default in refusing to permit the worker to exercise his right and any loss sustained by the worker as a result. Such an award does not include injury to feelings (*Gomes v Higher Level Care Ltd* UKEAT/0017/16/RN).

Where a tribunal finds a complaint under Reg 30(1)(b) that certain pay for leave entitlement has not been paid, it will order the employer to pay the worker the sums owing (Reg 30(5)).

Gross or net: N/A for Regs 10, 11, 12, 13, 24or 24A; Gross for Regs 14 and 16

Tax: The tax treatments is unclear for payments under Regs 10, 11, 12, 13, 24 or 24A. However, tax should be paid under s62 ITEPA 2003 for payments under Regs 14 and 16.

Written reasons for dismissal

An employee is entitled to a written statement of reasons for dismissal from his or her employer where the dismissal arises from either: a) the employer giving notice; b) the employer terminating without notice; or c) if a limited term contract terminates by virtue of its limiting event (s92(1) ERA 1996). Generally, the employee must have made a request for the written reasons and must have been continuously employed for 2 years (s92(2) and (3)). The exception is where someone is dismissed when she is pregnant or on maternity leave until dismissed (s92(4)), or he or she is on adoption leave until dismissed (s92(4A)).

An employee may make a complaint to a tribunal that his or her employer has unreasonably failed to provide the statement or that the particulars of the statement given are inadequate or untrue (s93(1)).

Remedy: Where a tribunal finds such a complaint well founded, it may make a declaration as to what it finds the employer's reasons were for dismissing the employee and will make an award of 2 weeks' pay.

Gross or net: Gross. A week's pay as defined in ss220 to 229 ERA 1996 applies (see *Week's pay*).

Limit on a week's pay: None

Limit on number of weeks: 2

Any maximum or minimum: The award is simply 2 weeks' pay.

Adjustments: None

Cap: The award will form part of the compensatory award and the cap will apply in non-discriminatory unfair dismissal cases.

Mitigation: N/A

Tax: Any payment made in connection with the termination of employment will be taxed under s401 ITEPA 2003, of which this award will form a part.

Recoupment: The award should not form part of the prescribed element.

Statutory authorities: ERA 1996 ss92 and 93

Written statement of particulars

Employees have the right to be given written particulars of their terms of employment within 2 months of starting their employment (ss1 to 7B ERA 1996), itemised pay statements (s8 and s9 ERA 1996) and a written statement in relation to rights not to work on Sunday (s41B and s41C ERA 1996).

An employee may bring a claim to a tribunal alleging that his or her employer has not complied with these obligations (s11(1)), and either party may bring a reference to a tribunal to determine what particulars ought to have been supplied (s11(2)).

Remedy (1): The tribunal has the power to determine the particulars of employment between the parties (s12(1) and (2)). Where an itemised pay statement has not been provided, or where deductions have been made which were not itemised on such a statement, the tribunal will make a declaration to that effect and may order the employer to pay the employee the value of the deductions (s12(3) and (4)).

Remedy (2): There is an additional right to a remedy from a tribunal where a claim has been brought within the list of jurisdictions in Sch 5 to EA 2002 (the list is extensive and includes many of the common, and not so common, claims). Where under such a claim the tribunal finds for the employee, whether or not it makes an award in respect of that claim, and where when the proceedings were brought the employer was in breach of the duty to give written particulars, the tribunal will make an award of 2 weeks' pay unless it would be unjust and inequitable to do so, and may if it considers it just and equitable in all the circumstances make an award of 4 weeks' pay (see s38(1) to (5) ERA 1996).

Gross or net: Gross. A week's pay as defined in ss220 to 229 ERA 1996 applies (see *Week's pay*).

Limit on a week's pay: The current weekly limit is £489 (see Table 1 for historical rates).

Limit on number of weeks: Minimum is 2; Maximum is 4 (s38(4) EA 2002).

Any maximum or minimum: Minimum is 2 weeks' pay, capped; Maximum is 4 weeks' pay, capped.

Adjustments: Contributory conduct applies. See *Adjustments and order of adjustments* for information about the order in which they apply when this head of loss is being claimed.

Cap: The award or increase of any award will fall within any applicable statutory cap for that award.

Mitigation: The usual rules of mitigation apply to the compensatory award.

Tax: The tax rules applicable to the particular award that has been made or increased will apply.

Recoupment: The award should not be included in the prescribed element.

Statutory authorities: EA 2002 s38, ERA 1996 ss1 to 12 and ss220 to 229

Wrongful dismissal: see Damages for wrongful dismissal

Zero-hours contracts

A zero-hours contract is one in which the employer does not guarantee the individual any hours of work. The employer offers the individual work when it arises, and the individual can either accept or decline the work offered on that occasion. Individuals on a zero-hours contract may have the employment status of a 'worker' or an 'employee'.

The term is a political rather than a legal concept, potentially covering a range of different contracts and working arrangements.

Regardless of how many hours are actually offered, the employer must pay at least the National Minimum Wage.

Section 27A(3) of the ERA 1996 (as inserted by the Small Business, Enterprise and Employment Act, section 153(1) and (2)) provides that, from 26 May 2015, a provision in a zero hours contract which prohibits the worker from doing work under any other arrangement is unenforceable.

Regulation 2 of the Exclusivity Terms in Zero Hours Contracts (Redress) Regulations 2015) makes provision in relation to the right for individuals on a zero hours contract not to be unfairly dismissed or subjected to a detriment (see Detriment) for a reason relating to a breach of a provision of a zero hours contract to which section 27A(3) of the 1996 Act applies.

There is no qualifying period for an employee

bringing such an unfair dismissal or detriment claim to the ET.

Remedy

Where an employment tribunal finds that a complaint is well founded, it must take such of the following steps as it considers just and equitable:

a) making a declaration as to the rights of the complainant and the employer in relation to the matters to which the complaint relates; and

b) ordering the employer to pay compensation to the complainant (Reg 4(1) Exclusivity Terms in Zero Hours Contracts (Redress) Regulations 2015) .

The amount of the compensation awarded must be such as the tribunal considers just and equitable in all the circumstances having regard to:

a) the infringement to which the complaint relates; and

b) any loss which is attributable to the act, or failure to act, which infringed the complainant's right (Reg 4(2) Exclusivity Terms in Zero Hours Contracts (Redress) Regulations 2015) .

The loss must be taken to include:

a) any expenses reasonably incurred by the complainant in consequence of the act, or failure to act, to which the complaint relates; and

b) loss of any benefit which the complainant might reasonably be expected to have had but for that act or failure to act (Reg 4(3) Exclusivity Terms in Zero Hours Contracts (Redress) Regulations 2015)

Gross or net: The basic award will be calculated gross and the compensatory award will be calculated on the basis of net loss.

Limit on a week's pay: £489 for the basic award element.

Any maximum or minimum: If the detriment to which the worker is subjected is the termination of the worker's contract, but that contract is not a contract of employment, the total award will not exceed the aggregate of the maximum basic award (£14,670) and the maximum compensatory award (£80,541) i.e. £95,211 (Reg 4(6) Exclusivity Terms in Zero Hours Contracts (Redress) Regulations 2015).

Adjustments: The award can be reduced for contributory fault (Reg 4(7) Exclusivity Terms in Zero Hours Contracts (Redress) Regulations 2015).

Mitigation: The individual is expected to mitigate their loss (Reg 4(4) Exclusivity Terms in Zero Hours Contracts (Redress) Regulations 2015).

Tax: If the combined sum of any basic and compensatory award is greater than £30,000 then the excess figure will be subject to tax (see Grossing up).

Recoupment: It is assumed that recoupment will be apply to immediate loss of earnings.

Statutory authorities: Exclusivity Terms in Zero Hours Contracts (Redress) Regulations 2015 Regs 2,3 and 4; Small Business, Enterprise and Employment Act 2015 s153; Employment Rights Act 1996 s27A

Caps and limits

Table 1: Statutory cap, maximum basic award and the limit on gross weekly pay

Date	Maximum Compensatory Award	Maximum Basic Award	Maximum Total	Gross Weekly Pay Limit
01/02/2012 to 31/01/2013	£72,300	£12,900	£85,200	£430
01/02/2013 to 28/07/2013	£74,200	£13,500	£87,700	£450
29/07/2013 to 05/04/2014	£74,200 or gross annual pay, whichever is the smaller	£13,500	£87,700	£450
06/04/2014 to 05/04/2015	£76,574 or gross annual pay, whichever is the smaller	£13,920	£90,494	£464
06/04/2015 to 05/04/2016	£78,335 or gross annual pay, whichever is the smaller	£14,250	£92,585	£475
06/04/2016 to 05/04/2017	£78,962 or gross annual pay, whichever is the smaller	£14,370	£93,332	£479
06/04/2017 to 05/04/2018	£80,541 or gross annual pay, whichever is the smaller	£14,670	£95,211	£489

Notes
1. The cap on gross weekly pay is only applicable to claims of Statutory redundancy pay, Basic award; Right to written particulars of employment; Right to be accompanied at a disciplinary hearing; Right to request flexible working; Insolvency provisions; Additional award
2. The Employment Rights (Increase of Limits) Order 2017 increased the limits to take effect from 06/04/2017. Limits will be increased in line with inflation every 6th April.

Table 2: Limits on awards (other) (see Employment Rights (Increase of Limits) Orders)

		06/04/2014 to 05/04/2015	06/04/2015 to 05/04/2016	06/04/2016 to 05/04/2017	06/04/2017 to 05/04/2018
s145E(3) TULR(C)A 1992	Amount of award for unlawful inducement relating to trade union membership or activities or for unlawful inducement relating to collective bargaining.	£3,715	£3,800	£3,830	£3,907
s156(1) TULR(C)A 1992	Minimum amount of basic award of compensation where dismissal is unfair by virtue of section 152(1) or 153 of the 1992 Act.	£5,676	£5,807	£5,853	£5,970
s176(6A) TULR(C)A 1992	Minimum amount of compensation where individual excluded or expelled from union in contravention of section 174 of the 1992 Act and not admitted or re-admitted by date of tribunal application.	£8,669	£8,868	£8,939	£9,118
s31(1) ERA 1996	Limit on amount of guarantee payment payable to an employee in respect of any day.	£25	£26	£26	£27
s120(1) ERA 1996	Minimum amount of basic award of compensation where dismissal is unfair by virtue of section 100(1)(a) and (b), 101A(d), 102(1) or 103 of the 1996 Act.	£5,676	£5,807	£5,853	£5,970

Table 3: Guarantee Payments

Date	Daily limit	Maximum amount in any 3 month period (5 days)
01/02/2013 to 05/04/2014	£24.20	£121.00
06/04/2014 to 05/04/2015	£25.00	£125.00
06/04/2015 to 05/04/2016	£26.00	£130.00
06/04/2016 to 05/04/2017	£26.00	£130.00
06/04/2017 to 05/04/2018	£27.00	£135.00

Table 4: Time limits for appeals

Review of ET decision	14 days
Appeal to EAT from ET	42 days
Review of EAT decision	14 days
Appeal to Court of Appeal from EAT	14 days

Table 5: Gross weekly pay: claims for which gross weekly pay is used in the calculation and the related calculation dates

Claim	Calculation date	Limit on a week's pay
Additional award	Date on which employee is given notice or the EDT.	£489
Basic award	If the employee is summarily dismissed or dismissed with less than the statutory notice, the calculation date is the date on which the employment ended. If the employee was dismissed with notice equal to or more than the statutory notice, the calculation date is found by subtracting the statutory notice period from the actual notice given. This means that if statutory notice is given, the calculation date is the date that notice was given. If statutory notice is 3 weeks and actual notice given is 4 weeks, the calculation date is the day after the end of the first week of notice.	£489
Guarantee pay	The day when the guarantee pay is due.	See separate limits
Insolvency	For arrears of pay and holiday, the date on which the employer became insolvent. For the Basic award the latest of (i) the date on which the employer became insolvent, (ii) the date of the termination of the employee's employment, and (iii) the date on which the award was made. In relation to any other debt whichever is the later of (i) the date on which the employer became insolvent, and (ii) the date of the termination of the employee's employment.	£489
Protective award	The date on which the protective award was made or, in the case of an employee who was dismissed before the date on which the protective award was made, the calculation date for the purpose of computing the amount of a redundancy payment.	Unlimited
Remuneration whilst suspended on medical grounds	The day before suspension began.	Unlimited
Right for union member not to be unjustifiably disciplined/expelled and blacklisting claims	N/A	£489 for the Basic award element
Time off to look for work or arrange training after being made redundant	The day on which the employer's notice was given.	Actual gross weekly pay is used but limited to 40% of a week's pay
Time off for antenatal care	The day of ante-natal appointment.	Unlimited

Table 5: Gross weekly pay: claims for which gross weekly pay is used in the calculation and the related calculation dates		
Claim	**Calculation date**	**Limit on a week's pay**
Time off for employee representatives (including ICE and OPPS); pension trustees; union duties, activities and union learning reps; study or training; young person for study or training; members of a European Works Council	Date on which time off was taken or should have been permitted.	No limit apart from for Study or training (not Young person study or training) where the limit is £489
TUPE claims	In the case of an employee who is dismissed by reason of redundancy the date which is the calculation date for the purposes of any entitlement of his to a redundancy payment. In the case of an employee who is dismissed for any other reason, the effective date of termination. In any other case, the date of the relevant transfer.	Unlimited
Right to be accompanied at a disciplinary or grievance meeting	Date of dismissal/EDT or if no dismissal the date of the hearing.	£489
Right to request flexible working	Date on which the application was made.	£489
Written reasons for dismissal	Date notice was given or if no notice the EDT.	Unlimited
Written statement of particulars	If the employee was employed by the employer on the date the proceedings were begun, that date. If he was not, the effective date of termination.	£489
Paid annual leave under the Working Time Regulations	Payment based on a normal week's pay on the first day of the period of leave in question.	Unlimited
Redundancy payments	Depends on the circumstances.	£489

Fees

(see Employment Tribunals and the Employment Appeal Tribunal Fees Order 2013 SI 2013/1893)

Table 6: Fees for individual claimants

Fee type	Type A claim	Type B claim
Issue fee	£160	£250
Hearing fee	£230	£950

Table 7: Fees for multiple claimants - Type A claims

	Number of claimants/ amount of fee		
Type of fee	2 to 10	11 to 200	Over 200
Issue fee	£320	£640	£960
Hearing fee	£460	£920	£1,380

Table 8: Fees for multiple claimants - Type B claims

	Number of claimants/fee amount		
Type of fee	2 to 10	11 to 200	Over 200
Issue fee	£500	£1,000	£1,500
Hearing fee	£1,900	£3,800	£5,700

Table 9: Specific Fees

Type of application	Type A Claim	Type B Claim	EAT fees
Reconsideration of a default judgment	£100	£100	N/A
Reconsideration of a judgment following a final hearing	£100	£350	N/A
Dismissal following withdrawal	£60	£60	N/A
An employer's contract claim made by way of application as part of the response to the employee's contract claim	£160	N/A	N/A
Issue fee (EAT)	N/A	N/A	£400
Hearing fee (EAT)	N/A	N/A	£1,200
Judicial mediation (payable by the respondent)	N/A	£600	N/A
Judicial assessment	N/A	Free	N/A

Table 10: Help with Fees 1: Disposable capital test (under 61 years old)

Court or tribunal fee	Disposable capital threshold
Up to £1,000	£3,000
£1,001 - £1,335	£4,000
£1,336 - £1,665	£5,000
£1,666 - £2,000	£6,000
£2,001 - £2,330	£7,000

Table 10: Help with Fees 1: Disposable capital test (under 61 years old)

Court or tribunal fee	Disposable capital threshold
£2,331 - £4,000	£8,000
£4,001 - £5,000	£10,000
£5,001 - £6,000	£12,000
£6,001 - £7,000	£14,000
£7001 or more	£16,000

For applicants 61 years old or older there is a single disposable capital threshold of £16,000 whatever the tribunal fee.

Table 11: Help with Fees 2: Gross monthly income thresholds – full remissions

Gross monthly income with:	Single	Couple
No children	£1,085	£1,245
One Child	£1,330	£1,490
Two Children	£1,575	£1,735

£245 for each additional child

For every £10 of income over the threshold set out in the table above, parties will be required to pay £5 towards the court or tribunal fee up until the thresholds below, in which case no remission will be given.

Table 12: Help with Fees: Gross monthly income cap thresholds – partial help

Gross monthly income with:	Single	Couple
No children	£5,085	£5,245
One Child	£5,330	£5,490
Two Children	£5,575	£5,735

£245 for each additional child

Table 13: Exempt from fees

From 31 January 2017, the following three types of proceedings in the ETs which relate to payments from the National Insurance Fund will be exempt from fees altogether:

References to the ETs related to a redundancy payment from the National Insurance Fund, under section 170 of the Employment Rights Act 1996

Complaints that the Secretary of State has failed to make any, or insufficient, payment out of the National Insurance Fund, under section 188 of the Employment Rights Act 1996

Complaints under section 128 of the Pension Schemes Act 1993

Table 14: Type A Claims (Type B claims are any claims not listed in this table) (Schedule 2, Table 2 Employment Tribunals and the Employment Appeal Tribunal Fees Order 2013)

Description of claim	Provision identifying the rights of the claimant	Provision conferring jurisdiction on tribunal
Application by the Secretary of State to prohibit a person from running an Employment Agency	Sections 3A EAA	Sections 3A EAA
Application by a person subject to a prohibition order to vary or set it aside	Section 3C EAA	Section 3C EAA
Appeal against improvement or prohibition notice	Section 24 HSWA	Section 24 HSWA

Table 14: Type A Claims (Type B claims are any claims not listed in this table) (Schedule 2, Table 2 Employment Tribunals and the Employment Appeal Tribunal Fees Order 2013)

Description of claim	Provision identifying the rights of the claimant	Provision conferring jurisdiction on tribunal
Appeal against assessment of training levy	Section 12 ITA	Section 12 ITA
Complaint of deduction of unauthorised subscriptions	Section 68 TULR(C)A	Section 68A TULR(C)A
Complaint relating to failure to deduct or refuse to deduct an amount to a political fund	Section 86 TULR(C)A	Section 87 TULR(C)A
Complaint that an employer has failed to permit time off for carrying out trade union duties	Section 168 TULR(C)A	Section 168 TULR(C)A
Complaint that an employer has failed to permit time off for union learning representatives	Section 168A TULR(C)A	Section 168A TULR(C)A
Complaint that an employer has failed to pay for time off for union learning representatives	Section 169 TULR(C)A	Section 169 TULR(C)A
Complaint that an employer has failed to permit time off for trade union activities	Section 170 TULR(C)A	Section 170 TULR(C)A
Complaint that employer has failed, wholly or in part, to pay remuneration under a protective award	Section 190 TULR(C)A	Section 192 TULR(C)A
Complaint that the Secretary of State has not paid, or has paid less than, the amount of relevant contributions which should have been paid into a pension scheme	Section 124 PSA	Section 126 PSA
Breach of contract, except where the employer's contract claim is made by way of application as part of the employer's response to the employee's contract claim (as to which, see instead article 4 and Schedule 1 to this Order)		Section 3 ETA; Articles 3 and 4 of each of the EJOs
Reference to determine what particulars ought to be included in a statement of employment particulars or changes to particulars	Sections 1 and 4 ERA	Section 11 ERA
Reference to determine what particulars ought to be included in an itemised pay statement	Section 8 ERA	Section 11 ERA
Complaint of unauthorised deductions from wages	Section 13 ERA	Section 23 ERA
Complaint that employer has received unauthorised payments	Section 15 ERA	Section 23 ERA
Complaint that employer has failed to pay guaranteed payment	Section 28 ERA	Section 34 ERA
Complaint that employer has failed to permit time off for public duties	Section 50 ERA	Section 51 ERA
Complaint that employer has refused to permit, or has failed to pay for, time off to look for work or arrange training	Sections 52 and 53 ERA	Section 54 ERA
Complaint that employer has refused to allow, or has failed to pay for, time off for ante-natal care	Sections 55, 56, 57ZA and 57ZB ERA	Sections 57 and 57ZC ERA
Complaint that employer has refused to allow time off for dependants	Section 57A ERA	Section 57B ERA

Table 14: Type A Claims (Type B claims are any claims not listed in this table) (Schedule 2, Table 2 Employment Tribunals and the Employment Appeal Tribunal Fees Order 2013)

Description of claim	Provision identifying the rights of the claimant	Provision conferring jurisdiction on tribunal
Complaint that employer has failed to allow, or to pay for, time off for trustee of pension scheme	Sections 58 and 59 ERA	Section 60 ERA
Complaint that employer has failed to allow, or to pay for, time off for employee representative	Sections 61 and 62 ERA	Section 63 ERA
Complaint that employer has failed to allow, or to pay for, time off for young people in Wales and Scotland	Section 63A and 63B ERA	Section 63C ERA
Complaint that employer has failed to pay for time off on medical or maternity grounds	Sections 64, 68 and 68C ERA	Sections 70 and 70A ERA
Complaint that employer has failed to deal with an application in relation to study or training in accordance with regulations or refused the application on the basis of incorrect facts	Sections 63D to 63H ERA	Section 63I ERA
Complaint that employer has unreasonably failed to provide a written statement of reasons for dismissal or the particulars are inadequate or untrue	Section 92 ERA	Section 93 ERA
Reference in respect of a right to redundancy payment	Section 135 ERA	Sections 163 and 177 ERA
Reference related to payment out of National Insurance Fund	Section 166 ERA	Section 170 ERA
References related to payments equivalent to redundancy payments	Sections 167, 168 and 177 ERA	Section 177 ERA
Complaint that the Secretary of State has failed to make any, or insufficient, payment of out the National Insurance Fund	Section 182 ERA	Section 188 ERA
Appeal against a notice of underpayment	Section 19C NMWA	Section 19C NMWA
Appeal against a notice issued by the Commission for Equality and Human Rights where the notice relates to an unlawful act	Section 21 EA 2006	Section 21 EA 2006
Complaint that prospective employer made enquiries about disability or health	Section 60 EA 2010	Section 120 EA 2010
Application in relation to the effect of a non-discrimination rule in an occupational pension scheme	Section 61 EA 2010	Section 120 EA 2010
Complaint in relation to a breach of a maternity equality clause	Section 73 EA 2010	Section 127 EA 2010
Complaint in relation to a breach of, or application in relation to the effect of, a maternity equality rule in an occupational pension scheme	Section 75 EA 2010	Section 127 EA 2010
Complaint in relation to terms prohibiting discussions about pay	Section 77 EA 2010	Section 120 EA 2010
Complaint that a term in a collective agreement is void or unenforceable	Section 145 EA 2010	Section 146 EA 2010
Appeal of decision of compensating authority	Regulation 42 CEC	Regulation 42 CEC
Complaint that employer has failed to pay for remunerated time off for safety representative	Regulation 4(2) of, and Schedule 2 to, the SRSC	Regulation 11 SRSC

Table 14: Type A Claims (Type B claims are any claims not listed in this table) (Schedule 2, Table 2 Employment Tribunals and the Employment Appeal Tribunal Fees Order 2013)

Description of claim	Provision identifying the rights of the claimant	Provision conferring jurisdiction on tribunal
Reference that there has been a failure to consult with employee representatives about contracting out of pension scheme	Regulation 4 OPS(CO)R and regulation 9 of OPS(DI)R	Regulation 4 OPS(CO)R and regulation 9 of OPS(DI)R
Complaint that employer has failed to pay for time off to carry out Safety Representative duties or undertake training	Regulation 7 of, and Schedule 1 to, the HSCE	Schedule 2 to the HSCE
Complaint that employer has refused to allow annual leave or make payment in respect of annual leave	Regulations 13, 13A,14 and 16 WTR	Regulation 30 WTR
Appeal against improvement or prohibition notice	Paragraph 6 of Schedule 3 to WTR	Paragraph 6 of Schedule 3 to WTR
Appeal against improvement or prohibition notice	Regulation 18 COMAH	Regulation 18 COMAH
Complaint in relation to refusal of annual leave or to make payment	Regulation 11 MSR	Regulation 18 MSR
Complaint in relation to refusal to provide paid annual leave	Regulation 4 CAR	Regulation 18 CAR
Complaint in relation to failure to provide free health assessments	Regulation 5 CAR	Regulation 18 CAR
Complaint in relation to refusal of annual leave or to make payment	Regulation 11 FVR	Regulation 19 FVR
Complaint that employer has refused to allow or failed to pay for time off for information and consultation or negotiating representatives	Regulations 27 and 28 ICR	Regulation 29 ICR
Appeal against improvement notice	Paragraph 6(2) of Schedule 2 to the RTR	Paragraph 6(2) of Schedule 2 to the RTR
Complaint in relation to failure to pay compensation in pursuance of tribunal order	Regulation 15(7) and 15(8) TUPE	Regulation 15(10) TUPE
Complaint that employer has failed to allow, or pay for, time off for functions as employee representative	Paragraphs 2 and 3 of the Schedule to OPR	Paragraph 4 of the Schedule to OPR
Complaint that employer has failed to allow, or pay for, time off for members of special negotiating body	Regulations 28 and 29 ECSR	Regulation 30 ECSR
Complaint that employer has failed to allow, or pay for, time off for members of special negotiating body	Regulations 43 and 44 CCBR	Regulation 45 CCBR
Appeal against notice from Health and Safety Executive or a local authority	Regulation 21 and Part 2 of Schedule 8 to REACHER	Regulation 21 and Part 2 of Schedule 8 to REACHER
Reference to determine what particulars ought to be included in an itemised statement of stipend	Regulation 6 EOR	Regulation 9 EOR
Reference to determine what particulars ought to be included in a statement of particulars or changes to particulars	Regulations 3 and 6 EOR	Regulation 9 EOR
Complaint that employer has failed to allow, or pay for, time off for members of special negotiating body	Regulations 26 and 27 ELLR	Regulation 28 ELLR
Appeal against a penalty notice	Section 37G ETA	Section 37G ETA
Complaint of unauthorised deductions from wages	Regulation 5 PWER	Regulation 6 PWER

Holiday

Table 15: Holiday Pay crib sheet (Holidays and holiday pay leaflet – ACAS)

Working Pattern	Before 1 April 2009	After 1 April 2009
Full-time (5 day week)	4.8 weeks (24 days)	5.6 weeks (28 days)
Part-time (4 day week)	4.8 weeks (19.2 days)	5.6 weeks (22.4 days)
Part-time (3 day week)	4.8 weeks (14.4 days)	5.6 weeks (16.8 days)
6 day week	4.8 weeks (28 days – the maximum statutory entitlement)	5.6 weeks (28 days – the maximum statutory entitlement)
Compressed hours e.g. 36 hours in 4 days	36 hours x 4.8 weeks = 172.8 hours per year	36 hours x 5.6 weeks = 201.6 hours per year
Annualised hours e.g. 1,600 hours at an average of 33.5 hours week	33.5 hours x 4.8 weeks = 160.8 hours per year	33.5 hours x 5.6 weeks = 187.6 hours per year
Bank Holidays	Can be included in the 4.8 weeks leave – check the contract	Can be included in the 5.6 weeks leave – check the contract

Income Tax and National Insurance

Table 16: Income Tax Rates and Taxable Bands

Rate	2015-2016	2016-2017	2017-2018
Starting rate for savings: 0%* (the rate was 10% prior to 6 April 2015)	£0 - £5,000	£0 - £5,000	£0 - £5,000
Basic rate: 20%	£0 - £31,785	£0 - £32,000	£0 - £33,500
Higher rate: 40%	£31,786 - £150,000	£32,001 - £150,000	£33,501 - £150,000
Additional rate: 45% from 6 April 2013	Over £150,000	Over £150,000	Over £150,000

Table 17: Income Tax Allowances

Income Tax allowances	2015-2016	2016-2017	2017-2018
Personal Allowance for those born after 5 April 1948	£10,600	£11,000	£11,500
Personal Allowance for those born between 6 April 1938 and 5 April 1948	£10,600	£11,000	£11,500
Personal Allowance for those born before 6 April 1938	£10,660	£11,000	£11,500
Income limit for Personal Allowance [1]	£100,000	£100,000	£100,000
Income limit for personal allowances (born before 6 April 1938) [2]	£27,700	£27,700	£28,000
Maximum amount of Married Couple's Allowance [3] [4]	£8,355	£8,355	£8,445
Minimum amount of Married Couple's Allowance [3] [5]	£3,220	£3,220	£3,260
Blind Person's Allowance	£2,290	£2,290	£2,320
Transferable Tax Allowance for married couples and civil partners [6]	£1,060	£1,100	£1,150

[1] The personal allowance reduces where the individual's income is above this limit by £1 for every £2 above the limit. This applies regardless of the individual's date of birth.

[2] This allowance reduces where the individual's income is above the income limit by £1 for every £2 above the income limit until it reaches the level of the personal allowance for someone born after 5 April 1948.

[3] Available to people born before 6 April 1935. Tax relief for this allowance is restricted to 10%.

[4] This allowance is reduced when the individual's income is above the income limit. This is at a rate of £1 for every £2 above the income limit until it reaches the minimum amount. Any reduction in the married couple's allowance applies after any reduction to the individual's personal allowance.

[5] This is also the maximum relief for maintenance payments where at least one of the parties is born before 6 April 1935.

Table 17: Income Tax Allowances

Income Tax allowances	2015-2016	2016-2017	2017-2018

(6) Available to spouses/ civil partners born after 5 April 1935. This allowance is 10% of the personal allowance for those born after 5 April 1938. It allows a spouse or civil partner who is not liable to income tax above the basic rate to transfer this amount of their personal allowance to their spouse/ civil partner. The recipient must not be liable to tax above the basic rate. The recipient is eligible to a tax reduction of 20% of the transferred amount.

Table 18: National Insurance Contributions - Rates and Allowances

	2015-2016	2016-2017	2017-2018
Lower earnings limit, primary Class 1	£112	£112	£113
Upper earnings limit, primary Class 1	£815	£827	£866
Upper accrual point	£770	£770	£770
Primary threshold (employee contribution)	£155	£155	£157
Secondary threshold (employer contribution)	£156	£156	£157
Employees' primary Class 1 rate between primary threshold and upper earnings limit (not contracted out)	12%	12%	12%
Employees' primary Class 1 rate above upper earnings limit	2%	2%	2%
Class 1A rate on employer provided benefits (1)	13.80%	13.80%	13.80%
Employers' secondary Class 1 rate above secondary threshold – no limit (not contracted out)	13.80%	13.80%	13.80%
Employers' contracted-out rebate, salary-related schemes	3.40%	-	-
Employment Allowance	£2,000 per year, per employer	£3,000 per year, per employer	£3,000 per year, per employer
Apprentice Upper Secondary Threshold (AUST) for under 25s(2)	-	£827	£866
Class 2 Rate	£2.80 per week	£2.80 per week	£2.85 per week
Class 2 small earnings exception/Small Profits Threshold	£5,965 per year	£5,965 per year	£6,025 per year
Special Class 2 rate for share fishermen	£3.45 per week	£3.45 per week	£3.50 per week
Special Class 2 rate for volunteer development workers	£5.60 per week	£5.60 per week	£5.65 per week
Class 3 rate	£14.10 per week	£14.10 per week	£14.25 per week
Class 4 lower profits limit	£8,060 per year	£8,060 per year	£8,164 per year
Class 4 upper profits limit	£42,385 per year	£43,000 per year	£45,000 per year
Class 4 rate between lower profits limit and upper profits limit	9%	9%	9%
Class 4 rate above upper profits limit	2%	2%	2%

(1) Class 1A NICs are payable in July and are calculated on the value of taxable benefits provided in the previous tax year, using the secondary Class 1 percentage rate appropriate to that tax year.
(2) Came into force 6 April 2016

Table 19: Class 1 NICs: Rates for employee (primary) contributions 2017-2018

Earnings (£ a week)	NIC rate
Below £113 (LEL)	0%
£113-157 (PT)	0%
£157.01-866	12%
Above £866	2%

Table 20: Class 1 NICs: Rates for employer (secondary) contributions 2017-2018

Earnings (£ a week)	NIC rate
Below £157 (ST)	0%
Above £157.01 (ST)	13.8%

Table 21: Class 3 NI Weekly Rates

Date	Weekly Rate
06/04/2012 to 05/04/2013	£13.25
06/04/2013 to 05/04/2014	£13.55
06/04/2014 to 05/04/2015	£13.90
06/04/2015 to 05/04/2016	£14.10
06/04/2016 to 05/04/2017	£14.10
06/04/2017 to 05/04/2018	£14.25

Table 22: Income tax and NI: Gross to Net Salaries 2017 – 2018 (Not contracted out of S2P for Class 1 NIC)

Gross (Annual)	Tax	NI	Net (Annual)
8,164	0.00	0.00	8,164.00
10,500	0.00	280.32	10,219.68
11,000	0.00	340.32	10,659.68
12,000	100.00	460.32	11,439.68
13,000	300.00	580.32	12,119.68
14,000	500.00	700.32	12,799.68
15,000	700.00	820.32	13,479.68
16,000	900.00	940.32	14,159.68
17,000	1,100.00	1,060.32	14,839.68
18,000	1,300.00	1,180.32	15,519.68
19,000	1,500.00	1,300.32	16,199.68
20,000	1,700.00	1,420.32	16,879.68
21,000	1,900.00	1,540.32	17,559.68
22,000	2,100.00	1,660.32	18,239.68
23,000	2,300.00	1,780.32	18,919.68
24,000	2,500.00	1,900.32	19,599.68
25,000	2,700.00	2,020.32	20,279.68
26,000	2,900.00	2,140.32	20,959.68
27,000	3,100.00	2,260.32	21,639.68
28,000	3,300.00	2,380.32	22,319.68
29,000	3,500.00	2,500.32	22,999.68
30,000	3,700.00	2,620.32	23,679.68
35,000	4,700.00	3,220.32	27,079.68
40,000	5,700.00	3,820.32	30,479.68
45,000	6,700.00	4,420.32	33,879.68
50,000	8,700.00	4,520.32	36,779.68
55,000	10,700.00	4,620.32	39,679.68
60,000	12,700.00	4,720.32	42,579.68

Table 22: Income tax and NI: Gross to Net Salaries 2017 – 2018 (Not contracted out of S2P for Class 1 NIC)

Gross (Annual)	Tax	NI	Net (Annual)
65,000	14,700.00	4,820.32	45,479.68
70,000	16,700.00	4,920.32	48,379.68
75,000	18,700.00	5,020.32	51,279.68
80,000	20,700.00	5,120.32	54,179.68
85,000	22,700.00	5,220.32	57,079.68
90,000	24,700.00	5,320.32	59,979.68
95,000	26,700.00	5,420.32	62,879.68
100,000	28,700.00	5,520.32	65,779.68
125,000	38,700.00	6,020.32	80,279.68
150,000	48,700.00	6,520.32	94,779.68
175,000	59,375.00	7,020.32	108,604.68
200,000	70,625.00	7,520.32	121,854.68

Assumption: the above figures are based on a tax code of 1150L (the personal allowance for 2017-18 is £11,500)

Table 23: Income tax and NI: Gross to Net Salaries 2017 - 2018 (Contracted out of S2P for Class 1 NIC and pension contribution of 3%)

Gross (Annual)	Tax	NI	Pension contribution	Net (Annual)
8,164	0.00	0.00	244.92	7,919.08
10,500	0.00	280.32	315	9,904.68
11,000	0.00	340.32	330	10,329.68
12,000	28.00	460.32	360	11,151.68
13,000	222.00	580.32	390	11,807.68
14,000	416.00	700.32	420	12,463.68
15,000	610.00	820.32	450	13,119.68
16,000	804.00	940.32	480	13,775.68
17,000	998.00	1,060.32	510	14,431.68
18,000	1,192.00	1,180.32	540	15,087.68
19,000	1,386.00	1,300.32	570	15,743.68
20,000	1,580.00	1,420.32	600	16,399.68
21,000	1,774.00	1,540.32	630	17,055.68
22,000	1,968.00	1,660.32	660	17,711.68
23,000	2,162.00	1,780.32	690	18,367.68
24,000	2,356.00	1,900.32	720	19,023.68
25,000	2,550.00	2,020.32	750	19,679.68
26,000	2,744.00	2,140.32	780	20,335.68
27,000	2,938.00	2,260.32	810	20,991.68
28,000	3,132.00	2,380.32	840	21,647.68
29,000	3,326.00	2,500.32	870	22,303.68
30,000	3,520.00	2,620.32	900	22,959.68
35,000	4,490.00	3,220.32	1,050	26,239.68
40,000	5,460.00	3,820.32	1,200	29,519.68
45,000	6,430.00	4,420.32	1,350	32,799.68
50,000	8,100.00	4,520.32	1,500	35,879.68
55,000	10,040.00	4,620.32	1,650	38,689.68

Table 23: Income tax and NI: Gross to Net Salaries 2017 - 2018 (Contracted out of S2P for Class 1 NIC and pension contribution of 3%)

Gross (Annual)	Tax	NI	Pension contribution	Net (Annual)
60,000	11,980.00	4,720.32	1,800	41,499.68
65,000	13,920.00	4,820.32	1,950	44,309.68
70,000	15,860.00	4,920.32	2,100	47,119.68
75,000	17,800.00	5,020.32	2,250	49,929.68
80,000	19,740.00	5,120.32	2,400	52,739.68
85,000	21,680.00	5,220.32	2,550	55,549.68
90,000	23,620.00	5,320.32	2,700	58,359.68
95,000	25,560.00	5,420.32	2,850	61,169.68
100,000	27,500.00	5,520.32	3,000	63,979.68
125,000	37,200.00	6,020.32	3,750	78,029.68
150,000	46,900.00	6,520.32	4,500	92,079.68
175,000	57,012.50	7,020.32	5,250	105,717.18
200,000	67,925.00	7,520.32	6,000	118,554.68

Assumption: the above figures are based on a tax code of 1150L (the personal allowance for 2017-18 is £11,500)

Interest

Table 24: Interest Rates

Until 29 July 2013 the interest rate to be applied in England and Wales was that prescribed for the special investment account under rule 27(1) of the Court Funds Rules 1987. The interest rate until 29 July 2013 was 0.5%. For claims presented on or after 29 July 2013 the relevant interest rate is that specified in s17 of the Judgments Act 1838. The interest rate now to be applied is 8% which is in line with Scotland.

From 01/08/1999	7%
From 01/02/2002	6%
From 01/02/2009	3%
From 01/06/2009	1.5%
From 01/07/2009	0.5%
From 29/07/2013	8%

Redundancy and statutory notice

Table 25: Statutory Redundancy

Age	

	\multicolumn{19}{Number of years' continuous service}

Age	2	3	4	5	6	7	8	9	10	11	12	13	14	15	16	17	18	19	20
17	1	-	-	-	-	-	-	-	-	-	-	-	-	-	-	-	-	-	-
18	1	1½	-	-	-	-	-	-	-	-	-	-	-	-	-	-	-	-	-
19	1	1½	2	-	-	-	-	-	-	-	-	-	-	-	-	-	-	-	-
20	1	1½	2	2½	-	-	-	-	-	-	-	-	-	-	-	-	-	-	-
21	1	1½	2	2½	3	-	-	-	-	-	-	-	-	-	-	-	-	-	-
22	1	1½	2	2½	3	3½	-	-	-	-	-	-	-	-	-	-	-	-	-
23	1½	2	2½	3	3½	4	4½	-	-	-	-	-	-	-	-	-	-	-	-
24	2	2½	3	3½	4	4½	5	5½	-	-	-	-	-	-	-	-	-	-	-

Table 25: Statutory Redundancy

| | Number of years' continuous service | | | | | | | | | | | | | | | | | | |
Age	2	3	4	5	6	7	8	9	10	11	12	13	14	15	16	17	18	19	20
25	2	3	3½	4	4½	5	5½	6	6½	-	-	-	-	-	-	-	-	-	-
26	2	3	4	4½	5	5½	6	6½	7	7½	-	-	-	-	-	-	-	-	-
27	2	3	4	5	5½	6	6½	7	7½	8	8½	-	-	-	-	-	-	-	-
28	2	3	4	5	6	6½	7	7½	8	8½	9	9½	-	-	-	-	-	-	-
29	2	3	4	5	6	7	7½	8	8½	9	9½	10	10½	-	-	-	-	-	-
30	2	3	4	5	6	7	8	8½	9	9½	10	10½	11	11½	-	-	-	-	-
31	2	3	4	5	6	7	8	9	9½	10	10½	11	11½	12	12½	-	-	-	-
32	2	3	4	5	6	7	8	9	10	10½	11	11½	12	12½	13	13½	-	-	-
33	2	3	4	5	6	7	8	9	10	11	11½	12	12½	13	13½	14	14½	-	-
34	2	3	4	5	6	7	8	9	10	11	12	12½	13	13½	14	14½	15	15½	-
35	2	3	4	5	6	7	8	9	10	11	12	13	13½	14	14½	15	15½	16	16½
36	2	3	4	5	6	7	8	9	10	11	12	13	14	14½	15	15½	16	16½	17
37	2	3	4	5	6	7	8	9	10	11	12	13	14	15	15½	16	16½	17	17½
38	2	3	4	5	6	7	8	9	10	11	12	13	14	15	16	16½	17	17½	18
39	2	3	4	5	6	7	8	9	10	11	12	13	14	15	16	17	17½	18	18½
40	2	3	4	5	6	7	8	9	10	11	12	13	14	15	16	17	18	18½	19
41	2	3	4	5	6	7	8	9	10	11	12	13	14	15	16	17	18	19	19½
42	2½	3½	4½	5½	6½	7½	8½	9½	10½	11½	12½	13½	14½	15½	16½	17½	18½	19½	20½
43	3	4	5	6	7	8	9	10	11	12	13	14	15	16	17	18	19	20	21
44	3	4½	5½	6½	7½	8½	9½	10½	11½	12½	13½	14½	15½	16½	17½	18½	19½	20½	21½
45	3	4½	6	7	8	9	10	11	12	13	14	15	16	17	18	19	20	21	22
46	3	4½	6	7½	8½	9½	10½	11½	12½	13½	14½	15½	16½	17½	18½	19½	20½	21½	22½
47	3	4½	6	7½	9	10	11	12	13	14	15	16	17	18	19	20	21	22	23
48	3	4½	6	7½	9	10½	11½	12½	13½	14½	15½	16½	17½	18½	19½	20½	21½	22½	23½
49	3	4½	6	7½	9	10½	12	13	14	15	16	17	18	19	20	21	22	23	24
50	3	4½	6	7½	9	10½	12	13½	14½	15½	16½	17½	18½	19½	20½	21½	22½	23½	24½
51	3	4½	6	7½	9	10½	12	13½	15	16	17	18	19	20	21	22	23	24	25
52	3	4½	6	7½	9	10½	12	13½	15	16½	17½	18½	19½	20½	21½	22½	23½	24½	25½
53	3	4½	6	7½	9	10½	12	13½	15	16½	18	19	20	21	22	23	24	25	26
54	3	4½	6	7½	9	10½	12	13½	15	16½	18	19½	20½	21½	22½	23½	24½	25½	26½
55	3	4½	6	7½	9	10½	12	13½	15	16½	18	19½	21	22	23	24	25	26	27
56	3	4½	6	7½	9	10½	12	13½	15	16½	18	19½	21	22½	23½	24½	25½	26½	27½
57	3	4½	6	7½	9	10½	12	13½	15	16½	18	19½	21	22½	24	25	26	27	28
58	3	4½	6	7½	9	10½	12	13½	15	16½	18	19½	21	22½	24	25½	26½	27½	28½
59	3	4½	6	7½	9	10½	12	13½	15	16½	18	19½	21	22½	24	25½	27	28	29
60	3	4½	6	7½	9	10½	12	13½	15	16½	18	19½	21	22½	24	25½	27	28½	29½
61+	3	4½	6	7½	9	10½	1 2	13½	15	16½	18	19½	21	22½	24	25½	27	28½	30

Table 26: Statutory Notice Periods

Period of continuous employment (years)	Minimum period of notice (weeks)
Less than 2 years (but more than 1 month)	1
At least 2 but less than 3	2
At least 3 but less than 4	3
At least 4 but less than 5	4
At least 5 but less than 6	5
At least 6 but less than 7	6
At least 7 but less than 8	7
At least 8 but less than 9	8
At least 9 but less than 10	9
At least 10 but less than 11	10
At least 11 but less than 12	11
More than 12	12

Statutory rates

Table 27: National Minimum and Living Wage Rates

Year	Living wage for adults aged 25 and over[2]	National Minimum Wage for workers between the ages of 21 and 24	Development Rate (for 18 to 20 year olds)	16-17 year olds rate	Apprentice rate[1]
01/10/2012 to 30/09/2013	-	£6.19	£4.98	£3.68	£2.65
01/10/2013 to 30/09/2014	-	£6.31	£5.03	£3.72	£2.68
01/10/2014 to 30/09/2015	-	£6.50	£5.13	£3.79	£2.73
01/10/2015 to 30/09/2016	£7.20 from 1 April 2016	£6.70	£5.30	£3.87	£3.30
01/10/2016 to 31/03/2017[3]	£7.20	£6.95	£5.55	£4.00	£3.40
01/04/2017 to 31/03/2018	£7.50	£7.05	£5.60	£4.05	£3.50
	[1] This rate is for apprentices under 19 or those in their first year. For anyone over the age of 19, and past their first year, the rate is applicable to the age [2] The National Living Wage came into effect for workers aged 25 and over on 1 April 2016 [3] The National Minimum Wage will be reviewed every April (instead of October) from 2017 to align it with the National Living Wage calendar				

Table 28: Statutory maternity, paternity, adoption, shared parental and sick pay rates					
	Statutory Maternity Pay (SMP)	Ordinary Statutory Paternity Pay (OSPP) (payable for up to 2 weeks) and Additional Statutory Paternity Pay (ASOO) (remaining weeks up to 39)	Statutory Adoption Pay (SAP) (payable for up to 39 weeks)	Statutory Shared Parental Pay (ShPP) (for parents of children due or adopted on or after 5 April 2015) (remaining weeks up to 39)	Statutory Sick Pay (SSP)
06/04/2015 to 05/04/2016	90% of average weekly gross pay for first 6 weeks; and then £139.58 or 90% of average gross weekly earnings (whichever is lower) for the next 33 weeks	£139.58 or 90% of average gross weekly earnings (whichever is lower)	90% of average weekly gross pay for first 6 weeks; and then £139.58 or 90% of average gross weekly earnings (whichever is lower) for the next 33 weeks	£139.58 or 90% of average gross weekly earnings (whichever is lower)	£88.45 per week
From 06/04/2016 to 05/04/2017 (No change from previous year)	90% of average weekly gross pay for first 6 weeks; and then £139.58 or 90% of average gross weekly earnings (whichever is lower) for the next 33 weeks	£139.58 or 90% of average gross weekly earnings (whichever is lower)	90% of average weekly gross pay for first 6 weeks; and then £139.58 or 90% of average gross weekly earnings (whichever is lower) for the next 33 weeks	£139.58 or 90% of average gross weekly earnings (whichever is lower)	£88.45 per week
06/04/2017 to 05/04/2018	90% of average weekly gross pay for first 6 weeks; and then £140.98 or 90% of average gross weekly earnings (whichever is lower) for the next 33 weeks	£140.98 or 90% of average gross weekly earnings (whichever is lower)	£140.98 or 90% of average gross weekly earnings (whichever is lower)	£140.98 or 90% of average gross weekly earnings (whichever is lower)	£89.35 per week

Legislation

Table 29: List of abbreviated statutes and statutory instruments	
AWR 2010	Agency Workers Regulations 2010
CAR 2004	Civil Aviation (Working Time) Regulations 2004
CCBR 2007	Companies (Cross-Border Mergers) Regulations 2007
CEC 1975	Colleges of Education (Compensation) Regulations 1975
COMAH 1999	Control of Major Accident Hazards Regulations 1999
CRA(TU)PE 2014	Collective Redundancies and Transfer of Undertakings (Protection of Employment) (Amendment) Regulations 2014
EA 2002	Employment Act 2002
EA 2010	Equality Act 2010
EA 2016	Enterprise Act 2016
EAA 1973	Employment Agencies Act 1973
ECSR 2006	European Cooperative Society (Involvement of Employees) Regulations 2006
EJOs 1994	Employment Tribunals Extension of Jurisdiction (England and Wales) Order 1994(13); and Employment Tribunals Extension of Jurisdiction (Scotland) Order 1994
EOR 2009	Ecclesiastical Offices (Terms of Service) Regulations 2009
ELLR 2009	European Public Limited-Liability Company (Employee Involvement) (Great Britain) Regulations 2009
EPA 1970	Equal Pay Act 1970
EP(RJAIS) Regs 1996	Employment Protection (Recoupment of Jobseeker's Allowance and Income Support) Regulations 1996
ERA 1996	Employment Rights Act 1996
ERelA 1999	Employment Relations Act 1999
ERR 2013	Enterprise and Regulatory Reform Act 2013
EST (PR) Regs 2010	Employee Study and Training (Procedural Requirements) Regulations 2010
EST (ECR) Regulations 2010	Employee Study and Training (Eligibility, Complaints and Remedies) Regulations 2010
ETA 1996	Employment Tribunals Act 1996
ET(I) Order 2013	Employment Tribunals (Interest) Order (Amendment) Order 2013
ET(IADC) Regs 2013	Employment Tribunals (Interest on Awards in Discrimination Cases)(Amendment) Regulations 2013
ETZH C (R) Regs 2015-	Exclusivity Terms in Zero Hours Contracts (Redress) Regulations 2015
FA 2017	Finance Act 2017
FTE(PLFT) Regs 2002	Fixed Term Employees (Prevention of less favourable treatment) Regulations 2002
FVR 2004	Fishing Vessels (Working Time: Sea-fishermen) Regulations 2004
FW(PR) Regs 2002	Flexible Working (Procedural Requirements) Regulations 2002
FW(ECR) Regs 2002	Flexible Working (Eligibility, Complaints and Remedies) Regulations 2002
HSCE 1996	Health and Safety (Consultation with Employees) Regulations 1996
HSWA 1974	Health and Safety at Work etc Act 1974
ICE Regs 2004	Information and Consultation of Employees Regulations 2004

Table 29: List of abbreviated statutes and statutory instruments

ICR 2004	Information and Consultation of Employees Regulations 2004
ITA 1982	Industrial Training Act 1982
IT(IADC) Regs 1996	Industrial Tribunals (Interest on Awards in Discrimination Cases) Regulations 1996
MSR 2003	Merchant Shipping (Working Time: Inland Waterways) Regulations 2003
NMWA 1998	National Minimum Wage Act 1998
OPPS Regs 2006	The Occupational and Personal Pension Schemes (Consultation by Employers and Miscellaneous Amendment) Regulations 2006
OPS(CO)R 1996	Occupational Pension Schemes (Contracting-Out) Regulations 1996
OPS(DI)R 1996	Occupational Pensions Schemes (Disclosure of Information) Regulations 1996
PSA 1993	Pension Schemes Act 1993
PTW(PLFT) Regs 2000	Part Time Workers (Prevention of less favourable treatment) Regulations 2000
PWER Regs 2016	The Posted Workers (Enforcement of Employment Rights) Regulations 2016
REACHER 2008	REACH Enforcement Regulations 2008
RTR 2005	Road Transport (Working Time) Regulations 2005
SBEE 2015	Small Business, Enterprise and Employment Act 2015
TICE 1999	Transnational Information and Consultation of Employees Regulations 1999
TULR(C)A 1992	Trade Union and Labour Relations (Consolidation) Act 1992
TUPE Regs 2006	The Transfer of Undertakings (Protection of Employment) Regulations 2006
WTR 1998	Working Time Regulations 1998

Table 30: Limitation periods and requisite minimum qualifying periods for claims

Claim	Limitation period (maximum length of time that can elapse for claim to be brought to ET)	Length of service required before a claim can be brought to ET
Discrimination (ss13, 15, 16, 18, 19, 21, 26, 27 EA 2010)	3 months (or 6 months if relating to armed forces service) (s123 EA 2010)	None
Right of union member not to be unjustifiably disciplined (s64 TULR(C)A)	3 months (s66 TULR(C)A)	None
Right of union member to compensation if declared to be unjustifiably disciplined (s67 TULR(C)A)	6 months, but not before 4 weeks (s67(3) TULR(C)A)	None
Right of union member not to suffer deduction of unauthorised or excessive subscriptions (s68 TULR(C)A)	3 months (s68A(1) TULR(C)A)	None
Right of union member not to suffer deduction of contributions to a political fund (s86 TULR(C)A)	3 months (s87(2) TULR(C)A)	None
Right of union member if employer has failed to comply with their right not to suffer deduction of contributions to a political fund (s87(5) TULR(C)A)	6 months but not before 4 weeks (s87(6) TULR(C)A)	None
Refusal of employment on grounds related to trade union membership (s137 TULR(C)A)	3 months (s139(1) TULR(C)A)	None
Right not to be offered inducements relating to union membership or activities (s145A TULR(C)A)	3 months (s145C TULR(C)A)	None
Right not to be offered inducements relating to collective bargaining (s145B TULR(C)A)	3 months (s145C TULR(C)A)	None
Protection from detriment (not dismissal) relating to union membership or activities (s146 TULR(C)A)	3 months (s147(1) TULR(C)A)	None

Table 30: Limitation periods and requisite minimum qualifying periods for claims

Claim	Limitation period (maximum length of time that can elapse for claim to be brought to ET)	Length of service required before a claim can be brought to ET
Time off for union duties (s168 TULR(C)A)	3 months (s171 TULR(C)A)	None
Time off for union learning representatives (s168A TULR(C)A)	3 months (s171 TULR(C)A)	None
Payment for time off for union duties and union learning reps (s169 TULR(C)A)	3 months (s171 TULR(C)A)	None
Time off for union activities (s170 TULR(C)A)	3 months (s171 TULR(C)A)	None
Right not to be excluded or expelled from union (s174 TULR(C)A)	6 months (s175 TULR(C)A)	None
Right to compensation if excluded or expelled from union (s176(2) TULR(C)A)	6 months (but not before 4 weeks) (s176(3) TULR(C)A)	None
Redundancy - right to be consulted (s188 TULR(C)A)	3 months (s189(5) TULR(C)A)	None
Redundancy - right to election of employee reps (s188A TULR(C)A)	3 months (s189(5) TULR(C)A)	None
Redundancy - right to be paid during protected period (s190 TULR(C)A)	3 months (s192(3) TULR(C)A)	None
Right to written statement of particulars (s1(1) ERA), or change in particulars (s4(1) ERA), or itemised pay statement (s8(1) ERA)	During employment or within 3 months of termination (s11(4) ERA)	1 month (s198 ERA) (none in the case of itemised statement)
Right not to suffer unauthorised deductions (normal) (s13(1) ERA), (retail) (s18(1)), not to make payments to employer (normal) (s15(1)), (retail) (s21(1))	3 months (s23 ERA)	None
Right to guarantee payments (s28(1) ERA)	3 months (s34(2) ERA)	1 month (s29 ERA)
Right not to suffer detriment (ss43M, 44, 45, 45A, 46, 47, 47A, 47B, 47C, 47D, 47E, 47F ERA; Reg 4 Exclusivity Terms in Zero Hours Contracts (Redress) Regulations 2015)	3 months (s48(3) ERA; Reg 3 Exclusivity Terms in Zero Hours Contracts (Redress) Regulations 2015 The time limit may be extended under the Exclusivity Terms Act in certain circumstances	None, except: 26 weeks in the case of Ordinary Adoption Leave (pre-5 April 2015 only), Additional Adoption Leave (pre-5 April 2015 only), Ordinary Paternity Leave (birth), Additional Paternity Leave (birth) (pre-5 April 2015 only), Paternity Leave (adoption), Shared Parental Leave; 1 year in the case of Parental Leave (reg 13 Maternity and Parental Leave etc Regs 1999)
Time off for public duties (s50(1) ERA)	3 months (s51(2) ERA)	None
Time off on redundancy to look for work or arrange training (s52(1) ERA) and payment for time off on redundancy to look for work or arrange training (ss53(1) and 53(4) ERA)	3 months (s54(2) ERA)	2 years (s52(2) ERA)
Time off for ante-natal care (s55(1) ERA) and payment for this time off (s56(1) ERA)	3 months (s57(2) ERA)	None
Time off for dependants (s57A ERA)	3 months (s57B(2) ERA)	None
Time off for pension scheme trustees (s58(1) ERA) and payment for this time off (s59(1) ERA)	3 months (s60(2) ERA)	None
Time off for employee representatives (s61(1) ERA) and payment for this time off (s62(1) ERA)	3 months (s63(2) ERA)	None
Time off for young person for study or training (s63A ERA) and payment for this time off (s63B ERA)	3 months (s63C(2) ERA)	None
Time off for study or training (s63D ERA)	3 months (s63I(5) ERA)	26 weeks (s63D(a) ERA)

Table 30: Limitation periods and requisite minimum qualifying periods for claims

Claim	Limitation period (maximum length of time that can elapse for claim to be brought to ET)	Length of service required before a claim can be brought to ET
Payment for suspension on medical grounds (s64(1) ERA) or maternity grounds (s68 ERA)	3 months (s70(2) ERA)	1 month (s65(1) ERA)
Offer of alternative work when suspended on maternity grounds (s67 ERA)	3 months (s70(5) ERA)	None
Right to request flexible working (s80F ERA)	3 months (s80H(5) ERA)	26 weeks (reg 13 Flexible Working (Eligibility etc) Regs 2002
Right of employee to minimum notice period (s86 ERA)	6 years under contract	1 month (s86 ERA 1996)
Right to written reasons for dismissal (s92(1) ERA)	3 months (s93(3) ERA)	1 year (s92(3) ERA)
Unfair dismissal (s94(1) ERA)	3 months (s111(2) ERA) The time limit may be extended in certain circumstances for claims under Reg 2 Exclusivity Terms in Zero Hours Contracts (Redress) Regulations 2015	1 year where period of continuous service started prior to 6 April 2012; 2 years where period of continuous service started on or after 6 April 2012. There is no qualifying period if the principal reasons for dismissal relates to: ERA ss98B; 99; 100 (1); 101; 101A(1); 102; 103; 103A; 104; s104A; 104B; 104C; 104E; 104F; 105; TULR(C)A Sch A1 para 161; ss238A; 152-153; ICE Reg 30 TICE Reg 28; OPPS 2006; Reg 7 PRW Regs; Reg 6 FTE Regs; s12 ERelA 1999; Sch 6 para 13(5) Exclusivity Terms in Zero Hours Contracts (Redress) Regulations 2015 Reg 2
Right to redundancy payment (s135(1) ERA)	6 months (s164 ERA)	2 years (s155 ERA)
Insolvency claim to Secretary of State (s182 ERA)	3 months (s188(2) ERA)	None
Time off for health and safety reps 1996 and payment for time off (Reg 7 HSC Regs)	3 months (Sch 2 HSC Regs 1996)	None
Claims under the Working Time Regulations (Regs 10, 11, 12, 13, 14, 16, 24, 24A, 25, 27, 27A WTR)	3 months (Reg 30(2) WTR)	None
Right to National Minimum Wage (s1(1) NMWA 1998)	3 months (s23(2) ERA) or 6 years under contract	None
Right to access to records in relation to (s10 NMWA)	3 months (s11 NMWA)	None
Right not to suffer detriment for asserting rights in connection with (s23 NMWA)	3 months (s24(2) NMWA)	None
Right to be accompanied at a grievance or disciplinary meeting (s10 ERelA 1999) and right not to suffer detriment in connection with this right (s12 ERelA)	3 months (s11(2) and s12(2) ERelA)	None
Time off for works body member and right to payment during this time off (Regs 25 and 26 TICE 1999)	3 months (Reg 27(2) TICE)	None
Part-time worker discrimination (Regs 5 and 7(2) PTW Regs 2000)	3 months (Reg 8(2) PTW Regs)	None
Fixed term worker discrimination (Regs 3 and 6(2) FTE Regs 2002)	3 months (Reg 7(2) FTE)	None

Table 30: Limitation periods and requisite minimum qualifying periods for claims

Claim	Limitation period (maximum length of time that can elapse for claim to be brought to ET)	Length of service required before a claim can be brought to ET
Right to be accompanied at, or postponement of, flexible working meeting (Reg 14(2) and 14(4) FW(PR) Regs 2002)	3 months (Reg 15(2) FW(PR) Regs)	None
Time off for employee reps (reg 27 ICE Regs 2004) and payment for time off (Reg 28 ICE)	3 months (Reg 29(2) ICE)	None
Right to be informed and /or consulted over TUPE (Reg 13 TUPE 2006) and right to election of employee reps (Reg 14 TUPE)	3 months (Reg 15(12) TUPE)	None
Time off for employee reps (Sch paragraph 2 OPPS Regs 2006) and payment for time off (Sch paragraph 3 OPPS)	3 months (Schedule paragraph 4(2) OPPS)	None
Right not to suffer detriment in connection with employee reps (Schedule paragraph 7 OPPS)	3 months (Schedule paragraph 8(2) OPPS)	None
Breach of Sex Equality Clause (s66 EA 2010) or Maternity Equality Clause (s73 EA 2010)	6 months (or 9 months if relating to armed forces service) (s129 EA 2010)	None
Right to be accompanied to a meeting concerning study and training (Reg 16 EST (PR) Regs 2010)	3 months (Reg 17(2) EST (PR) Regs)	None

Table 31: Matters to which the prescribed element is attributable (Schedule to Employment Protection (Recoupment of Jobseeker's Allowance and Income Support) Regulations 1996)

Payment	Proceedings	Matter to which prescribed element is attributable
Guarantee payments under section 28.	Complaint under section 34.	Any amount found to be due to the employee and ordered to be paid under section 34(3) for a period before the conclusion of the tribunal proceedings.
Payments under any collective agreement having regard to which the appropriate Minister has made an exemption order under section 35.	Complaint under section 35(4).	Any amount found to be due to the employee and ordered to be paid under section 34(3), as applied by section 35(4), for a period before the conclusion of the tribunal proceedings.
Payments of remuneration in respect of a period of suspension on medical grounds under section 64 and section 108(2).	Complaint under section 70.	Any amount found to be due to the employee and ordered to be paid under section 70(3) for a period before the conclusion of the tribunal proceedings.
Payments of remuneration in respect of a period of suspension on maternity grounds under section 68.	Complaint under section 70.	Any amount found to be due to the employee and ordered to be paid under section 70(3) for a period before the conclusion of the tribunal proceedings.
Payments under an order for reinstatement under section 114(1).	Complaint of unfair dismissal under section 111(1).	Any amount ordered to be paid under section 114(2)(a) in respect of arrears of pay for a period before the conclusion of the tribunal proceedings.
Payments under an order for re-engagement under section 117(8).	Complaint of unfair dismissal under section 111(1).	Any amount ordered to be paid under section 115(2)(d) in respect of arrears of pay for a period before the conclusion of the tribunal proceedings.
Payments under an award of compensation for unfair dismissal in cases falling under section 112(4) (cases where no order for reinstatement or re-engagement has been made).	Complaint of unfair dismissal under section 111(1).	Any amount ordered to be paid and calculated under section 123 in respect of compensation for loss of wages for a period before the conclusion of the tribunal proceedings.
Payments under an award of compensation for unfair dismissal under section 117(3) where reinstatement order not complied with.	Proceedings in respect of non-compliance with order.	Any amount ordered to be paid and calculated under section 123 in respect of compensation for loss of wages for a period before the conclusion of the tribunal proceedings.
Payments under an award of compensation for unfair dismissal under section 117(3) where re-engagement order not complied with.	Proceedings in respect of non-compliance with order	Any amount ordered to be paid and calculated under section 123 in respect of compensation for loss of wages for a period before the conclusion of the tribunal proceedings.
Payments under an interim order for reinstatement under section 163(4) of the 1992 Act.	Proceedings on an application for an order for interim relief under section 161(1) of the	Any amount found to be due to the complainant and ordered to be paid in respect of arrears of pay for the period between the date of termination of employment and the conclusion of the tribunal proceedings.
Payments under an interim order for re-engagement under section 163(5)(a) of the 1992 Act.	Proceedings on an application for an order for interim relief under section 161(1) of the	Any amount found to be due to the complainant and ordered to be paid in respect of arrears of pay for the period between the date of termination of employment and the conclusion of the tribunal proceedings.
Payments under an order for the continuation of a contract of employment under section 163(5)(b) of the 1992 Act where employee reasonably refuses re-engagement.	Proceedings on an application for an order for interim relief under section 161(1) of the	Any amount found to be due to the complainant and ordered to be paid in respect of arrears of pay for the period between the date of termination of employment and the conclusion of the tribunal proceedings.
Payments under an order for the continuation of a contract of employment under section 163(6) of the 1992 Act where employer fails to attend or is unwilling to reinstate or re-engage.	Proceedings on an application for an order for interim relief under section 161(1) of the	Any amount found to be due to the complainant and ordered to be paid in respect of arrears of pay for the period between the date of termination of employment and the conclusion of the tribunal proceedings.
Payments under an order for the continuation of a contract of employment under sections 166(1) and (2) of the 1992 Act where reinstatement or re-engagement order not complied with.	Proceedings in respect of non-compliance with order.	Any amount ordered to be paid to the employee by way of compensation under section 166(1)(b) of the 1992 Act for loss of wages for the period between the date of termination of employment and the conclusion of the tribunal proceedings.

Table 31: Matters to which the prescribed element is attributable (Schedule to Employment Protection (Recoupment of Jobseeker's Allowance and Income Support) Regulations 1996)

Payment	Proceedings	Matter to which prescribed element is attributable
Payments under an order for compensation under sections 166(3)–(5) of the 1992 Act where order for the continuation of contract of employment not complied with.	Proceedings in respect of non-compliance with order.	Any amount ordered to be paid to the employee by way of compensation under section 166(3)–(4) of the 1992 Act for loss of wages for the period between the date of termination of employment and the conclusion of the tribunal proceedings.
Payments under an order under section 192(3) of the 1992 Act on employer's default in respect of remuneration due to employee under protective award.	Complaint under section 192(1) of the 1992 Act.	Any amount ordered to be paid to the employee in respect of so much of the relevant protected period as falls before the date of the conclusion of the tribunal proceedings.

Pensions and Ogden Tables

Table 32: State pension age for women born on or before 5 December 1953

For women born	Date State Pension age reached
On or before 5 April 1950	Age 60
6 April 1950 to 5 May 1950	6 May 2010
6 May 1950 to 5 June 1950	6 July 2010
6 June 1950 to 5 July 1950	6 September 2010
6 July 1950 to 5 August 1950	6 November 2010
6 August 1950 to 5 September 1950	6 January 2011
6 September 1950 to 5 October 1950	6 March 2011
6 October 1950 to 5 November 1950	6 May 2011
6 November 1950 to 5 December 1950	6 July 2011
6 December 1950 to 5 January 1951	6 September 2011
6 January 1951 to 5 February 1951	6 November 2011
6 February 1951 to 5 March 1951	6 January 2012
6 March 1951 to 5 April 1951	6 March 2012
6 April 1951 to 5 May 1951	6 May 2012
6 May 1951 to 5 June 1951	6 July 2012
6 June 1951 to 5 July 1951	6 September 2012
6 July 1951 to 5 August 1951	6 November 2012
6 August 1951 to 5 September 1951	6 January 2013
6 September 1951 to 5 October 1951	6 March 2013
6 October 1951 to 5 November 1951	6 May 2013
6 November 1951 to 5 December 1951	6 July 2013
6 December 1951 to 5 January 1952	6 September 2013
6 January 1952 to 5 February 1952	6 November 2013
6 February 1952 to 5 March 1952	6 January 2014
6 March 1952 to 5 April 1952	6 March 2014
6 April 1952 to 5 May 1952	6 May 2014
6 May 1952 to 5 June 1952	6 July 2014
6 June 1952 to 5 July 1952	6 September 2014
6 July 1952 to 5 August 1952	6 November 2014
6 August 1952 to 5 September 1952	6 January 2015
6 September 1952 to 5 October 1952	6 March 2015
6 October 1952 to 5 November 1952	6 May 2015
6 November 1952 to 5 December 1952	6 July 2015
6 December 1952 to 5 January 1953	6 September 2015
6 January 1953 to 5 February 1953	6 November 2015

6 February 1953 to 5 March 1953	6 January 2016
6 March 1953 to 5 April 1953	6 March 2016
6 April 1953 to 5 May 1953	6 July 2016
6 May 1953 to 5 June 1953	6 November 2016
6 June 1953 to 5 July 1953	6 March 2017
6 July 1953 to 5 August 1953	6 July 2017
6 August 1953 to 5 September 1953	6 November 2017
6 September 1953 to 5 October 1953	6 March 2018
6 October 1953 to 5 November 1953	6 July 2018
6 November 1953 to 5 December 1953	6 November 2018

Table 33: State pension age for men and women born after 5 December 1953

For men and women born	Date State Pension age reached
6 December 1953 to 5 January 1954	6 March 2019
6 January 1954 to 5 February 1954	6 May 2019
6 February 1954 to 5 March 1954	6 July 2019
6 March 1954 to 5 April 1954	6 September 2019
6 April 1954 to 5 May 1954	6 November 2019
6 May 1954 to 5 June 1954	6 January 2020
6 June 1954 to 5 July 1954	6 March 2020
6 July 1954 to 5 August 1954	6 May 2020
6 August 1954 to 5 September 1954	6 July 2020
6 September 1954 to 5 October 1954	6 September 2020
6 October 1954 to 5 April 1960	66th birthday
6 April 1960 to 5 May 1960	Age 66 and 1 month
6 May 1960 to 5 June 1960	Age 66 and 2 months
6 June 1960 to 5 July 1960	Age 66 and 3 months
6 July 1960 to 5 August 1960	Age 66 and 4 months
6 August 1960 to 5 September 1960	Age 66 and 5 months
6 September 1960 to 5 October 1960	Age 66 and 6 months
6 October to 5 November 1960	Age 66 and 7 months
6 November 1960 to 5 December 1960	Age 66 and 8 months
6 December 1960 to 5 January 1961	Age 66 and 9 months
6 January 1961 to 5 February 1961	Age 66 and 10 months
6 February 1961 to 5 March 1961	Age 66 and 11 months
6 March 1961 to 5 April 1977	67th birthday
6 April 1977 and 5 May 1977	6 May 2044
6 May 1977 and 5 June 1977	6 July 2044
6 June 1977 and 5 July 1977	6 September 2044
6 July 1977 and 5 August 1977	6 November 2044
6 August 1977 and 5 September 1977	6 January 2045
6 September 1977 and 5 October 1977	6 March 2045
6 October 1977 and 5 November 1977	6 May 2045
6 November 1977 and 5 December 1977	6 July 2045
6 December 1977 and 5 January 1978	6 September 2045
6 January 1978 and 5 February 1978	6 November 2045
6 February 1978 and 5 March 1978	6 January 2046
6 March 1978 and 5 April 1978	6 March 2046
On or after 6 April 1978	68th birthday

Ogden Table 15: Multipliers for loss of pension commencing age 50 (males)

Age at date of trial	Multiplier calculated with allowance for projected mortality from the 2008-based population projections and rate of return of												Age at date of trial
	-2.0%	-1.5%	-1.0%	-0.75%	-0.5%	0.0%	0.5%	1.0%	1.5%	2.0%	2.5%	3.0%	
0	179.64	121.70	83.09	68.85	57.16	39.61	27.64	19.42	13.74	9.78	7.00	5.04	0
1	176.24	120.05	82.40	68.47	56.99	39.70	27.85	19.67	13.99	10.01	7.20	5.21	1
2	172.05	117.83	81.32	67.74	56.54	39.59	27.92	19.83	14.17	10.19	7.37	5.36	2
3	167.93	115.64	80.24	67.02	56.09	39.49	27.99	19.98	14.35	10.37	7.54	5.51	3
4	163.90	113.48	79.16	66.30	55.63	39.37	28.06	20.13	14.53	10.56	7.72	5.67	4
5	159.97	111.36	78.10	65.59	55.18	39.26	28.12	20.28	14.72	10.75	7.89	5.83	5
6	156.12	109.27	77.05	64.88	54.73	39.14	28.19	20.43	14.91	10.94	8.08	5.99	6
7	152.36	107.22	76.01	64.18	54.28	39.03	28.25	20.59	15.10	11.14	8.26	6.16	7
8	148.69	105.21	74.99	63.48	53.83	38.91	28.32	20.74	15.29	11.33	8.45	6.34	8
9	145.10	103.23	73.98	62.79	53.39	38.80	28.38	20.90	15.48	11.54	8.65	6.52	9
10	141.59	101.28	72.97	62.10	52.95	38.68	28.44	21.05	15.68	11.74	8.84	6.70	10
11	138.17	99.37	71.98	61.42	52.51	38.56	28.51	21.21	15.87	11.95	9.05	6.89	11
12	134.83	97.50	71.01	60.75	52.07	38.44	28.57	21.36	16.07	12.16	9.26	7.08	12
13	131.57	95.66	70.04	60.09	51.64	38.33	28.63	21.52	16.28	12.38	9.47	7.28	13
14	128.40	93.86	69.10	59.44	51.21	38.21	28.70	21.68	16.48	12.60	9.69	7.48	14
15	125.31	92.10	68.16	58.79	50.79	38.10	28.76	21.85	16.69	12.82	9.91	7.69	15
16	122.29	90.37	67.24	58.15	50.38	37.99	28.83	22.01	16.90	13.05	10.14	7.91	16
17	119.35	88.68	66.34	57.53	49.96	37.88	28.89	22.17	17.12	13.29	10.37	8.13	17
18	116.49	87.02	65.46	56.91	49.56	37.77	28.96	22.34	17.34	13.53	10.61	8.36	18
19	113.71	85.41	64.59	56.30	49.16	37.67	29.03	22.52	17.56	13.77	10.86	8.60	19
20	111.01	83.83	63.74	55.71	48.78	37.57	29.11	22.69	17.79	14.02	11.11	8.85	20
21	108.37	82.28	62.90	55.12	48.39	37.46	29.18	22.87	18.02	14.28	11.37	9.10	21
22	105.78	80.76	62.06	54.54	48.00	37.36	29.26	23.04	18.25	14.53	11.63	9.36	22
23	103.25	79.25	61.24	53.96	47.62	37.26	29.33	23.22	18.49	14.80	11.90	9.62	23
24	100.79	77.78	60.42	53.38	47.24	37.16	29.40	23.40	18.73	15.06	12.18	9.90	24
25	98.39	76.35	59.63	52.82	46.86	37.06	29.48	23.58	18.97	15.34	12.46	10.18	25
26	96.06	74.95	58.85	52.27	46.50	36.96	29.56	23.77	19.22	15.62	12.76	10.47	26
27	93.80	73.57	58.08	51.73	46.14	36.87	29.64	23.96	19.47	15.90	13.06	10.77	27
28	91.57	72.22	57.32	51.18	45.77	36.77	29.71	24.14	19.72	16.19	13.36	11.08	28
29	89.39	70.88	56.56	50.64	45.41	36.68	29.79	24.33	19.98	16.49	13.67	11.39	29
30	87.27	69.58	55.82	50.11	45.06	36.58	29.87	24.52	20.24	16.79	13.99	11.72	30
31	85.23	68.32	55.10	49.60	44.71	36.50	29.96	24.72	20.51	17.10	14.33	12.05	31
32	83.24	67.09	54.41	49.10	44.38	36.42	30.05	24.93	20.79	17.42	14.67	12.40	32
33	81.32	65.90	53.73	48.62	44.06	36.35	30.15	25.14	21.07	17.75	15.02	12.77	33
34	79.44	64.72	53.05	48.14	43.74	36.27	30.24	25.35	21.36	18.08	15.38	13.14	34
35	77.60	63.57	52.39	47.66	43.42	36.20	30.34	25.56	21.65	18.42	15.75	13.52	35
36	75.82	62.44	51.74	47.19	43.11	36.13	30.44	25.78	21.95	18.77	16.13	13.92	36
37	74.08	61.34	51.09	46.73	42.81	36.06	30.54	26.00	22.25	19.12	16.51	14.32	37
38	72.37	60.25	50.46	46.28	42.50	35.99	30.64	26.22	22.55	19.49	16.91	14.74	38
39	70.70	59.18	49.83	45.82	42.19	35.92	30.74	26.45	22.86	19.85	17.32	15.17	39
40	69.07	58.13	49.21	45.37	41.89	35.85	30.85	26.67	23.18	20.23	17.74	15.62	40
41	67.49	57.11	48.61	44.93	41.60	35.79	30.96	26.91	23.50	20.62	18.17	16.08	41
42	65.95	56.11	48.01	44.51	41.31	35.73	31.07	27.14	23.83	21.01	18.61	16.55	42
43	64.46	55.14	47.44	44.09	41.03	35.68	31.18	27.39	24.16	21.42	19.07	17.04	43
44	63.01	54.19	46.87	43.68	40.76	35.63	31.30	27.63	24.51	21.84	19.54	17.55	44

Ogden Table 15: Multipliers for loss of pension commencing age 50 (males)

Age at date of trial	Multiplier calculated with allowance for projected mortality from the 2008-based population projections and rate of return of												Age at date of trial
	-2.0%	-1.5%	-1.0%	-0.75%	-0.5%	0.0%	0.5%	1.0%	1.5%	2.0%	2.5%	3.0%	
45	61.60	53.26	46.32	43.28	40.49	35.58	31.42	27.89	24.86	22.26	20.02	18.07	45
46	60.22	52.36	45.77	42.88	40.23	35.54	31.55	28.14	25.22	22.70	20.52	18.62	46
47	58.88	51.47	45.24	42.50	39.98	35.50	31.68	28.41	25.59	23.15	21.03	19.18	47
48	57.59	50.62	44.73	42.13	39.73	35.47	31.83	28.69	25.97	23.62	21.56	19.76	48
49	56.34	49.79	44.23	41.78	39.50	35.46	31.98	28.97	26.37	24.10	22.11	20.37	49
50	55.14	48.99	43.76	41.44	39.29	35.45	32.14	29.27	26.78	24.60	22.69	21.01	50

Ogden Table 16: Multipliers for loss of pension commencing age 50 (females)

Age at date of trial	Multiplier calculated with allowance for projected mortality from the 2008-based population projections and rate of return of												Age at date of trial
	-2.0%	-1.5%	-1.0%	-0.75%	-0.5%	0.0%	0.5%	1.0%	1.5%	2.0%	2.5%	3.0%	
0	199.59	134.37	91.19	75.34	62.37	42.98	29.85	20.87	14.70	10.42	7.43	5.33	0
1	195.74	132.49	90.40	74.89	62.16	43.07	30.06	21.13	14.95	10.65	7.64	5.51	1
2	191.18	130.11	89.25	74.13	61.69	42.97	30.15	21.30	15.16	10.85	7.82	5.67	2
3	186.71	127.75	88.10	73.38	61.23	42.87	30.24	21.48	15.36	11.05	8.00	5.83	3
4	182.34	125.44	86.97	72.63	60.76	42.77	30.32	21.65	15.56	11.26	8.19	6.00	4
5	178.06	123.16	85.85	71.88	60.30	42.67	30.41	21.82	15.77	11.46	8.39	6.17	5
6	173.88	120.92	84.74	71.14	59.84	42.56	30.49	22.00	15.97	11.67	8.58	6.35	6
7	169.79	118.72	83.65	70.41	59.38	42.46	30.58	22.17	16.18	11.89	8.78	6.53	7
8	165.80	116.55	82.56	69.68	58.92	42.36	30.66	22.35	16.40	12.10	8.99	6.72	8
9	161.89	114.43	81.49	68.96	58.47	42.25	30.75	22.53	16.61	12.33	9.20	6.91	9
10	158.08	112.34	80.43	68.25	58.02	42.15	30.83	22.70	16.83	12.55	9.42	7.11	10
11	154.36	110.29	79.39	67.54	57.57	42.04	30.92	22.89	17.05	12.78	9.64	7.31	11
12	150.73	108.28	78.36	66.84	57.12	41.94	31.00	23.07	17.27	13.01	9.86	7.52	12
13	147.17	106.30	77.34	66.15	56.68	41.83	31.08	23.25	17.50	13.25	10.09	7.73	13
14	143.71	104.36	76.34	65.47	56.24	41.73	31.17	23.43	17.73	13.49	10.33	7.95	14
15	140.33	102.45	75.35	64.79	55.81	41.62	31.25	23.62	17.96	13.74	10.57	8.18	15
16	137.02	100.58	74.37	64.12	55.38	41.52	31.34	23.81	18.20	13.99	10.82	8.41	16
17	133.80	98.75	73.41	63.46	54.95	41.42	31.42	24.00	18.44	14.25	11.07	8.65	17
18	130.66	96.95	72.46	62.80	54.53	41.32	31.51	24.19	18.68	14.51	11.33	8.90	18
19	127.60	95.19	71.52	62.16	54.11	41.22	31.60	24.38	18.92	14.78	11.60	9.16	19
20	124.61	93.47	70.61	61.53	53.70	41.12	31.69	24.58	19.18	15.05	11.87	9.42	20
21	121.70	91.78	69.70	60.90	53.30	41.03	31.78	24.78	19.43	15.32	12.15	9.69	21
22	118.85	90.11	68.80	60.27	52.89	40.93	31.87	24.97	19.69	15.61	12.44	9.97	22
23	116.05	88.47	67.91	59.65	52.48	40.82	31.96	25.17	19.94	15.89	12.73	10.25	23
24	113.32	86.85	67.03	59.03	52.08	40.72	32.05	25.37	20.21	16.18	13.03	10.54	24
25	110.66	85.27	66.16	58.43	51.68	40.62	32.14	25.57	20.47	16.48	13.33	10.85	25
26	108.06	83.73	65.31	57.83	51.28	40.53	32.23	25.78	20.74	16.78	13.65	11.16	26
27	105.53	82.21	64.47	57.24	50.89	40.43	32.32	25.99	21.02	17.09	13.97	11.48	27
28	103.06	80.72	63.64	56.65	50.50	40.33	32.41	26.19	21.29	17.40	14.30	11.81	28
29	100.65	79.26	62.82	56.07	50.12	40.24	32.50	26.41	21.58	17.72	14.64	12.14	29
30	98.30	77.82	62.02	55.50	49.74	40.15	32.60	26.62	21.86	18.05	14.98	12.49	30

Ogden Table 16: Multipliers for loss of pension commencing age 50 (females)

Age at date of trial	Multiplier calculated with allowance for projected mortality from the 2008-based population projections and rate of return of												Age at date of trial
	-2.0%	-1.5%	-1.0%	-0.75%	-0.5%	0.0%	0.5%	1.0%	1.5%	2.0%	2.5%	3.0%	
31	96.01	76.42	61.23	54.94	49.37	40.06	32.69	26.84	22.15	18.38	15.33	12.85	31
32	93.78	75.05	60.46	54.39	49.00	39.97	32.79	27.06	22.45	18.73	15.70	13.22	32
33	91.61	73.71	59.69	53.84	48.64	39.88	32.89	27.28	22.75	19.07	16.07	13.61	33
34	89.48	72.38	58.93	53.30	48.28	39.79	32.99	27.50	23.05	19.43	16.45	14.00	34
35	87.39	71.08	58.18	52.76	47.92	39.70	33.09	27.73	23.36	19.79	16.84	14.40	35
36	85.37	69.81	57.45	52.24	47.57	39.62	33.19	27.96	23.68	20.16	17.24	14.82	36
37	83.40	68.57	56.73	51.72	47.22	39.54	33.29	28.19	24.00	20.53	17.65	15.25	37
38	81.47	67.35	56.02	51.20	46.87	39.45	33.40	28.43	24.32	20.92	18.07	15.69	38
39	79.59	66.15	55.31	50.70	46.53	39.37	33.50	28.66	24.65	21.31	18.50	16.14	39
40	77.75	64.97	54.62	50.19	46.19	39.29	33.61	28.90	24.99	21.71	18.95	16.61	40
41	75.96	63.82	53.94	49.70	45.86	39.22	33.72	29.15	25.33	22.11	19.40	17.10	41
42	74.22	62.69	53.27	49.22	45.54	39.14	33.83	29.40	25.67	22.53	19.87	17.60	42
43	72.53	61.59	52.62	48.74	45.22	39.07	33.95	29.65	26.03	22.96	20.35	18.11	43
44	70.88	60.52	51.98	48.28	44.90	39.01	34.07	29.91	26.39	23.40	20.84	18.64	44
45	69.28	59.47	51.35	47.82	44.60	38.94	34.19	30.17	26.76	23.85	21.35	19.19	45
46	67.72	58.45	50.74	47.38	44.30	38.89	34.32	30.44	27.14	24.31	21.87	19.76	46
47	66.20	57.45	50.14	46.94	44.01	38.83	34.45	30.72	27.53	24.78	22.41	20.35	47
48	64.73	56.48	49.56	46.52	43.73	38.79	34.59	31.01	27.93	25.27	22.97	20.96	48
49	63.31	55.54	48.99	46.11	43.46	38.76	34.74	31.30	28.34	25.77	23.54	21.59	49
50	61.93	54.62	48.44	45.71	43.20	38.73	34.90	31.61	28.76	26.29	24.14	22.25	50

Ogden Table 17: Multipliers for loss of pension commencing age 55 (males)

Age at date of trial	Multiplier calculated with allowance for projected mortality from the 2008-based population projections and rate of return of												Age at date of trial
	-2.0%	-1.5%	-1.0%	-0.75%	-0.5%	0.0%	0.5%	1.0%	1.5%	2.0%	2.5%	3.0%	
0	165.74	111.07	74.94	61.71	50.90	34.80	23.94	16.57	11.54	8.08	5.69	4.02	0
1	162.56	109.52	74.30	61.34	50.73	34.87	24.11	16.78	11.74	8.26	5.85	4.16	1
2	158.64	107.46	73.29	60.68	50.31	34.76	24.17	16.90	11.89	8.41	5.98	4.27	2
3	154.79	105.43	72.29	60.01	49.89	34.65	24.22	17.02	12.04	8.56	6.12	4.39	3
4	151.03	103.43	71.30	59.34	49.47	34.54	24.27	17.15	12.19	8.71	6.26	4.52	4
5	147.35	101.46	70.32	58.68	49.05	34.43	24.31	17.27	12.34	8.86	6.40	4.64	5
6	143.76	99.52	69.35	58.03	48.63	34.32	24.36	17.39	12.49	9.02	6.54	4.77	6
7	140.25	97.62	68.39	57.38	48.22	34.20	24.41	17.52	12.64	9.17	6.69	4.90	7
8	136.83	95.76	67.44	56.74	47.80	34.09	24.45	17.64	12.80	9.33	6.84	5.04	8
9	133.48	93.92	66.51	56.10	47.39	33.97	24.50	17.77	12.96	9.50	7.00	5.18	9
10	130.21	92.11	65.58	55.46	46.98	33.86	24.54	17.89	13.11	9.66	7.15	5.32	10
11	127.02	90.34	64.67	54.84	46.57	33.74	24.59	18.02	13.27	9.83	7.32	5.47	11
12	123.91	88.61	63.77	54.22	46.17	33.63	24.63	18.14	13.44	10.00	7.48	5.62	12
13	120.87	86.91	62.88	53.61	45.77	33.51	24.68	18.27	13.60	10.18	7.65	5.78	13
14	117.91	85.24	62.00	53.00	45.37	33.40	24.72	18.40	13.77	10.35	7.82	5.94	14
15	115.03	83.61	61.14	52.41	44.98	33.29	24.77	18.53	13.94	10.53	8.00	6.10	15
16	112.22	82.01	60.30	51.82	44.60	33.17	24.81	18.66	14.11	10.72	8.18	6.27	16

Ogden Table 17: Multipliers for loss of pension commencing age 55 (males)

Age at date of trial	Multiplier calculated with allowance for projected mortality from the 2008-based population projections and rate of return of												Age at date of trial
	-2.0%	-1.5%	-1.0%	-0.75%	-0.5%	0.0%	0.5%	1.0%	1.5%	2.0%	2.5%	3.0%	
17	109.49	80.45	59.47	51.24	44.22	33.06	24.86	18.79	14.28	10.90	8.37	6.45	17
18	106.83	78.92	58.65	50.67	43.84	32.96	24.91	18.93	14.46	11.10	8.56	6.63	18
19	104.24	77.42	57.85	50.11	43.47	32.85	24.96	19.07	14.64	11.29	8.75	6.81	19
20	101.73	75.97	57.07	49.57	43.11	32.75	25.02	19.21	14.82	11.49	8.95	7.00	20
21	99.28	74.54	56.29	49.02	42.76	32.65	25.07	19.35	15.01	11.70	9.16	7.20	21
22	96.87	73.13	55.52	48.48	42.40	32.55	25.12	19.49	15.19	11.90	9.37	7.40	22
23	94.52	71.74	54.76	47.95	42.04	32.45	25.17	19.63	15.38	12.11	9.58	7.61	23
24	92.23	70.38	54.02	47.42	41.69	32.34	25.23	19.77	15.58	12.33	9.80	7.82	24
25	90.00	69.05	53.28	46.90	41.34	32.24	25.28	19.92	15.77	12.54	10.02	8.04	25
26	87.84	67.76	52.56	46.39	41.00	32.15	25.34	20.07	15.97	12.77	10.25	8.27	26
27	85.73	66.49	51.86	45.89	40.67	32.06	25.40	20.22	16.17	13.00	10.49	8.50	27
28	83.67	65.24	51.16	45.39	40.33	31.96	25.45	20.37	16.38	13.23	10.73	8.74	28
29	81.64	64.01	50.46	44.89	39.99	31.86	25.51	20.52	16.58	13.46	10.97	8.98	29
30	79.68	62.81	49.78	44.41	39.66	31.76	25.56	20.67	16.79	13.70	11.23	9.24	30
31	77.78	61.65	49.12	43.93	39.35	31.68	25.63	20.83	17.01	13.95	11.49	9.50	31
32	75.95	60.52	48.48	43.48	39.04	31.60	25.69	20.99	17.23	14.20	11.76	9.77	32
33	74.17	59.42	47.86	43.03	38.74	31.52	25.77	21.16	17.46	14.46	12.03	10.05	33
34	72.42	58.34	47.24	42.59	38.44	31.44	25.84	21.33	17.69	14.73	12.32	10.34	34
35	70.72	57.27	46.62	42.15	38.15	31.36	25.91	21.50	17.92	15.00	12.61	10.64	35
36	69.07	56.24	46.03	41.72	37.86	31.29	25.98	21.68	18.16	15.28	12.90	10.94	36
37	67.45	55.22	45.44	41.29	37.57	31.22	26.06	21.85	18.40	15.56	13.21	11.26	37
38	65.87	54.22	44.85	40.87	37.29	31.14	26.13	22.03	18.65	15.85	13.52	11.58	38
39	64.33	53.23	44.27	40.45	37.00	31.07	26.21	22.21	18.89	16.14	13.84	11.91	39
40	62.82	52.27	43.70	40.04	36.72	31.00	26.28	22.38	19.14	16.44	14.17	12.26	40
41	61.36	51.33	43.15	39.63	36.45	30.93	26.36	22.57	19.40	16.74	14.50	12.61	41
42	59.93	50.41	42.60	39.24	36.18	30.86	26.45	22.76	19.66	17.06	14.85	12.98	42
43	58.55	49.51	42.07	38.85	35.92	30.80	26.53	22.95	19.93	17.38	15.21	13.36	43
44	57.21	48.64	41.55	38.47	35.66	30.74	26.62	23.15	20.21	17.71	15.57	13.75	44
45	55.90	47.78	41.04	38.10	35.41	30.69	26.71	23.35	20.49	18.04	15.95	14.15	45
46	54.63	46.95	40.54	37.74	35.16	30.64	26.81	23.55	20.77	18.39	16.34	14.57	46
47	53.39	46.14	40.05	37.38	34.93	30.59	26.91	23.76	21.06	18.74	16.74	15.00	47
48	52.20	45.35	39.58	37.04	34.70	30.55	27.01	23.98	21.37	19.11	17.15	15.45	48
49	51.04	44.58	39.12	36.71	34.48	30.52	27.12	24.20	21.68	19.49	17.58	15.92	49
50	49.93	43.85	38.68	36.39	34.27	30.50	27.25	24.44	22.00	19.88	18.03	16.40	50
51	48.86	43.14	38.26	36.09	34.08	30.49	27.38	24.69	22.34	20.29	18.49	16.91	51
52	47.83	42.46	37.86	35.81	33.91	30.49	27.53	24.95	22.69	20.72	18.98	17.44	52
53	46.84	41.81	37.48	35.55	33.74	30.50	27.68	25.22	23.06	21.16	19.48	17.99	53
54	45.90	41.19	37.12	35.30	33.60	30.53	27.86	25.51	23.44	21.62	20.01	18.57	54
55	44.99	40.60	36.79	35.07	33.47	30.58	28.04	25.81	23.85	22.11	20.56	19.18	55

Ogden Table 18: Multipliers for loss of pension commencing age 55 (females)

Age at date of trial	Multiplier calculated with allowance for projected mortality from the 2008-based population projections and rate of return of												Age at date of trial
	-2.0%	-1.5%	-1.0%	-0.75%	-0.5%	0.0%	0.5%	1.0%	1.5%	2.0%	2.5%	3.0%	
0	185.47	123.56	82.90	68.08	56.01	38.10	26.08	17.97	12.46	8.69	6.09	4.30	0
1	181.85	121.80	82.16	67.66	55.81	38.16	26.26	18.19	12.68	8.88	6.26	4.44	1
2	177.57	119.58	81.09	66.95	55.37	38.06	26.33	18.33	12.84	9.05	6.41	4.57	2
3	173.37	117.38	80.03	66.25	54.94	37.96	26.40	18.48	13.01	9.21	6.56	4.69	3
4	169.26	115.23	78.98	65.56	54.51	37.86	26.47	18.62	13.18	9.38	6.71	4.83	4
5	165.25	113.10	77.94	64.87	54.08	37.76	26.54	18.76	13.35	9.55	6.87	4.97	5
6	161.33	111.01	76.92	64.18	53.65	37.66	26.60	18.91	13.52	9.72	7.03	5.11	6
7	157.49	108.96	75.90	63.50	53.22	37.56	26.67	19.05	13.69	9.89	7.19	5.25	7
8	153.74	106.95	74.89	62.83	52.79	37.45	26.73	19.20	13.87	10.07	7.36	5.40	8
9	150.08	104.96	73.90	62.16	52.37	37.35	26.80	19.35	14.04	10.25	7.53	5.55	9
10	146.51	103.02	72.92	61.50	51.95	37.24	26.86	19.49	14.22	10.44	7.70	5.71	10
11	143.02	101.11	71.95	60.85	51.53	37.14	26.93	19.64	14.41	10.63	7.88	5.87	11
12	139.61	99.24	71.00	60.20	51.12	37.04	26.99	19.79	14.59	10.82	8.06	6.04	12
13	136.29	97.39	70.05	59.55	50.71	36.93	27.06	19.94	14.78	11.01	8.25	6.21	13
14	133.04	95.59	69.12	58.92	50.30	36.83	27.12	20.09	14.97	11.21	8.44	6.38	14
15	129.87	93.82	68.21	58.29	49.90	36.72	27.19	20.25	15.16	11.41	8.63	6.56	15
16	126.78	92.08	67.30	57.67	49.50	36.62	27.26	20.40	15.35	11.61	8.83	6.75	16
17	123.76	90.37	66.41	57.06	49.10	36.52	27.32	20.55	15.55	11.82	9.03	6.94	17
18	120.82	88.70	65.53	56.45	48.71	36.42	27.39	20.71	15.75	12.03	9.24	7.13	18
19	117.96	87.07	64.67	55.86	48.32	36.32	27.46	20.87	15.95	12.25	9.46	7.34	19
20	115.17	85.47	63.82	55.27	47.94	36.23	27.53	21.03	16.16	12.47	9.68	7.54	20
21	112.45	83.90	62.98	54.69	47.56	36.13	27.60	21.20	16.37	12.70	9.90	7.76	21
22	109.78	82.35	62.15	54.11	47.19	36.03	27.67	21.36	16.58	12.93	10.13	7.98	22
23	107.16	80.82	61.33	53.54	46.81	35.93	27.73	21.52	16.79	13.16	10.37	8.20	23
24	104.61	79.32	60.51	52.97	46.43	35.83	27.80	21.68	17.00	13.40	10.61	8.43	24
25	102.12	77.86	59.71	52.40	46.06	35.73	27.87	21.85	17.22	13.64	10.85	8.67	25
26	99.70	76.42	58.92	51.85	45.69	35.63	27.94	22.02	17.44	13.88	11.10	8.92	26
27	97.34	75.01	58.15	51.30	45.33	35.54	28.01	22.19	17.67	14.13	11.36	9.17	27
28	95.02	73.63	57.38	50.76	44.97	35.44	28.08	22.36	17.89	14.39	11.62	9.43	28
29	92.77	72.27	56.62	50.23	44.61	35.34	28.15	22.53	18.12	14.65	11.89	9.70	29
30	90.58	70.94	55.88	49.70	44.26	35.25	28.22	22.71	18.36	14.91	12.17	9.97	30
31	88.45	69.65	55.15	49.18	43.92	35.16	28.29	22.88	18.60	15.18	12.45	10.26	31
32	86.37	68.38	54.44	48.67	43.58	35.07	28.37	23.06	18.84	15.46	12.74	10.55	32
33	84.34	67.13	53.73	48.17	43.24	34.98	28.45	23.24	19.09	15.74	13.04	10.85	33
34	82.35	65.90	53.03	47.67	42.90	34.89	28.52	23.43	19.33	16.03	13.35	11.16	34
35	80.41	64.70	52.34	47.17	42.57	34.80	28.60	23.61	19.59	16.32	13.66	11.48	35
36	78.53	63.52	51.66	46.68	42.24	34.72	28.67	23.80	19.84	16.62	13.98	11.80	36
37	76.69	62.37	51.00	46.20	41.92	34.63	28.75	23.99	20.10	16.92	14.30	12.14	37
38	74.89	61.24	50.34	45.73	41.60	34.55	28.83	24.18	20.37	17.23	14.64	12.49	38
39	73.14	60.13	49.69	45.26	41.28	34.46	28.91	24.37	20.64	17.55	14.98	12.85	39
40	71.43	59.04	49.05	44.80	40.97	34.38	29.00	24.57	20.91	17.87	15.34	13.22	40
41	69.76	57.97	48.43	44.34	40.66	34.30	29.08	24.77	21.19	18.20	15.70	13.60	41
42	68.14	56.93	47.81	43.90	40.35	34.23	29.17	24.97	21.47	18.54	16.07	13.99	42

Ogden Table 18: Multipliers for loss of pension commencing age 55 (females)

Age at date of trial	Multiplier calculated with allowance for projected mortality from the 2008-based population projections and rate of return of												Age at date of trial
	-2.0%	-1.5%	-1.0%	-0.75%	-0.5%	0.0%	0.5%	1.0%	1.5%	2.0%	2.5%	3.0%	
43	66.56	55.91	47.21	43.46	40.05	34.15	29.25	25.17	21.76	18.88	16.45	14.39	43
44	65.03	54.92	46.62	43.03	39.76	34.08	29.35	25.38	22.05	19.23	16.84	14.81	44
45	63.54	53.95	46.04	42.61	39.48	34.02	29.44	25.60	22.35	19.60	17.25	15.24	45
46	62.09	53.00	45.47	42.19	39.20	33.95	29.54	25.82	22.66	19.97	17.66	15.68	46
47	60.68	52.07	44.91	41.79	38.93	33.89	29.64	26.04	22.97	20.35	18.09	16.14	47
48	59.31	51.18	44.38	41.40	38.66	33.84	29.75	26.27	23.30	20.74	18.53	16.62	48
49	57.99	50.31	43.85	41.02	38.41	33.80	29.87	26.51	23.63	21.14	18.99	17.12	49
50	56.70	49.46	43.35	40.65	38.17	33.76	29.99	26.76	23.97	21.56	19.46	17.63	50
51	55.46	48.63	42.85	40.29	37.93	33.73	30.12	27.01	24.32	21.99	19.95	18.16	51
52	54.25	47.83	42.37	39.94	37.70	33.70	30.25	27.27	24.68	22.43	20.45	18.71	52
53	53.08	47.05	41.90	39.61	37.49	33.68	30.40	27.54	25.06	22.88	20.97	19.29	53
54	51.95	46.30	41.45	39.29	37.28	33.68	30.55	27.83	25.44	23.35	21.51	19.88	54
55	50.86	45.57	41.02	38.99	37.09	33.68	30.71	28.12	25.84	23.84	22.07	20.51	55

Ogden Table 19: Multipliers for loss of pension commencing age 60 (males)

Age at date of trial	Multiplier calculated with allowance for projected mortality from the 2008-based population projections and rate of return of												Age at date of trial
	-2.0%	-1.5%	-1.0%	-0.75%	-0.5%	0.0%	0.5%	1.0%	1.5%	2.0%	2.5%	3.0%	
0	150.59	99.76	66.49	54.40	44.58	30.06	20.38	13.89	9.52	6.56	4.54	3.16	0
1	147.63	98.33	65.89	54.05	44.41	30.10	20.52	14.06	9.69	6.70	4.66	3.26	1
2	144.02	96.44	64.97	53.44	44.02	30.00	20.55	14.16	9.80	6.82	4.77	3.35	2
3	140.47	94.58	64.06	52.83	43.63	29.89	20.59	14.26	9.92	6.94	4.88	3.44	3
4	137.00	92.74	63.15	52.22	43.25	29.78	20.62	14.35	10.04	7.06	4.98	3.54	4
5	133.61	90.93	62.25	51.62	42.86	29.67	20.65	14.45	10.16	7.18	5.10	3.63	5
6	130.29	89.16	61.36	51.02	42.47	29.56	20.68	14.54	10.28	7.30	5.21	3.73	6
7	127.06	87.42	60.49	50.42	42.09	29.45	20.71	14.64	10.40	7.42	5.32	3.83	7
8	123.91	85.71	59.63	49.84	41.71	29.34	20.74	14.74	10.52	7.55	5.44	3.94	8
9	120.82	84.03	58.77	49.25	41.33	29.22	20.77	14.84	10.65	7.68	5.56	4.05	9
10	117.81	82.38	57.93	48.67	40.95	29.11	20.80	14.93	10.77	7.81	5.68	4.16	10
11	114.87	80.76	57.09	48.10	40.58	29.00	20.82	15.03	10.90	7.94	5.81	4.27	11
12	112.01	79.17	56.27	47.54	40.21	28.88	20.85	15.13	11.03	8.07	5.94	4.39	12
13	109.22	77.62	55.46	46.98	39.84	28.77	20.88	15.23	11.16	8.21	6.07	4.50	13
14	106.50	76.10	54.67	46.43	39.48	28.66	20.91	15.33	11.29	8.35	6.20	4.63	14
15	103.85	74.61	53.88	45.88	39.12	28.55	20.94	15.43	11.42	8.49	6.34	4.75	15
16	101.27	73.15	53.11	45.35	38.77	28.44	20.96	15.53	11.55	8.63	6.48	4.88	16
17	98.76	71.72	52.36	44.82	38.42	28.33	20.99	15.63	11.69	8.78	6.62	5.02	17
18	96.32	70.32	51.61	44.30	38.07	28.23	21.03	15.74	11.83	8.93	6.77	5.15	18
19	93.94	68.96	50.88	43.79	37.74	28.12	21.06	15.84	11.97	9.08	6.92	5.30	19
20	91.64	67.63	50.17	43.29	37.41	28.02	21.09	15.95	12.11	9.24	7.08	5.44	20
21	89.39	66.33	49.47	42.80	37.08	27.92	21.13	16.06	12.26	9.40	7.23	5.59	21
22	87.18	65.04	48.77	42.31	36.75	27.82	21.16	16.17	12.41	9.56	7.40	5.74	22
23	85.02	63.77	48.08	41.82	36.42	27.72	21.19	16.28	12.55	9.72	7.56	5.90	23

Ogden Table 19: Multipliers for loss of pension commencing age 60 (males)

Age at date of trial	Multiplier calculated with allowance for projected mortality from the 2008-based population projections and rate of return of												Age at date of trial
	-2.0%	-1.5%	-1.0%	-0.75%	-0.5%	0.0%	0.5%	1.0%	1.5%	2.0%	2.5%	3.0%	
24	82.92	62.54	47.40	41.34	36.09	27.62	21.23	16.39	12.70	9.89	7.73	6.06	24
25	80.88	61.33	46.73	40.86	35.78	27.52	21.26	16.50	12.86	10.06	7.90	6.23	25
26	78.91	60.15	46.08	40.40	35.46	27.42	21.30	16.61	13.01	10.23	8.08	6.40	26
27	76.98	59.00	45.44	39.95	35.16	27.33	21.34	16.73	13.17	10.41	8.26	6.58	27
28	75.09	57.86	44.80	39.49	34.85	27.23	21.37	16.84	13.33	10.59	8.45	6.76	28
29	73.23	56.74	44.17	39.03	34.54	27.13	21.41	16.96	13.49	10.77	8.63	6.95	29
30	71.44	55.65	43.55	38.59	34.24	27.04	21.44	17.08	13.65	10.96	8.83	7.14	30
31	69.70	54.59	42.95	38.16	33.95	26.95	21.48	17.20	13.82	11.15	9.03	7.34	31
32	68.02	53.56	42.37	37.74	33.66	26.86	21.53	17.32	13.99	11.35	9.23	7.54	32
33	66.40	52.56	41.80	37.34	33.39	26.79	21.58	17.45	14.17	11.55	9.45	7.75	33
34	64.81	51.58	41.24	36.93	33.12	26.71	21.63	17.58	14.35	11.76	9.66	7.97	34
35	63.25	50.61	40.68	36.53	32.84	26.63	21.67	17.71	14.53	11.96	9.89	8.20	35
36	61.74	49.67	40.14	36.14	32.58	26.55	21.72	17.85	14.72	12.18	10.11	8.43	36
37	60.27	48.75	39.60	35.75	32.31	26.47	21.78	17.98	14.90	12.40	10.35	8.66	37
38	58.83	47.84	39.07	35.37	32.05	26.40	21.83	18.12	15.09	12.62	10.58	8.91	38
39	57.42	46.95	38.55	34.99	31.79	26.32	21.88	18.25	15.28	12.84	10.83	9.16	39
40	56.04	46.07	38.03	34.61	31.53	26.24	21.93	18.39	15.48	13.07	11.08	9.42	40
41	54.71	45.22	37.53	34.24	31.28	26.17	21.98	18.53	15.68	13.31	11.33	9.68	41
42	53.42	44.38	37.04	33.88	31.03	26.10	22.03	18.67	15.88	13.55	11.60	9.96	42
43	52.16	43.57	36.55	33.53	30.79	26.03	22.09	18.82	16.09	13.80	11.87	10.24	43
44	50.93	42.78	36.08	33.18	30.55	25.97	22.15	18.97	16.30	14.05	12.15	10.54	44
45	49.74	42.01	35.62	32.85	30.32	25.91	22.22	19.12	16.51	14.31	12.44	10.84	45
46	48.58	41.25	35.16	32.51	30.09	25.85	22.28	19.28	16.73	14.57	12.73	11.15	46
47	47.46	40.51	34.72	32.19	29.87	25.79	22.35	19.44	16.96	14.84	13.03	11.48	47
48	46.37	39.80	34.29	31.87	29.65	25.74	22.42	19.60	17.19	15.12	13.35	11.81	48
49	45.32	39.10	33.87	31.57	29.45	25.70	22.50	19.77	17.43	15.41	13.67	12.16	49
50	44.30	38.43	33.47	31.28	29.26	25.66	22.59	19.95	17.68	15.71	14.01	12.52	50
51	43.33	37.79	33.09	31.00	29.07	25.64	22.69	20.14	17.94	16.03	14.36	12.90	51
52	42.39	37.17	32.72	30.74	28.91	25.62	22.79	20.34	18.21	16.35	14.72	13.30	52
53	41.49	36.58	32.37	30.49	28.75	25.62	22.91	20.55	18.49	16.69	15.11	13.71	53
54	40.63	36.01	32.04	30.26	28.61	25.63	23.04	20.77	18.79	17.04	15.50	14.14	54
55	39.81	35.48	31.73	30.05	28.48	25.65	23.18	21.01	19.10	17.41	15.92	14.60	55
56	39.03	34.97	31.45	29.86	28.37	25.69	23.33	21.26	19.43	17.80	16.36	15.07	56
57	38.29	34.49	31.18	29.68	28.28	25.74	23.50	21.52	19.77	18.21	16.82	15.57	57
58	37.56	34.02	30.92	29.51	28.20	25.80	23.68	21.79	20.12	18.63	17.29	16.09	58
59	36.86	33.56	30.67	29.35	28.12	25.86	23.86	22.07	20.49	19.06	17.79	16.64	59
60	36.17	33.12	30.42	29.19	28.04	25.92	24.04	22.36	20.86	19.51	18.30	17.20	60

Ogden Table 20: Multipliers for loss of pension commencing age 60 (females)

Age at date of trial	Multiplier calculated with allowance for projected mortality from the 2008-based population projections and rate of return of												Age at date of trial
	-2.0%	-1.5%	-1.0%	-0.75%	-0.5%	0.0%	0.5%	1.0%	1.5%	2.0%	2.5%	3.0%	
0	169.99	112.01	74.27	60.62	49.55	33.26	22.45	15.24	10.40	7.14	4.92	3.41	0
1	166.62	110.38	73.58	60.22	49.35	33.30	22.59	15.42	10.58	7.30	5.06	3.52	1
2	162.64	108.33	72.60	59.57	48.95	33.20	22.65	15.53	10.71	7.43	5.17	3.62	2
3	158.74	106.30	71.62	58.93	48.55	33.10	22.70	15.65	10.85	7.56	5.29	3.72	3
4	154.93	104.31	70.66	58.29	48.15	33.00	22.75	15.77	10.98	7.69	5.41	3.83	4
5	151.21	102.36	69.71	57.65	47.75	32.90	22.80	15.88	11.12	7.83	5.54	3.93	5
6	147.57	100.43	68.76	57.02	47.36	32.80	22.85	16.00	11.26	7.97	5.66	4.04	6
7	144.01	98.54	67.83	56.40	46.96	32.70	22.89	16.11	11.40	8.11	5.79	4.16	7
8	140.54	96.68	66.91	55.78	46.57	32.60	22.94	16.23	11.54	8.25	5.92	4.27	8
9	137.14	94.85	65.99	55.16	46.18	32.49	22.99	16.35	11.69	8.39	6.06	4.39	9
10	133.83	93.06	65.09	54.56	45.79	32.39	23.03	16.47	11.83	8.54	6.20	4.51	10
11	130.60	91.31	64.21	53.96	45.41	32.29	23.08	16.59	11.98	8.69	6.34	4.64	11
12	127.45	89.58	63.33	53.36	45.02	32.18	23.13	16.71	12.13	8.84	6.48	4.77	12
13	124.36	87.89	62.47	52.77	44.65	32.08	23.17	16.83	12.28	9.00	6.63	4.90	13
14	121.36	86.23	61.62	52.19	44.27	31.98	23.22	16.95	12.43	9.16	6.78	5.04	14
15	118.43	84.60	60.77	51.62	43.90	31.88	23.27	17.07	12.58	9.32	6.93	5.18	15
16	115.57	83.00	59.95	51.05	43.53	31.78	23.31	17.19	12.74	9.48	7.09	5.32	16
17	112.78	81.44	59.13	50.49	43.16	31.67	23.36	17.32	12.90	9.65	7.25	5.47	17
18	110.06	79.90	58.33	49.93	42.80	31.58	23.41	17.44	13.06	9.82	7.42	5.62	18
19	107.41	78.40	57.53	49.39	42.45	31.48	23.46	17.57	13.22	9.99	7.58	5.78	19
20	104.83	76.93	56.76	48.85	42.10	31.38	23.51	17.70	13.38	10.17	7.76	5.94	20
21	102.32	75.49	55.99	48.32	41.75	31.29	23.56	17.83	13.55	10.35	7.93	6.11	21
22	99.85	74.07	55.23	47.79	41.40	31.19	23.61	17.96	13.72	10.53	8.12	6.28	22
23	97.44	72.67	54.48	47.26	41.05	31.09	23.66	18.09	13.89	10.71	8.30	6.45	23
24	95.08	71.29	53.73	46.74	40.70	30.99	23.70	18.22	14.06	10.90	8.49	6.63	24
25	92.79	69.95	53.00	46.22	40.36	30.89	23.75	18.35	14.24	11.09	8.68	6.82	25
26	90.55	68.63	52.28	45.72	40.03	30.79	23.80	18.48	14.41	11.29	8.88	7.01	26
27	88.37	67.34	51.57	45.22	39.69	30.70	23.85	18.62	14.59	11.49	9.08	7.20	27
28	86.24	66.07	50.87	44.72	39.36	30.60	23.90	18.75	14.77	11.69	9.29	7.41	28
29	84.17	64.83	50.18	44.23	39.03	30.51	23.95	18.89	14.96	11.90	9.50	7.61	29
30	82.15	63.61	49.50	43.75	38.71	30.41	24.00	19.03	15.15	12.11	9.71	7.83	30
31	80.18	62.43	48.84	43.28	38.39	30.32	24.05	19.17	15.34	12.32	9.94	8.04	31
32	78.27	61.26	48.19	42.81	38.08	30.23	24.11	19.31	15.53	12.54	10.16	8.27	32
33	76.40	60.12	47.54	42.35	37.77	30.14	24.16	19.45	15.72	12.76	10.40	8.50	33
34	74.57	59.00	46.90	41.89	37.46	30.05	24.22	19.60	15.92	12.99	10.64	8.74	34
35	72.79	57.90	46.27	41.44	37.15	29.96	24.27	19.74	16.12	13.22	10.88	8.99	35
36	71.05	56.82	45.66	40.99	36.85	29.88	24.33	19.89	16.33	13.45	11.13	9.24	36
37	69.36	55.77	45.05	40.56	36.55	29.79	24.38	20.04	16.53	13.69	11.38	9.50	37
38	67.71	54.73	44.45	40.12	36.26	29.71	24.44	20.19	16.74	13.94	11.65	9.77	38
39	66.10	53.72	43.86	39.70	35.97	29.62	24.50	20.34	16.96	14.19	11.92	10.04	39
40	64.53	52.73	43.28	39.27	35.68	29.54	24.56	20.50	17.17	14.44	12.19	10.32	40
41	63.00	51.75	42.70	38.86	35.39	29.46	24.62	20.65	17.39	14.70	12.47	10.62	41
42	61.51	50.80	42.14	38.45	35.11	29.38	24.68	20.81	17.62	14.97	12.76	10.92	42

Ogden Table 20: Multipliers for loss of pension commencing age 60 (females)

Age at date of trial	Multiplier calculated with allowance for projected mortality from the 2008-based population projections and rate of return of												Age at date of trial
	-2.0%	-1.5%	-1.0%	-0.75%	-0.5%	0.0%	0.5%	1.0%	1.5%	2.0%	2.5%	3.0%	
43	60.06	49.87	41.59	38.05	34.84	29.30	24.74	20.97	17.85	15.24	13.06	11.23	43
44	58.65	48.97	41.06	37.65	34.57	29.23	24.81	21.14	18.08	15.52	13.36	11.55	44
45	57.28	48.08	40.53	37.27	34.31	29.16	24.88	21.31	18.32	15.80	13.68	11.88	45
46	55.95	47.21	40.01	36.89	34.05	29.09	24.95	21.48	18.56	16.09	14.00	12.22	46
47	54.65	46.37	39.50	36.52	33.79	29.02	25.02	21.65	18.81	16.39	14.33	12.57	47
48	53.40	45.55	39.01	36.16	33.55	28.97	25.10	21.84	19.06	16.70	14.67	12.94	48
49	52.19	44.75	38.54	35.81	33.32	28.92	25.19	22.03	19.33	17.01	15.03	13.32	49
50	51.01	43.98	38.07	35.47	33.09	28.87	25.28	22.22	19.60	17.34	15.39	13.71	50
51	49.86	43.22	37.62	35.14	32.87	28.83	25.38	22.42	19.87	17.67	15.77	14.11	51
52	48.76	42.49	37.17	34.82	32.65	28.79	25.47	22.62	20.16	18.02	16.16	14.53	52
53	47.68	41.78	36.75	34.52	32.45	28.76	25.58	22.83	20.45	18.38	16.56	14.97	53
54	46.65	41.09	36.34	34.22	32.26	28.74	25.70	23.06	20.76	18.74	16.98	15.43	54
55	45.65	40.43	35.94	33.94	32.08	28.73	25.82	23.29	21.07	19.13	17.41	15.90	55
56	44.69	39.79	35.57	33.67	31.91	28.73	25.95	23.53	21.40	19.52	17.86	16.39	56
57	43.76	39.18	35.20	33.41	31.75	28.73	26.09	23.78	21.74	19.93	18.33	16.91	57
58	42.86	38.57	34.85	33.16	31.59	28.74	26.24	24.04	22.09	20.35	18.81	17.44	58
59	41.98	37.99	34.50	32.92	31.44	28.76	26.39	24.30	22.44	20.79	19.31	17.99	59
60	41.12	37.41	34.16	32.68	31.30	28.78	26.55	24.57	22.81	21.24	19.83	18.57	60

Ogden Table 21: Multipliers for loss of pension commencing age 65 (males)

Age at date of trial	Multiplier calculated with allowance for projected mortality from the 2008-based population projections and rate of return of												Age at date of trial
	-2.0%	-1.5%	-1.0%	-0.75%	-0.5%	0.0%	0.5%	1.0%	1.5%	2.0%	2.5%	3.0%	
0	134.16	87.81	57.78	46.96	38.22	25.41	16.98	11.40	7.69	5.21	3.54	2.42	0
1	131.46	86.50	57.23	46.64	38.06	25.44	17.08	11.53	7.82	5.32	3.64	2.50	1
2	128.17	84.80	56.40	46.08	37.70	25.33	17.10	11.60	7.91	5.41	3.72	2.57	2
3	124.95	83.11	55.57	45.53	37.35	25.23	17.12	11.67	8.00	5.50	3.80	2.64	3
4	121.80	81.45	54.76	44.98	37.00	25.12	17.14	11.75	8.09	5.59	3.88	2.71	4
5	118.72	79.82	53.95	44.43	36.64	25.01	17.15	11.82	8.18	5.68	3.97	2.78	5
6	115.71	78.22	53.15	43.89	36.29	24.90	17.17	11.89	8.27	5.78	4.05	2.85	6
7	112.78	76.65	52.36	43.36	35.95	24.80	17.18	11.96	8.36	5.87	4.14	2.93	7
8	109.92	75.11	51.59	42.83	35.60	24.69	17.20	12.03	8.46	5.97	4.23	3.01	8
9	107.13	73.60	50.82	42.30	35.26	24.58	17.21	12.11	8.55	6.07	4.32	3.09	9
10	104.40	72.11	50.06	41.78	34.91	24.47	17.22	12.18	8.65	6.17	4.41	3.17	10
11	101.74	70.65	49.31	41.26	34.57	24.36	17.23	12.25	8.74	6.27	4.51	3.26	11
12	99.15	69.23	48.57	40.76	34.24	24.25	17.25	12.32	8.84	6.37	4.60	3.34	12
13	96.62	67.83	47.84	40.25	33.91	24.14	17.26	12.39	8.94	6.47	4.70	3.43	13
14	94.16	66.46	47.13	39.76	33.58	24.03	17.27	12.47	9.04	6.58	4.80	3.52	14
15	91.77	65.12	46.43	39.27	33.25	23.92	17.28	12.54	9.14	6.68	4.91	3.62	15
16	89.44	63.81	45.74	38.79	32.93	23.82	17.30	12.62	9.24	6.79	5.01	3.71	16
17	87.17	62.53	45.06	38.31	32.61	23.71	17.31	12.69	9.34	6.90	5.12	3.81	17
18	84.97	61.27	44.39	37.85	32.30	23.61	17.33	12.77	9.45	7.02	5.23	3.91	18

Ogden Table 21: Multipliers for loss of pension commencing age 65 (males)

Age at date of trial	Multiplier calculated with allowance for projected mortality from the 2008-based population projections and rate of return of												Age at date of trial
	-2.0%	-1.5%	-1.0%	-0.75%	-0.5%	0.0%	0.5%	1.0%	1.5%	2.0%	2.5%	3.0%	
19	82.83	60.05	43.74	37.39	32.00	23.51	17.34	12.85	9.55	7.13	5.34	4.02	19
20	80.75	58.86	43.10	36.94	31.70	23.41	17.36	12.93	9.66	7.25	5.46	4.13	20
21	78.72	57.69	42.47	36.50	31.40	23.31	17.38	13.01	9.77	7.37	5.58	4.24	21
22	76.73	56.54	41.84	36.05	31.10	23.21	17.39	13.09	9.88	7.49	5.70	4.35	22
23	74.79	55.40	41.22	35.61	30.80	23.11	17.41	13.17	9.99	7.61	5.82	4.47	23
24	72.90	54.29	40.61	35.18	30.51	23.01	17.42	13.25	10.11	7.74	5.95	4.59	24
25	71.06	53.21	40.01	34.76	30.22	22.91	17.44	13.33	10.22	7.87	6.08	4.71	25
26	69.28	52.16	39.43	34.34	29.94	22.82	17.46	13.41	10.34	8.00	6.21	4.83	26
27	67.55	51.13	38.86	33.93	29.66	22.73	17.48	13.50	10.46	8.13	6.34	4.97	27
28	65.85	50.11	38.29	33.52	29.38	22.63	17.50	13.58	10.58	8.26	6.48	5.10	28
29	64.18	49.10	37.72	33.11	29.10	22.53	17.51	13.66	10.69	8.40	6.62	5.23	29
30	62.57	48.13	37.17	32.72	28.82	22.44	17.53	13.75	10.82	8.54	6.76	5.38	30
31	61.01	47.18	36.64	32.33	28.56	22.35	17.55	13.83	10.94	8.68	6.91	5.52	31
32	59.50	46.27	36.12	31.96	28.30	22.26	17.58	13.93	11.07	8.83	7.07	5.67	32
33	58.05	45.38	35.61	31.59	28.06	22.18	17.61	14.02	11.20	8.98	7.22	5.83	33
34	56.62	44.50	35.11	31.23	27.81	22.10	17.63	14.12	11.34	9.14	7.38	5.99	34
35	55.23	43.64	34.61	30.87	27.56	22.02	17.66	14.21	11.47	9.29	7.55	6.15	35
36	53.87	42.80	34.13	30.52	27.32	21.94	17.69	14.31	11.61	9.45	7.72	6.32	36
37	52.56	41.97	33.65	30.17	27.08	21.87	17.72	14.41	11.75	9.61	7.89	6.49	37
38	51.26	41.16	33.18	29.83	26.84	21.79	17.75	14.50	11.89	9.78	8.07	6.67	38
39	50.00	40.37	32.71	29.48	26.60	21.71	17.77	14.60	12.03	9.95	8.24	6.85	39
40	48.77	39.59	32.25	29.15	26.36	21.63	17.80	14.70	12.18	10.12	8.43	7.04	40
41	47.58	38.83	31.80	28.82	26.13	21.55	17.83	14.80	12.32	10.29	8.62	7.24	41
42	46.42	38.09	31.36	28.49	25.91	21.48	17.86	14.90	12.47	10.47	8.81	7.44	42
43	45.30	37.36	30.93	28.18	25.69	21.41	17.90	15.01	12.63	10.65	9.01	7.64	43
44	44.21	36.66	30.51	27.87	25.47	21.34	17.93	15.12	12.78	10.84	9.21	7.86	44
45	43.15	35.97	30.09	27.56	25.26	21.27	17.97	15.23	12.94	11.03	9.43	8.08	45
46	42.11	35.30	29.69	27.26	25.05	21.21	18.01	15.34	13.10	11.22	9.64	8.30	46
47	41.11	34.64	29.29	26.97	24.85	21.15	18.05	15.46	13.27	11.42	9.86	8.54	47
48	40.14	34.01	28.91	26.68	24.65	21.09	18.10	15.57	13.44	11.63	10.09	8.78	48
49	39.20	33.39	28.53	26.41	24.46	21.04	18.15	15.70	13.62	11.84	10.33	9.03	49
50	38.29	32.79	28.18	26.15	24.28	20.99	18.20	15.83	13.80	12.07	10.58	9.29	50
51	37.42	32.22	27.83	25.90	24.11	20.96	18.27	15.97	13.99	12.29	10.83	9.56	51
52	36.58	31.67	27.50	25.66	23.96	20.93	18.34	16.11	14.19	12.53	11.10	9.85	52
53	35.78	31.14	27.19	25.43	23.81	20.91	18.41	16.26	14.40	12.78	11.37	10.15	53
54	35.01	30.64	26.89	25.22	23.67	20.90	18.50	16.42	14.62	13.04	11.66	10.46	54
55	34.28	30.15	26.61	25.02	23.55	20.90	18.60	16.59	14.85	13.31	11.97	10.78	55
56	33.59	29.70	26.35	24.84	23.44	20.91	18.71	16.78	15.09	13.60	12.29	11.13	56
57	32.92	29.27	26.10	24.68	23.35	20.94	18.83	16.97	15.34	13.90	12.62	11.49	57
58	32.28	28.85	25.87	24.52	23.26	20.97	18.95	17.18	15.60	14.21	12.97	11.86	58
59	31.65	28.44	25.64	24.36	23.17	21.00	19.08	17.38	15.87	14.53	13.32	12.25	59
60	31.03	28.04	25.41	24.21	23.09	21.03	19.21	17.59	16.14	14.85	13.69	12.65	60
61	30.43	27.65	25.19	24.06	23.01	21.07	19.35	17.81	16.43	15.19	14.08	13.07	61

Ogden Table 21: Multipliers for loss of pension commencing age 65 (males)

Age at date of trial	Multiplier calculated with allowance for projected mortality from the 2008-based population projections and rate of return of												Age at date of trial
	-2.0%	-1.5%	-1.0%	-0.75%	-0.5%	0.0%	0.5%	1.0%	1.5%	2.0%	2.5%	3.0%	
62	29.87	27.28	24.99	23.94	22.94	21.12	19.50	18.04	16.73	15.55	14.48	13.51	62
63	29.34	26.94	24.81	23.83	22.90	21.20	19.67	18.29	17.05	15.93	14.91	13.98	63
64	28.85	26.63	24.65	23.74	22.88	21.29	19.86	18.56	17.39	16.33	15.37	14.49	64
65	28.40	26.37	24.54	23.70	22.90	21.42	20.08	18.87	17.77	16.77	15.86	15.03	65

Ogden Table 22: Multipliers for loss of pension commencing age 65 (females)

Age at date of trial	Multiplier calculated with allowance for projected mortality from the 2008-based population projections and rate of return of												Age at date of trial
	-2.0%	-1.5%	-1.0%	-0.75%	-0.5%	0.0%	0.5%	1.0%	1.5%	2.0%	2.5%	3.0%	
0	153.09	99.71	65.31	52.96	43.01	28.47	18.95	12.67	8.52	5.75	3.90	2.66	0
1	149.98	98.22	64.68	52.59	42.82	28.50	19.06	12.81	8.66	5.87	4.00	2.74	1
2	146.34	96.35	63.78	52.00	42.45	28.40	19.10	12.90	8.76	5.98	4.09	2.82	2
3	142.77	94.51	62.90	51.42	42.08	28.30	19.13	12.99	8.87	6.08	4.19	2.90	3
4	139.29	92.70	62.02	50.84	41.72	28.21	19.16	13.08	8.98	6.18	4.28	2.98	4
5	135.88	90.92	61.16	50.26	41.36	28.11	19.20	13.17	9.08	6.29	4.38	3.06	5
6	132.55	89.17	60.30	49.69	40.99	28.01	19.23	13.26	9.19	6.40	4.47	3.14	6
7	129.30	87.45	59.46	49.12	40.63	27.91	19.26	13.35	9.30	6.51	4.57	3.23	7
8	126.13	85.76	58.62	48.56	40.27	27.81	19.29	13.45	9.41	6.62	4.68	3.32	8
9	123.03	84.10	57.80	48.00	39.92	27.70	19.32	13.54	9.53	6.73	4.78	3.41	9
10	120.00	82.48	56.98	47.45	39.56	27.60	19.35	13.63	9.64	6.85	4.89	3.50	10
11	117.06	80.89	56.18	46.91	39.21	27.50	19.38	13.72	9.75	6.97	4.99	3.60	11
12	114.18	79.32	55.39	46.37	38.87	27.40	19.41	13.81	9.87	7.08	5.11	3.69	12
13	111.37	77.79	54.61	45.83	38.52	27.30	19.44	13.90	9.99	7.20	5.22	3.79	13
14	108.63	76.28	53.84	45.31	38.18	27.20	19.47	14.00	10.11	7.33	5.33	3.90	14
15	105.96	74.81	53.08	44.79	37.84	27.10	19.50	14.09	10.23	7.45	5.45	4.00	15
16	103.35	73.36	52.33	44.27	37.50	27.00	19.53	14.19	10.35	7.58	5.57	4.11	16
17	100.81	71.94	51.59	43.76	37.17	26.90	19.56	14.28	10.47	7.71	5.70	4.23	17
18	98.33	70.55	50.86	43.26	36.84	26.80	19.59	14.38	10.60	7.84	5.82	4.34	18
19	95.92	69.19	50.15	42.77	36.52	26.71	19.62	14.47	10.72	7.97	5.95	4.46	19
20	93.58	67.87	49.45	42.28	36.20	26.61	19.65	14.57	10.85	8.11	6.09	4.58	20
21	91.29	66.56	48.76	41.80	35.88	26.52	19.69	14.67	10.98	8.25	6.22	4.71	21
22	89.05	65.28	48.07	41.33	35.56	26.42	19.72	14.77	11.11	8.39	6.36	4.84	22
23	86.86	64.01	47.39	40.85	35.24	26.32	19.74	14.87	11.24	8.53	6.50	4.97	23
24	84.71	62.77	46.72	40.37	34.93	26.23	19.77	14.97	11.38	8.68	6.65	5.11	24
25	82.63	61.55	46.06	39.91	34.62	26.13	19.80	15.07	11.51	8.83	6.79	5.25	25
26	80.60	60.37	45.41	39.45	34.31	26.03	19.83	15.17	11.65	8.98	6.94	5.39	26
27	78.62	59.20	44.77	39.00	34.01	25.94	19.86	15.27	11.79	9.13	7.10	5.54	27
28	76.69	58.06	44.14	38.55	33.71	25.84	19.89	15.38	11.93	9.29	7.26	5.69	28
29	74.81	56.94	43.52	38.11	33.41	25.75	19.93	15.48	12.07	9.44	7.42	5.84	29
30	72.98	55.84	42.91	37.68	33.12	25.66	19.96	15.58	12.21	9.61	7.58	6.00	30
31	71.20	54.77	42.32	37.25	32.83	25.57	19.99	15.69	12.36	9.77	7.75	6.17	31
32	69.46	53.73	41.73	36.83	32.54	25.48	20.03	15.80	12.51	9.94	7.92	6.34	32

Ogden Table 22: Multipliers for loss of pension commencing age 65 (females)

Age at date of trial	Multiplier calculated with allowance for projected mortality from the 2008-based population projections and rate of return of												Age at date of trial
	-2.0%	-1.5%	-1.0%	-0.75%	-0.5%	0.0%	0.5%	1.0%	1.5%	2.0%	2.5%	3.0%	
33	67.77	52.70	41.15	36.42	32.26	25.39	20.06	15.91	12.66	10.11	8.10	6.51	33
34	66.12	51.69	40.58	36.00	31.98	25.30	20.09	16.02	12.81	10.28	8.28	6.69	34
35	64.50	50.70	40.01	35.60	31.70	25.21	20.13	16.13	12.97	10.46	8.47	6.88	35
36	62.93	49.73	39.45	35.19	31.43	25.13	20.16	16.24	13.12	10.64	8.66	7.06	36
37	61.41	48.78	38.91	34.80	31.15	25.04	20.20	16.35	13.28	10.83	8.85	7.26	37
38	59.91	47.85	38.37	34.41	30.89	24.95	20.23	16.47	13.44	11.01	9.05	7.46	38
39	58.46	46.94	37.84	34.02	30.62	24.87	20.27	16.58	13.61	11.20	9.25	7.67	39
40	57.04	46.05	37.32	33.64	30.36	24.79	20.31	16.70	13.77	11.40	9.46	7.88	40
41	55.66	45.17	36.80	33.27	30.10	24.70	20.35	16.81	13.94	11.60	9.67	8.10	41
42	54.31	44.32	36.30	32.90	29.84	24.62	20.38	16.93	14.11	11.80	9.89	8.32	42
43	53.01	43.48	35.81	32.54	29.59	24.54	20.43	17.05	14.29	12.00	10.12	8.55	43
44	51.74	42.67	35.33	32.18	29.35	24.47	20.47	17.18	14.46	12.22	10.35	8.79	44
45	50.50	41.88	34.85	31.84	29.11	24.40	20.51	17.31	14.65	12.43	10.58	9.04	45
46	49.30	41.10	34.39	31.50	28.87	24.32	20.56	17.44	14.83	12.65	10.83	9.29	46
47	48.13	40.34	33.93	31.16	28.64	24.26	20.61	17.57	15.02	12.88	11.08	9.55	47
48	47.00	39.61	33.49	30.84	28.42	24.19	20.66	17.70	15.22	13.11	11.33	9.82	48
49	45.91	38.89	33.06	30.52	28.20	24.14	20.72	17.85	15.42	13.35	11.60	10.10	49
50	44.85	38.20	32.64	30.22	27.99	24.08	20.78	17.99	15.62	13.60	11.88	10.40	50
51	43.82	37.52	32.23	29.92	27.79	24.03	20.85	18.14	15.83	13.85	12.16	10.70	51
52	42.82	36.86	31.84	29.63	27.59	23.99	20.92	18.29	16.05	14.12	12.45	11.01	52
53	41.85	36.22	31.45	29.35	27.40	23.95	20.99	18.45	16.27	14.38	12.75	11.33	53
54	40.92	35.60	31.08	29.08	27.22	23.91	21.07	18.62	16.50	14.66	13.06	11.67	54
55	40.02	35.01	30.73	28.82	27.05	23.89	21.16	18.80	16.74	14.95	13.39	12.02	55
56	39.16	34.44	30.38	28.57	26.89	23.87	21.26	18.98	16.99	15.25	13.73	12.38	56
57	38.32	33.88	30.05	28.34	26.74	23.86	21.36	19.17	17.25	15.56	14.08	12.76	57
58	37.51	33.34	29.73	28.11	26.59	23.86	21.46	19.36	17.51	15.88	14.44	13.16	58
59	36.72	32.81	29.42	27.88	26.45	23.85	21.57	19.56	17.78	16.21	14.81	13.56	59
60	35.94	32.29	29.10	27.66	26.31	23.85	21.68	19.76	18.06	16.54	15.19	13.98	60
61	35.18	31.78	28.80	27.44	26.17	23.85	21.79	19.97	18.34	16.89	15.59	14.42	61
62	34.46	31.29	28.51	27.24	26.04	23.86	21.91	20.18	18.63	17.25	16.00	14.87	62
63	33.76	30.83	28.23	27.04	25.93	23.88	22.05	20.41	18.94	17.62	16.43	15.35	63
64	33.10	30.39	27.98	26.88	25.83	23.92	22.20	20.66	19.27	18.02	16.89	15.86	64
65	32.50	29.99	27.76	26.74	25.77	23.98	22.38	20.93	19.63	18.45	17.38	16.40	65

Ogden Table 23: Multipliers for loss of pension commencing age 70 (males)

Age at date of trial	Multiplier calculated with allowance for projected mortality from the 2008-based population projections and rate of return of												Age at date of trial
	-2.0%	-1.5%	-1.0%	-0.75%	-0.5%	0.0%	0.5%	1.0%	1.5%	2.0%	2.5%	3.0%	
0	116.52	75.30	48.89	39.47	31.89	20.90	13.76	9.09	6.04	4.02	2.69	1.81	0
1	114.10	74.13	48.39	39.17	31.74	20.91	13.83	9.19	6.13	4.11	2.76	1.87	1
2	111.17	72.62	47.66	38.67	31.42	20.81	13.84	9.24	6.20	4.17	2.82	1.91	2
3	108.30	71.12	46.93	38.18	31.10	20.70	13.84	9.29	6.27	4.24	2.88	1.96	3

Ogden Table 23: Multipliers for loss of pension commencing age 70 (males)

Age at date of trial	Multiplier calculated with allowance for projected mortality from the 2008-based population projections and rate of return of												Age at date of trial
	-2.0%	-1.5%	-1.0%	-0.75%	-0.5%	0.0%	0.5%	1.0%	1.5%	2.0%	2.5%	3.0%	
4	105.50	69.65	46.20	37.69	30.78	20.60	13.85	9.34	6.33	4.31	2.94	2.02	4
5	102.76	68.21	45.49	37.21	30.47	20.50	13.85	9.39	6.40	4.37	3.00	2.07	5
6	100.08	66.80	44.78	36.73	30.16	20.39	13.85	9.44	6.46	4.44	3.06	2.12	6
7	97.48	65.41	44.09	36.25	29.84	20.29	13.85	9.49	6.53	4.51	3.13	2.18	7
8	94.95	64.05	43.40	35.79	29.54	20.19	13.85	9.54	6.60	4.58	3.19	2.23	8
9	92.47	62.71	42.72	35.32	29.23	20.08	13.85	9.59	6.67	4.65	3.26	2.29	9
10	90.04	61.40	42.05	34.86	28.92	19.97	13.85	9.64	6.74	4.73	3.33	2.35	10
11	87.69	60.11	41.39	34.40	28.62	19.87	13.85	9.69	6.81	4.80	3.39	2.41	11
12	85.39	58.86	40.74	33.95	28.32	19.76	13.85	9.74	6.88	4.87	3.46	2.47	12
13	83.16	57.63	40.10	33.51	28.02	19.66	13.85	9.79	6.95	4.95	3.54	2.54	13
14	80.98	56.42	39.47	33.07	27.73	19.56	13.85	9.84	7.02	5.02	3.61	2.60	14
15	78.87	55.24	38.85	32.64	27.44	19.45	13.85	9.89	7.09	5.10	3.68	2.67	15
16	76.81	54.09	38.25	32.21	27.15	19.35	13.85	9.94	7.16	5.18	3.76	2.74	16
17	74.80	52.96	37.65	31.79	26.87	19.25	13.85	9.99	7.24	5.26	3.84	2.81	17
18	72.86	51.86	37.06	31.38	26.59	19.15	13.85	10.05	7.31	5.34	3.92	2.88	18
19	70.97	50.79	36.49	30.98	26.32	19.06	13.85	10.10	7.39	5.43	4.00	2.95	19
20	69.13	49.74	35.93	30.58	26.05	18.96	13.85	10.15	7.47	5.51	4.08	3.03	20
21	67.34	48.71	35.38	30.19	25.79	18.87	13.85	10.21	7.55	5.60	4.17	3.11	21
22	65.59	47.70	34.82	29.80	25.52	18.77	13.85	10.26	7.63	5.69	4.25	3.19	22
23	63.88	46.71	34.28	29.41	25.25	18.67	13.85	10.31	7.70	5.77	4.34	3.27	23
24	62.22	45.74	33.75	29.03	24.99	18.58	13.85	10.37	7.78	5.86	4.43	3.36	24
25	60.60	44.79	33.22	28.65	24.74	18.48	13.86	10.42	7.87	5.96	4.52	3.44	25
26	59.04	43.87	32.71	28.29	24.48	18.39	13.86	10.48	7.95	6.05	4.62	3.53	26
27	57.52	42.97	32.21	27.93	24.24	18.30	13.86	10.54	8.03	6.14	4.71	3.63	27
28	56.02	42.07	31.71	27.57	23.99	18.21	13.86	10.59	8.12	6.24	4.81	3.72	28
29	54.56	41.20	31.22	27.21	23.74	18.11	13.86	10.65	8.20	6.34	4.91	3.82	29
30	53.15	40.34	30.73	26.86	23.49	18.02	13.87	10.70	8.29	6.44	5.01	3.92	30
31	51.78	39.52	30.27	26.52	23.26	17.93	13.87	10.76	8.38	6.54	5.12	4.02	31
32	50.46	38.72	29.81	26.19	23.03	17.85	13.88	10.82	8.47	6.64	5.23	4.12	32
33	49.19	37.94	29.37	25.87	22.81	17.77	13.89	10.89	8.56	6.75	5.34	4.23	33
34	47.94	37.18	28.93	25.55	22.59	17.69	13.90	10.95	8.66	6.86	5.45	4.35	34
35	46.72	36.43	28.50	25.24	22.37	17.61	13.91	11.02	8.75	6.97	5.57	4.46	35
36	45.54	35.70	28.08	24.93	22.15	17.53	13.92	11.08	8.85	7.08	5.69	4.58	36
37	44.39	34.98	27.66	24.62	21.94	17.45	13.93	11.15	8.95	7.20	5.81	4.70	37
38	43.26	34.27	27.24	24.32	21.72	17.37	13.94	11.21	9.04	7.32	5.93	4.82	38
39	42.16	33.58	26.84	24.02	21.51	17.30	13.95	11.28	9.14	7.43	6.06	4.95	39
40	41.09	32.90	26.43	23.72	21.30	17.22	13.95	11.34	9.24	7.55	6.19	5.08	40
41	40.05	32.24	26.04	23.43	21.10	17.14	13.97	11.41	9.35	7.68	6.32	5.22	41
42	39.04	31.60	25.66	23.15	20.90	17.07	13.98	11.48	9.45	7.80	6.46	5.36	42
43	38.06	30.97	25.28	22.87	20.70	16.99	13.99	11.55	9.56	7.93	6.60	5.50	43
44	37.11	30.36	24.92	22.60	20.51	16.92	14.01	11.62	9.67	8.06	6.74	5.65	44
45	36.18	29.76	24.56	22.33	20.32	16.85	14.02	11.69	9.78	8.20	6.89	5.80	45
46	35.28	29.18	24.20	22.06	20.13	16.79	14.04	11.77	9.89	8.33	7.04	5.96	46

Ogden Table 23: Multipliers for loss of pension commencing age 70 (males)

Age at date of trial	Multiplier calculated with allowance for projected mortality from the 2008-based population projections and rate of return of												Age at date of trial
	-2.0%	-1.5%	-1.0%	-0.75%	-0.5%	0.0%	0.5%	1.0%	1.5%	2.0%	2.5%	3.0%	
47	34.41	28.61	23.86	21.81	19.95	16.72	14.06	11.85	10.01	8.47	7.19	6.12	47
48	33.57	28.06	23.52	21.56	19.77	16.66	14.08	11.92	10.13	8.62	7.35	6.29	48
49	32.75	27.52	23.19	21.31	19.60	16.60	14.10	12.01	10.25	8.77	7.52	6.46	49
50	31.96	27.01	22.88	21.08	19.43	16.55	14.13	12.09	10.38	8.92	7.69	6.64	50
51	31.21	26.51	22.58	20.86	19.28	16.51	14.17	12.19	10.51	9.08	7.87	6.83	51
52	30.48	26.03	22.29	20.64	19.13	16.47	14.21	12.28	10.65	9.25	8.05	7.02	52
53	29.79	25.57	22.01	20.44	19.00	16.43	14.25	12.39	10.79	9.42	8.24	7.23	53
54	29.12	25.13	21.75	20.25	18.87	16.41	14.30	12.50	10.94	9.60	8.44	7.44	54
55	28.48	24.71	21.50	20.07	18.75	16.39	14.36	12.61	11.10	9.79	8.65	7.66	55
56	27.88	24.32	21.27	19.91	18.65	16.39	14.43	12.74	11.27	9.99	8.88	7.90	56
57	27.30	23.94	21.05	19.76	18.55	16.39	14.51	12.88	11.45	10.20	9.11	8.15	57
58	26.74	23.58	20.84	19.61	18.46	16.40	14.59	13.02	11.63	10.42	9.35	8.40	58
59	26.19	23.22	20.63	19.47	18.38	16.40	14.68	13.16	11.82	10.64	9.59	8.67	59
60	25.65	22.86	20.42	19.32	18.29	16.41	14.76	13.30	12.01	10.86	9.85	8.94	60
61	25.13	22.52	20.22	19.18	18.20	16.42	14.84	13.44	12.20	11.10	10.11	9.23	61
62	24.63	22.19	20.03	19.05	18.13	16.44	14.94	13.60	12.41	11.34	10.38	9.52	62
63	24.16	21.88	19.86	18.94	18.07	16.47	15.04	13.77	12.63	11.60	10.67	9.84	63
64	23.72	21.60	19.71	18.84	18.03	16.52	15.17	13.95	12.86	11.87	10.98	10.18	64
65	23.33	21.35	19.59	18.78	18.01	16.59	15.31	14.16	13.12	12.17	11.32	10.54	65
66	22.97	21.14	19.50	18.74	18.02	16.69	15.48	14.39	13.40	12.50	11.68	10.93	66
67	22.66	20.96	19.44	18.73	18.06	16.81	15.68	14.65	13.71	12.86	12.07	11.36	67
68	22.38	20.82	19.40	18.75	18.12	16.96	15.90	14.93	14.05	13.24	12.50	11.82	68
69	22.13	20.70	19.40	18.79	18.21	17.13	16.15	15.24	14.42	13.66	12.96	12.31	69
70	21.91	20.60	19.41	18.85	18.32	17.32	16.41	15.58	14.81	14.10	13.44	12.84	70

Ogden Table 24: Multipliers for loss of pension commencing age 70 (females)

Age at date of trial	Multiplier calculated with allowance for projected mortality from the 2008-based population projections and rate of return of												Age at date of trial
	-2.0%	-1.5%	-1.0%	-0.75%	-0.5%	0.0%	0.5%	1.0%	1.5%	2.0%	2.5%	3.0%	
0	134.74	86.70	56.06	45.17	36.43	23.78	15.60	10.28	6.80	4.52	3.01	2.02	0
1	131.93	85.35	55.49	44.82	36.25	23.79	15.68	10.38	6.91	4.61	3.09	2.08	1
2	128.66	83.68	54.69	44.29	35.92	23.69	15.70	10.45	6.99	4.69	3.16	2.14	2
3	125.45	82.03	53.90	43.77	35.58	23.60	15.72	10.52	7.07	4.77	3.23	2.20	3
4	122.32	80.42	53.12	43.25	35.25	23.50	15.74	10.58	7.15	4.85	3.30	2.25	4
5	119.26	78.83	52.35	42.74	34.93	23.41	15.76	10.65	7.23	4.93	3.37	2.32	5
6	116.28	77.27	51.59	42.22	34.60	23.31	15.77	10.72	7.31	5.01	3.44	2.38	6
7	113.36	75.74	50.83	41.72	34.27	23.21	15.79	10.78	7.39	5.09	3.52	2.44	7
8	110.51	74.23	50.09	41.22	33.95	23.11	15.80	10.85	7.48	5.18	3.59	2.51	8
9	107.73	72.75	49.35	40.72	33.63	23.01	15.82	10.92	7.56	5.26	3.67	2.57	9
10	105.03	71.30	48.63	40.23	33.31	22.92	15.83	10.98	7.65	5.35	3.75	2.64	10
11	102.39	69.89	47.92	39.74	33.00	22.82	15.85	11.05	7.73	5.43	3.83	2.71	11
12	99.81	68.49	47.21	39.26	32.68	22.72	15.86	11.12	7.82	5.52	3.92	2.79	12

Ogden Table 24: Multipliers for loss of pension commencing age 70 (females)

Age at date of trial	Multiplier calculated with allowance for projected mortality from the 2008-based population projections and rate of return of												Age at date of trial
	-2.0%	-1.5%	-1.0%	-0.75%	-0.5%	0.0%	0.5%	1.0%	1.5%	2.0%	2.5%	3.0%	
13	97.30	67.13	46.52	38.78	32.37	22.62	15.87	11.18	7.91	5.61	4.00	2.86	13
14	94.85	65.79	45.83	38.32	32.07	22.53	15.89	11.25	8.00	5.71	4.09	2.94	14
15	92.46	64.48	45.16	37.85	31.76	22.43	15.90	11.32	8.09	5.80	4.17	3.01	15
16	90.13	63.19	44.49	37.39	31.46	22.33	15.92	11.39	8.18	5.89	4.26	3.09	16
17	87.86	61.93	43.84	36.94	31.16	22.24	15.93	11.46	8.27	5.99	4.36	3.18	17
18	85.65	60.70	43.19	36.49	30.86	22.14	15.95	11.53	8.36	6.09	4.45	3.26	18
19	83.51	59.49	42.56	36.05	30.57	22.05	15.96	11.60	8.46	6.19	4.55	3.35	19
20	81.42	58.32	41.94	35.62	30.29	21.96	15.98	11.67	8.55	6.29	4.64	3.44	20
21	79.38	57.16	41.33	35.20	30.00	21.86	15.99	11.74	8.65	6.40	4.74	3.53	21
22	77.38	56.02	40.72	34.77	29.72	21.77	16.01	11.81	8.75	6.50	4.85	3.62	22
23	75.43	54.90	40.12	34.35	29.43	21.67	16.02	11.88	8.85	6.61	4.95	3.72	23
24	73.52	53.80	39.52	33.93	29.15	21.58	16.03	11.95	8.94	6.71	5.06	3.82	24
25	71.67	52.72	38.94	33.51	28.87	21.48	16.05	12.03	9.04	6.82	5.16	3.92	25
26	69.86	51.67	38.37	33.11	28.60	21.39	16.06	12.10	9.14	6.93	5.28	4.03	26
27	68.11	50.64	37.80	32.71	28.32	21.30	16.07	12.17	9.25	7.05	5.39	4.13	27
28	66.39	49.63	37.25	32.31	28.05	21.21	16.09	12.24	9.35	7.16	5.50	4.24	28
29	64.72	48.64	36.70	31.92	27.79	21.11	16.10	12.32	9.46	7.28	5.62	4.36	29
30	63.09	47.68	36.16	31.53	27.52	21.03	16.12	12.39	9.56	7.40	5.74	4.47	30
31	61.51	46.73	35.63	31.16	27.27	20.94	16.13	12.47	9.67	7.52	5.87	4.59	31
32	59.98	45.81	35.11	30.78	27.01	20.85	16.15	12.55	9.78	7.65	6.00	4.72	32
33	58.48	44.91	34.60	30.42	26.76	20.76	16.16	12.62	9.89	7.77	6.13	4.84	33
34	57.02	44.02	34.10	30.05	26.51	20.68	16.18	12.70	10.00	7.90	6.26	4.97	34
35	55.59	43.14	33.60	29.69	26.26	20.59	16.20	12.78	10.12	8.03	6.39	5.10	35
36	54.20	42.29	33.11	29.34	26.01	20.50	16.21	12.86	10.23	8.16	6.53	5.24	36
37	52.85	41.45	32.63	28.99	25.77	20.42	16.23	12.94	10.35	8.30	6.67	5.38	37
38	51.53	40.64	32.16	28.64	25.53	20.33	16.25	13.02	10.46	8.44	6.82	5.53	38
39	50.24	39.83	31.69	28.30	25.29	20.25	16.26	13.10	10.58	8.57	6.97	5.67	39
40	48.99	39.05	31.23	27.96	25.06	20.17	16.28	13.18	10.70	8.72	7.12	5.83	40
41	47.77	38.28	30.78	27.63	24.82	20.08	16.30	13.27	10.83	8.86	7.27	5.98	41
42	46.58	37.53	30.34	27.31	24.60	20.00	16.32	13.35	10.95	9.01	7.43	6.14	42
43	45.43	36.80	29.90	26.99	24.37	19.93	16.34	13.44	11.08	9.16	7.59	6.31	43
44	44.31	36.08	29.48	26.67	24.15	19.85	16.36	13.52	11.21	9.31	7.76	6.48	44
45	43.23	35.39	29.06	26.37	23.94	19.78	16.39	13.61	11.34	9.47	7.93	6.66	45
46	42.17	34.70	28.65	26.06	23.73	19.70	16.41	13.70	11.47	9.63	8.11	6.84	46
47	41.14	34.04	28.25	25.77	23.52	19.63	16.44	13.80	11.61	9.80	8.29	7.03	47
48	40.14	33.39	27.86	25.48	23.32	19.57	16.47	13.89	11.75	9.97	8.47	7.22	48
49	39.18	32.77	27.49	25.20	23.12	19.51	16.50	13.99	11.90	10.14	8.67	7.42	49
50	38.25	32.16	27.12	24.93	22.93	19.45	16.54	14.10	12.05	10.32	8.86	7.63	50
51	37.34	31.56	26.76	24.66	22.75	19.39	16.57	14.20	12.20	10.51	9.07	7.84	51
52	36.46	30.99	26.41	24.40	22.57	19.34	16.62	14.31	12.36	10.69	9.28	8.06	52
53	35.61	30.43	26.07	24.15	22.40	19.29	16.66	14.42	12.52	10.89	9.49	8.30	53
54	34.79	29.89	25.74	23.91	22.23	19.25	16.71	14.54	12.69	11.09	9.72	8.53	54
55	34.00	29.36	25.43	23.68	22.08	19.21	16.77	14.67	12.86	11.30	9.95	8.78	55

Ogden Table 24: Multipliers for loss of pension commencing age 70 (females)

Age at date of trial	Multiplier calculated with allowance for projected mortality from the 2008-based population projections and rate of return of												Age at date of trial
	-2.0%	-1.5%	-1.0%	-0.75%	-0.5%	0.0%	0.5%	1.0%	1.5%	2.0%	2.5%	3.0%	
56	33.24	28.86	25.12	23.46	21.93	19.19	16.83	14.80	13.04	11.52	10.19	9.04	56
57	32.51	28.37	24.83	23.25	21.79	19.16	16.89	14.93	13.23	11.74	10.44	9.31	57
58	31.79	27.90	24.54	23.04	21.65	19.14	16.96	15.07	13.42	11.97	10.70	9.59	58
59	31.10	27.43	24.26	22.84	21.51	19.12	17.03	15.21	13.61	12.21	10.97	9.88	59
60	30.41	26.97	23.98	22.63	21.37	19.10	17.10	15.35	13.81	12.44	11.24	10.17	60
61	29.74	26.52	23.71	22.43	21.24	19.08	17.17	15.49	14.01	12.69	11.52	10.48	61
62	29.10	26.09	23.44	22.24	21.11	19.06	17.25	15.64	14.22	12.94	11.81	10.80	62
63	28.48	25.67	23.19	22.06	21.00	19.06	17.33	15.80	14.43	13.21	12.11	11.13	63
64	27.90	25.28	22.96	21.90	20.90	19.07	17.43	15.97	14.67	13.49	12.43	11.48	64
65	27.36	24.92	22.75	21.76	20.82	19.10	17.55	16.17	14.92	13.79	12.78	11.86	65
66	26.86	24.60	22.58	21.65	20.77	19.15	17.69	16.38	15.19	14.12	13.15	12.26	66
67	26.40	24.30	22.43	21.56	20.74	19.22	17.85	16.61	15.49	14.47	13.54	12.69	67
68	25.97	24.04	22.30	21.50	20.73	19.32	18.03	16.87	15.81	14.84	13.96	13.15	68
69	25.57	23.79	22.19	21.45	20.74	19.43	18.23	17.14	16.15	15.24	14.40	13.64	69
70	25.19	23.57	22.10	21.41	20.76	19.55	18.44	17.43	16.50	15.65	14.87	14.15	70

Ogden Table 25: Multipliers for loss of pension commencing age 75 (males)

Age at date of trial	Multiplier calculated with allowance for projected mortality from the 2008-based population projections and rate of return of												Age at date of trial
	-2.0%	-1.5%	-1.0%	-0.75%	-0.5%	0.0%	0.5%	1.0%	1.5%	2.0%	2.5%	3.0%	
0	97.81	62.36	39.93	32.00	25.68	16.58	10.74	6.99	4.57	2.99	1.97	1.30	0
1	95.69	61.34	39.49	31.73	25.52	16.56	10.79	7.06	4.63	3.05	2.02	1.34	1
2	93.15	60.03	38.85	31.30	25.24	16.47	10.79	7.09	4.68	3.10	2.06	1.37	2
3	90.66	58.74	38.22	30.87	24.97	16.37	10.78	7.12	4.73	3.15	2.10	1.41	3
4	88.23	57.47	37.59	30.45	24.69	16.28	10.77	7.16	4.77	3.19	2.14	1.44	4
5	85.86	56.23	36.98	30.03	24.41	16.18	10.76	7.19	4.82	3.24	2.19	1.48	5
6	83.55	55.01	36.37	29.61	24.14	16.08	10.75	7.22	4.86	3.29	2.23	1.52	6
7	81.31	53.82	35.77	29.20	23.86	15.98	10.74	7.25	4.91	3.33	2.27	1.55	7
8	79.12	52.65	35.18	28.80	23.59	15.88	10.73	7.28	4.95	3.38	2.32	1.59	8
9	76.97	51.50	34.59	28.39	23.32	15.79	10.72	7.31	5.00	3.43	2.36	1.63	9
10	74.89	50.37	34.02	27.99	23.06	15.69	10.71	7.34	5.05	3.48	2.41	1.67	10
11	72.85	49.27	33.45	27.60	22.79	15.59	10.70	7.37	5.09	3.53	2.46	1.71	11
12	70.88	48.19	32.89	27.21	22.53	15.49	10.69	7.40	5.14	3.58	2.50	1.76	12
13	68.96	47.14	32.34	26.83	22.27	15.39	10.67	7.43	5.19	3.63	2.55	1.80	13
14	67.09	46.10	31.80	26.45	22.02	15.29	10.66	7.46	5.23	3.68	2.60	1.84	14
15	65.27	45.10	31.27	26.08	21.76	15.20	10.65	7.49	5.28	3.74	2.65	1.89	15
16	63.50	44.11	30.75	25.71	21.51	15.10	10.64	7.52	5.33	3.79	2.71	1.94	16
17	61.78	43.15	30.24	25.35	21.27	15.01	10.63	7.55	5.38	3.85	2.76	1.98	17
18	60.12	42.21	29.74	24.99	21.03	14.92	10.62	7.58	5.43	3.90	2.81	2.03	18
19	58.50	41.29	29.25	24.65	20.79	14.82	10.61	7.61	5.48	3.96	2.87	2.08	19
20	56.93	40.40	28.77	24.31	20.55	14.74	10.60	7.65	5.53	4.02	2.92	2.13	20
21	55.40	39.52	28.29	23.97	20.32	14.65	10.59	7.68	5.59	4.08	2.98	2.19	21

Ogden Table 25: Multipliers for loss of pension commencing age 75 (males)

Age at date of trial	\-2.0%	\-1.5%	\-1.0%	\-0.75%	\-0.5%	0.0%	0.5%	1.0%	1.5%	2.0%	2.5%	3.0%	Age at date of trial
Multiplier calculated with allowance for projected mortality from the 2008-based population projections and rate of return of													
22	53.90	38.66	27.82	23.63	20.09	14.55	10.58	7.71	5.64	4.13	3.04	2.24	22
23	52.44	37.81	27.36	23.30	19.86	14.46	10.57	7.74	5.69	4.19	3.10	2.30	23
24	51.02	36.99	26.90	22.97	19.63	14.37	10.55	7.77	5.74	4.25	3.16	2.35	24
25	49.64	36.18	26.46	22.65	19.41	14.28	10.54	7.81	5.80	4.31	3.22	2.41	25
26	48.31	35.40	26.02	22.34	19.19	14.20	10.53	7.84	5.85	4.38	3.29	2.47	26
27	47.02	34.64	25.60	22.03	18.98	14.11	10.52	7.87	5.91	4.44	3.35	2.53	27
28	45.74	33.88	25.17	21.72	18.76	14.02	10.51	7.90	5.96	4.51	3.42	2.60	28
29	44.50	33.14	24.75	21.41	18.54	13.93	10.50	7.94	6.01	4.57	3.48	2.66	29
30	43.30	32.41	24.34	21.11	18.33	13.85	10.49	7.97	6.07	4.64	3.55	2.73	30
31	42.14	31.71	23.94	20.82	18.13	13.76	10.48	8.00	6.13	4.70	3.62	2.79	31
32	41.02	31.04	23.56	20.54	17.93	13.69	10.48	8.04	6.19	4.77	3.69	2.86	32
33	39.94	30.38	23.18	20.27	17.74	13.61	10.47	8.08	6.25	4.85	3.77	2.94	33
34	38.89	29.74	22.81	20.00	17.54	13.53	10.47	8.12	6.31	4.92	3.84	3.01	34
35	37.86	29.10	22.44	19.73	17.35	13.45	10.46	8.15	6.37	4.99	3.92	3.09	35
36	36.86	28.49	22.08	19.46	17.16	13.38	10.46	8.19	6.43	5.07	4.00	3.16	36
37	35.88	27.88	21.73	19.20	16.98	13.30	10.45	8.23	6.50	5.14	4.08	3.24	37
38	34.93	27.29	21.38	18.94	16.79	13.23	10.44	8.27	6.56	5.22	4.16	3.33	38
39	34.00	26.71	21.03	18.68	16.61	13.15	10.44	8.31	6.62	5.30	4.24	3.41	39
40	33.10	26.14	20.69	18.43	16.43	13.07	10.43	8.34	6.69	5.38	4.33	3.49	40
41	32.22	25.58	20.36	18.18	16.25	13.00	10.43	8.38	6.75	5.46	4.42	3.58	41
42	31.38	25.04	20.04	17.94	16.07	12.93	10.42	8.42	6.82	5.54	4.51	3.67	42
43	30.55	24.51	19.72	17.70	15.90	12.86	10.42	8.46	6.89	5.62	4.60	3.77	43
44	29.75	24.00	19.41	17.47	15.73	12.79	10.42	8.50	6.96	5.71	4.69	3.86	44
45	28.98	23.50	19.10	17.24	15.57	12.72	10.41	8.55	7.03	5.79	4.79	3.96	45
46	28.22	23.01	18.80	17.01	15.41	12.65	10.41	8.59	7.10	5.88	4.88	4.06	46
47	27.49	22.53	18.51	16.79	15.25	12.59	10.41	8.63	7.17	5.97	4.99	4.17	47
48	26.78	22.07	18.23	16.58	15.09	12.52	10.41	8.68	7.25	6.07	5.09	4.28	48
49	26.10	21.62	17.95	16.37	14.94	12.46	10.42	8.73	7.33	6.16	5.20	4.39	49
50	25.44	21.18	17.68	16.17	14.80	12.41	10.43	8.78	7.41	6.26	5.31	4.50	50
51	24.80	20.77	17.43	15.98	14.66	12.36	10.44	8.83	7.49	6.37	5.42	4.62	51
52	24.20	20.37	17.18	15.80	14.53	12.31	10.45	8.89	7.58	6.48	5.54	4.75	52
53	23.61	19.98	16.95	15.62	14.41	12.27	10.47	8.96	7.67	6.59	5.67	4.88	53
54	23.05	19.61	16.72	15.45	14.29	12.23	10.50	9.02	7.77	6.70	5.80	5.02	54
55	22.52	19.26	16.51	15.30	14.18	12.20	10.53	9.09	7.87	6.83	5.93	5.16	55
56	22.01	18.93	16.31	15.15	14.08	12.18	10.56	9.17	7.98	6.96	6.08	5.31	56
57	21.53	18.61	16.12	15.02	13.99	12.17	10.60	9.26	8.10	7.09	6.23	5.47	57
58	21.06	18.30	15.94	14.88	13.91	12.16	10.65	9.34	8.21	7.23	6.38	5.64	58
59	20.60	18.00	15.76	14.75	13.82	12.15	10.69	9.43	8.33	7.38	6.54	5.81	59
60	20.15	17.70	15.58	14.62	13.73	12.13	10.74	9.52	8.45	7.52	6.70	5.98	60
61	19.71	17.41	15.40	14.49	13.65	12.12	10.78	9.61	8.58	7.67	6.87	6.16	61
62	19.29	17.13	15.23	14.38	13.57	12.12	10.84	9.71	8.71	7.83	7.04	6.35	62
63	18.89	16.86	15.08	14.27	13.51	12.12	10.89	9.81	8.85	7.99	7.23	6.55	63
64	18.52	16.62	14.94	14.17	13.45	12.13	10.96	9.92	8.99	8.16	7.42	6.76	64

Ogden Table 25: Multipliers for loss of pension commencing age 75 (males)

Age at date of trial	Multiplier calculated with allowance for projected mortality from the 2008-based population projections and rate of return of												Age at date of trial
	-2.0%	-1.5%	-1.0%	-0.75%	-0.5%	0.0%	0.5%	1.0%	1.5%	2.0%	2.5%	3.0%	
65	18.18	16.40	14.82	14.10	13.41	12.16	11.05	10.05	9.16	8.35	7.63	6.99	65
66	17.87	16.21	14.73	14.04	13.40	12.21	11.15	10.20	9.34	8.56	7.86	7.23	66
67	17.60	16.04	14.65	14.01	13.40	12.28	11.27	10.36	9.53	8.79	8.11	7.50	67
68	17.35	15.90	14.60	14.00	13.42	12.37	11.41	10.54	9.75	9.03	8.38	7.78	68
69	17.12	15.78	14.56	14.00	13.46	12.47	11.56	10.73	9.98	9.30	8.67	8.09	69
70	16.92	15.67	14.54	14.02	13.51	12.58	11.72	10.94	10.23	9.58	8.97	8.42	70
71	16.72	15.57	14.53	14.04	13.57	12.70	11.90	11.17	10.49	9.87	9.30	8.77	71
72	16.53	15.48	14.52	14.07	13.64	12.83	12.08	11.40	10.77	10.18	9.64	9.14	72
73	16.36	15.40	14.52	14.11	13.71	12.97	12.28	11.64	11.05	10.51	10.00	9.53	73
74	16.19	15.33	14.53	14.16	13.80	13.12	12.49	11.90	11.36	10.86	10.39	9.95	74
75	16.04	15.27	14.56	14.22	13.90	13.29	12.72	12.19	11.70	11.24	10.81	10.40	75

Ogden Table 26: Multipliers for loss of pension commencing age 75 (females)

Age at date of trial	Multiplier calculated with allowance for projected mortality from the 2008-based population projections and rate of return of												Age at date of trial
	-2.0%	-1.5%	-1.0%	-0.75%	-0.5%	0.0%	0.5%	1.0%	1.5%	2.0%	2.5%	3.0%	
0	114.99	73.05	46.61	37.29	29.87	19.22	12.42	8.06	5.25	3.43	2.25	1.48	0
1	112.51	71.86	46.09	36.97	29.69	19.21	12.48	8.13	5.33	3.50	2.31	1.53	1
2	109.64	70.40	45.40	36.51	29.40	19.12	12.48	8.18	5.38	3.56	2.36	1.57	2
3	106.83	68.96	44.71	36.05	29.10	19.02	12.49	8.23	5.44	3.61	2.41	1.61	3
4	104.08	67.55	44.02	35.60	28.81	18.93	12.49	8.27	5.50	3.67	2.46	1.65	4
5	101.41	66.16	43.35	35.15	28.52	18.84	12.49	8.32	5.56	3.73	2.51	1.69	5
6	98.79	64.80	42.69	34.70	28.23	18.75	12.50	8.36	5.62	3.79	2.56	1.74	6
7	96.24	63.47	42.03	34.25	27.94	18.65	12.50	8.41	5.67	3.84	2.61	1.78	7
8	93.75	62.16	41.38	33.81	27.66	18.56	12.50	8.45	5.73	3.90	2.67	1.83	8
9	91.32	60.87	40.74	33.38	27.37	18.46	12.50	8.50	5.79	3.97	2.72	1.88	9
10	88.95	59.61	40.11	32.95	27.09	18.37	12.50	8.54	5.85	4.03	2.78	1.92	10
11	86.65	58.38	39.49	32.53	26.82	18.28	12.50	8.59	5.92	4.09	2.84	1.97	11
12	84.41	57.17	38.88	32.11	26.54	18.18	12.51	8.63	5.98	4.15	2.90	2.03	12
13	82.21	55.99	38.27	31.69	26.26	18.09	12.51	8.68	6.04	4.22	2.96	2.08	13
14	80.08	54.83	37.68	31.28	25.99	18.00	12.51	8.72	6.10	4.28	3.02	2.13	14
15	78.00	53.69	37.09	30.88	25.73	17.91	12.51	8.77	6.16	4.35	3.08	2.19	15
16	75.98	52.58	36.52	30.48	25.46	17.81	12.51	8.81	6.23	4.42	3.14	2.24	16
17	74.00	51.48	35.95	30.08	25.20	17.72	12.51	8.86	6.29	4.49	3.21	2.30	17
18	72.08	50.42	35.39	29.69	24.94	17.63	12.51	8.90	6.36	4.55	3.27	2.36	18
19	70.22	49.37	34.84	29.31	24.68	17.54	12.51	8.95	6.42	4.63	3.34	2.42	19
20	68.41	48.36	34.31	28.94	24.43	17.45	12.51	9.00	6.49	4.70	3.41	2.48	20
21	66.64	47.36	33.78	28.57	24.18	17.36	12.51	9.05	6.56	4.77	3.48	2.55	21
22	64.91	46.38	33.26	28.20	23.93	17.27	12.51	9.09	6.63	4.85	3.55	2.61	22
23	63.22	45.41	32.73	27.83	23.68	17.18	12.51	9.14	6.69	4.92	3.63	2.68	23
24	61.56	44.46	32.22	27.46	23.43	17.09	12.51	9.18	6.76	4.99	3.70	2.75	24
25	59.96	43.53	31.71	27.10	23.18	17.00	12.51	9.23	6.83	5.07	3.78	2.82	25

Ogden Table 26: Multipliers for loss of pension commencing age 75 (females)

Age at date of trial	Multiplier calculated with allowance for projected mortality from the 2008-based population projections and rate of return of												Age at date of trial
	-2.0%	-1.5%	-1.0%	-0.75%	-0.5%	0.0%	0.5%	1.0%	1.5%	2.0%	2.5%	3.0%	
26	58.40	42.63	31.22	26.75	22.94	16.91	12.51	9.28	6.90	5.15	3.85	2.89	26
27	56.88	41.74	30.73	26.40	22.70	16.82	12.51	9.32	6.97	5.23	3.93	2.97	27
28	55.40	40.87	30.25	26.06	22.47	16.74	12.50	9.37	7.04	5.31	4.01	3.04	28
29	53.96	40.02	29.78	25.72	22.23	16.65	12.50	9.42	7.12	5.39	4.10	3.12	29
30	52.56	39.19	29.32	25.39	22.00	16.56	12.50	9.47	7.19	5.47	4.18	3.20	30
31	51.20	38.38	28.86	25.06	21.78	16.48	12.50	9.52	7.26	5.56	4.27	3.28	31
32	49.88	37.59	28.42	24.74	21.55	16.39	12.51	9.57	7.34	5.65	4.35	3.37	32
33	48.59	36.82	27.98	24.42	21.33	16.31	12.51	9.62	7.42	5.73	4.44	3.45	33
34	47.33	36.05	27.55	24.11	21.11	16.23	12.51	9.67	7.49	5.82	4.54	3.54	34
35	46.10	35.30	27.12	23.79	20.89	16.14	12.51	9.72	7.57	5.91	4.63	3.63	35
36	44.91	34.57	26.70	23.49	20.68	16.06	12.51	9.77	7.65	6.00	4.73	3.73	36
37	43.75	33.86	26.29	23.19	20.47	15.98	12.51	9.82	7.73	6.10	4.82	3.82	37
38	42.62	33.16	25.88	22.89	20.26	15.90	12.51	9.87	7.81	6.19	4.92	3.92	38
39	41.52	32.48	25.48	22.59	20.05	15.82	12.51	9.92	7.89	6.29	5.02	4.02	39
40	40.44	31.81	25.09	22.30	19.84	15.73	12.51	9.97	7.97	6.39	5.13	4.13	40
41	39.40	31.15	24.70	22.02	19.64	15.66	12.51	10.03	8.05	6.49	5.23	4.23	41
42	38.38	30.51	24.32	21.74	19.44	15.58	12.52	10.08	8.14	6.59	5.34	4.34	42
43	37.40	29.89	23.95	21.46	19.24	15.50	12.52	10.13	8.22	6.69	5.45	4.46	43
44	36.44	29.28	23.59	21.19	19.05	15.43	12.52	10.19	8.31	6.80	5.57	4.57	44
45	35.52	28.69	23.23	20.93	18.86	15.35	12.53	10.25	8.40	6.90	5.69	4.69	45
46	34.61	28.10	22.88	20.66	18.68	15.28	12.53	10.31	8.49	7.01	5.81	4.82	46
47	33.73	27.54	22.54	20.41	18.49	15.21	12.54	10.36	8.58	7.13	5.93	4.94	47
48	32.89	26.99	22.21	20.16	18.32	15.14	12.55	10.43	8.68	7.24	6.06	5.07	48
49	32.07	26.46	21.88	19.92	18.15	15.08	12.56	10.49	8.78	7.36	6.19	5.21	49
50	31.27	25.94	21.57	19.69	17.98	15.02	12.58	10.56	8.88	7.48	6.32	5.35	50
51	30.50	25.43	21.26	19.45	17.81	14.96	12.59	10.62	8.98	7.61	6.46	5.49	51
52	29.75	24.94	20.96	19.23	17.65	14.90	12.61	10.69	9.09	7.74	6.60	5.64	52
53	29.03	24.47	20.67	19.01	17.50	14.85	12.63	10.77	9.20	7.87	6.75	5.80	53
54	28.33	24.01	20.39	18.80	17.35	14.80	12.66	10.84	9.31	8.01	6.90	5.96	54
55	27.66	23.56	20.12	18.60	17.21	14.76	12.69	10.92	9.43	8.15	7.06	6.12	55
56	27.02	23.14	19.86	18.41	17.08	14.72	12.72	11.01	9.55	8.30	7.22	6.30	56
57	26.39	22.72	19.60	18.22	16.95	14.69	12.75	11.10	9.67	8.45	7.39	6.48	57
58	25.78	22.32	19.36	18.04	16.83	14.66	12.79	11.19	9.80	8.60	7.56	6.66	58
59	25.19	21.92	19.11	17.86	16.70	14.62	12.83	11.28	9.93	8.76	7.74	6.85	59
60	24.61	21.53	18.87	17.68	16.57	14.59	12.86	11.37	10.06	8.92	7.92	7.05	60
61	24.04	21.14	18.63	17.50	16.45	14.55	12.90	11.46	10.19	9.08	8.11	7.25	61
62	23.49	20.77	18.40	17.33	16.33	14.52	12.94	11.55	10.33	9.25	8.30	7.46	62
63	22.96	20.41	18.17	17.16	16.22	14.50	12.99	11.65	10.47	9.43	8.50	7.68	63
64	22.46	20.07	17.97	17.01	16.12	14.48	13.04	11.76	10.63	9.62	8.71	7.91	64
65	22.00	19.76	17.78	16.88	16.04	14.49	13.11	11.89	10.79	9.82	8.94	8.16	65
66	21.56	19.48	17.62	16.77	15.97	14.51	13.20	12.03	10.98	10.03	9.19	8.42	66
67	21.16	19.22	17.48	16.68	15.93	14.54	13.30	12.18	11.17	10.27	9.45	8.71	67
68	20.79	18.98	17.36	16.61	15.90	14.59	13.41	12.35	11.39	10.51	9.72	9.01	68

Ogden Table 26: Multipliers for loss of pension commencing age 75 (females)

Age at date of trial	Multiplier calculated with allowance for projected mortality from the 2008-based population projections and rate of return of												Age at date of trial
	-2.0%	-1.5%	-1.0%	-0.75%	-0.5%	0.0%	0.5%	1.0%	1.5%	2.0%	2.5%	3.0%	
69	20.44	18.76	17.25	16.55	15.88	14.65	13.54	12.53	11.61	10.78	10.02	9.33	69
70	20.11	18.55	17.15	16.49	15.87	14.72	13.67	12.72	11.85	11.05	10.33	9.66	70
71	19.78	18.35	17.05	16.44	15.87	14.79	13.81	12.91	12.09	11.34	10.65	10.01	71
72	19.46	18.14	16.95	16.39	15.86	14.86	13.95	13.11	12.34	11.63	10.98	10.38	72
73	19.13	17.93	16.84	16.33	15.84	14.93	14.08	13.31	12.59	11.93	11.32	10.75	73
74	18.80	17.72	16.74	16.28	15.83	15.00	14.23	13.51	12.86	12.24	11.68	11.15	74
75	18.48	17.53	16.64	16.23	15.83	15.08	14.38	13.74	13.14	12.58	12.06	11.58	75

Ogden Table 27: Factors to be applied for calculating deduction for accelerated payment

Term	-2.0%	-1.5%	-1.0%	-0.75%	-0.5%	0.0%	0.5%	1.0%	1.5%	2.0%	2.5%	3.0%	Term
1	1.0204	1.0152	1.0101	1.0076	1.005	1	0.995	0.9901	0.9852	0.9804	0.9756	0.9709	1
2	1.0412	1.0307	1.0203	1.0152	1.0101	1	0.9901	0.9803	0.9707	0.9612	0.9518	0.9426	2
3	1.0625	1.0464	1.0306	1.0228	1.0152	1	0.9851	0.9706	0.9563	0.9423	0.9286	0.9151	3
4	1.0842	1.0623	1.041	1.0306	1.0203	1	0.9802	0.961	0.9422	0.9238	0.906	0.8885	4
5	1.1063	1.0785	1.0515	1.0384	1.0254	1	0.9754	0.9515	0.9283	0.9057	0.8839	0.8626	5
6	1.1289	1.0949	1.0622	1.0462	1.0305	1	0.9705	0.942	0.9145	0.888	0.8623	0.8375	6
7	1.1519	1.1116	1.0729	1.0541	1.0357	1	0.9657	0.9327	0.901	0.8706	0.8413	0.8131	7
8	1.1754	1.1285	1.0837	1.0621	1.0409	1	0.9609	0.9235	0.8877	0.8535	0.8207	0.7894	8
9	1.1994	1.1457	1.0947	1.0701	1.0461	1	0.9561	0.9143	0.8746	0.8368	0.8007	0.7664	9
10	1.2239	1.1632	1.1057	1.0782	1.0514	1	0.9513	0.9053	0.8617	0.8203	0.7812	0.7441	10
11	1.2489	1.1809	1.1169	1.0863	1.0567	1	0.9466	0.8963	0.8489	0.8043	0.7621	0.7224	11
12	1.2743	1.1989	1.1282	1.0945	1.062	1	0.9419	0.8874	0.8364	0.7885	0.7436	0.7014	12
13	1.3004	1.2171	1.1396	1.1028	1.0673	1	0.9372	0.8787	0.824	0.773	0.7254	0.681	13
14	1.3269	1.2356	1.1511	1.1112	1.0727	1	0.9326	0.87	0.8118	0.7579	0.7077	0.6611	14
15	1.354	1.2545	1.1627	1.1195	1.0781	1	0.9279	0.8613	0.7999	0.743	0.6905	0.6419	15
16	1.3816	1.2736	1.1745	1.1280	1.0835	1	0.9233	0.8528	0.788	0.7284	0.6736	0.6232	16
17	1.4098	1.293	1.1863	1.1365	1.0889	1	0.9187	0.8444	0.7764	0.7142	0.6572	0.605	17
18	1.4386	1.3126	1.1983	1.1451	1.0944	1	0.9141	0.836	0.7649	0.7002	0.6412	0.5874	18
19	1.4679	1.3326	1.2104	1.1538	1.0999	1	0.9096	0.8277	0.7536	0.6864	0.6255	0.5703	19
20	1.4979	1.3529	1.2226	1.1625	1.1054	1	0.9051	0.8195	0.7425	0.673	0.6103	0.5537	20
21	1.5285	1.3735	1.235	1.1713	1.111	1	0.9006	0.8114	0.7315	0.6598	0.5954	0.5375	21
22	1.5596	1.3944	1.2475	1.1801	1.1166	1	0.8961	0.8034	0.7207	0.6468	0.5809	0.5219	22
23	1.5915	1.4157	1.2601	1.1890	1.1222	1	0.8916	0.7954	0.71	0.6342	0.5667	0.5067	23
24	1.624	1.4372	1.2728	1.1980	1.1278	1	0.8872	0.7876	0.6995	0.6217	0.5529	0.4919	24
25	1.6571	1.4591	1.2856	1.2071	1.1335	1	0.8828	0.7798	0.6892	0.6095	0.5394	0.4776	25
26	1.6909	1.4814	1.2986	1.2162	1.1392	1	0.8784	0.772	0.679	0.5976	0.5262	0.4637	26

Ogden Table 27: Factors to be applied for calculating deduction for accelerated payment

Term	−2.0%	−1.5%	−1.0%	−0.75%	−0.5%	0.0%	0.5%	1.0%	1.5%	2.0%	2.5%	3.0%	Term
27	1.7254	1.5039	1.3117	1.2254	1.1449	1	0.874	0.7644	0.669	0.5859	0.5134	0.4502	27
28	1.7606	1.5268	1.325	1.2347	1.1507	1	0.8697	0.7568	0.6591	0.5744	0.5009	0.4371	28
29	1.7966	1.5501	1.3384	1.2440	1.1565	1	0.8653	0.7493	0.6494	0.5631	0.4887	0.4243	29
30	1.8332	1.5737	1.3519	1.2534	1.1623	1	0.861	0.7419	0.6398	0.5521	0.4767	0.412	30
31	1.8706	1.5976	1.3656	1.2629	1.1681	1	0.8567	0.7346	0.6303	0.5412	0.4651	0.4	31
32	1.9088	1.622	1.3793	1.2724	1.174	1	0.8525	0.7273	0.621	0.5306	0.4538	0.3883	32
33	1.9478	1.6467	1.3933	1.2820	1.1799	1	0.8482	0.7201	0.6118	0.5202	0.4427	0.377	33
34	1.9875	1.6717	1.4074	1.2917	1.1858	1	0.844	0.713	0.6028	0.51	0.4319	0.366	34
35	2.0281	1.6972	1.4216	1.3015	1.1918	1	0.8398	0.7059	0.5939	0.5	0.4214	0.3554	35
36	2.0695	1.723	1.4359	1.3113	1.1978	1	0.8356	0.6989	0.5851	0.4902	0.4111	0.345	36
37	2.1117	1.7493	1.4504	1.3212	1.2038	1	0.8315	0.692	0.5764	0.4806	0.4011	0.335	37
38	2.1548	1.7759	1.4651	1.3312	1.2098	1	0.8274	0.6852	0.5679	0.4712	0.3913	0.3252	38
39	2.1988	1.803	1.4799	1.3413	1.2159	1	0.8232	0.6784	0.5595	0.4619	0.3817	0.3158	39
40	2.2437	1.8304	1.4948	1.3514	1.222	1	0.8191	0.6717	0.5513	0.4529	0.3724	0.3066	40
41	2.2894	1.8583	1.5099	1.3616	1.2282	1	0.8151	0.665	0.5431	0.444	0.3633	0.2976	41
42	2.3362	1.8866	1.5252	1.3719	1.2343	1	0.811	0.6584	0.5351	0.4353	0.3545	0.289	42
43	2.3838	1.9153	1.5406	1.3823	1.2405	1	0.807	0.6519	0.5272	0.4268	0.3458	0.2805	43
44	2.4325	1.9445	1.5561	1.3927	1.2468	1	0.803	0.6454	0.5194	0.4184	0.3374	0.2724	44
45	2.4821	1.9741	1.5719	1.4032	1.253	1	0.799	0.6391	0.5117	0.4102	0.3292	0.2644	45
46	2.5328	2.0042	1.5877	1.4138	1.2593	1	0.795	0.6327	0.5042	0.4022	0.3211	0.2567	46
47	2.5845	2.0347	1.6038	1.4245	1.2657	1	0.791	0.6265	0.4967	0.3943	0.3133	0.2493	47
48	2.6372	2.0657	1.62	1.4353	1.272	1	0.7871	0.6203	0.4894	0.3865	0.3057	0.242	48
49	2.6911	2.0971	1.6363	1.4461	1.2784	1	0.7832	0.6141	0.4821	0.379	0.2982	0.235	49
50	2.746	2.1291	1.6529	1.4570	1.2848	1	0.7793	0.608	0.475	0.3715	0.2909	0.2281	50
51	2.802	2.1615	1.6696	1.4681	1.2913	1	0.7754	0.602	0.468	0.3642	0.2838	0.2215	51
52	2.8592	2.1944	1.6864	1.4792	1.2978	1	0.7716	0.5961	0.4611	0.3571	0.2769	0.215	52
53	2.9175	2.2278	1.7035	1.4903	1.3043	1	0.7677	0.5902	0.4543	0.3501	0.2702	0.2088	53
54	2.9771	2.2617	1.7207	1.5016	1.3109	1	0.7639	0.5843	0.4475	0.3432	0.2636	0.2027	54
55	3.0378	2.2962	1.7381	1.5129	1.3174	1	0.7601	0.5785	0.4409	0.3365	0.2572	0.1968	55
56	3.0998	2.3312	1.7556	1.5244	1.3241	1	0.7563	0.5728	0.4344	0.3299	0.2509	0.191	56
57	3.1631	2.3667	1.7733	1.5359	1.3307	1	0.7525	0.5671	0.428	0.3234	0.2448	0.1855	57
58	3.2277	2.4027	1.7913	1.5475	1.3374	1	0.7488	0.5615	0.4217	0.3171	0.2388	0.1801	58
59	3.2935	2.4393	1.8094	1.5592	1.3441	1	0.7451	0.556	0.4154	0.3109	0.233	0.1748	59
60	3.3607	2.4764	1.8276	1.5710	1.3509	1	0.7414	0.5504	0.4093	0.3048	0.2273	0.1697	60
61	3.4293	2.5141	1.8461	1.5828	1.3577	1	0.7377	0.545	0.4032	0.2988	0.2217	0.1648	61

Ogden Table 27: Factors to be applied for calculating deduction for accelerated payment

Term	−2.0%	−1.5%	−1.0%	−0.75%	−0.5%	0.0%	0.5%	1.0%	1.5%	2.0%	2.5%	3.0%	Term
62	3.4993	2.5524	1.8647	1.5948	1.3645	1	0.734	0.5396	0.3973	0.2929	0.2163	0.16	62
63	3.5707	2.5913	1.8836	1.6069	1.3713	1	0.7304	0.5343	0.3914	0.2872	0.2111	0.1553	63
64	3.6436	2.6308	1.9026	1.6190	1.3782	1	0.7267	0.529	0.3856	0.2816	0.2059	0.1508	64
65	3.718	2.6708	1.9218	1.6312	1.3852	1	0.7231	0.5237	0.3799	0.2761	0.2009	0.1464	65
66	3.7938	2.7115	1.9412	1.6436	1.3921	1	0.7195	0.5185	0.3743	0.2706	0.196	0.1421	66
67	3.8713	2.7528	1.9608	1.6560	1.3991	1	0.7159	0.5134	0.3688	0.2653	0.1912	0.138	67
68	3.9503	2.7947	1.9806	1.6685	1.4061	1	0.7124	0.5083	0.3633	0.2601	0.1865	0.134	68
69	4.0309	2.8373	2.0007	1.6811	1.4132	1	0.7088	0.5033	0.358	0.255	0.182	0.1301	69
70	4.1132	2.8805	2.0209	1.6938	1.4203	1	0.7053	0.4983	0.3527	0.25	0.1776	0.1263	70
71	4.1971	2.9243	2.0413	1.7066	1.4275	1	0.7018	0.4934	0.3475	0.2451	0.1732	0.1226	71
72	4.2827	2.9689	2.0619	1.7195	1.4346	1	0.6983	0.4885	0.3423	0.2403	0.169	0.119	72
73	4.3702	3.0141	2.0827	1.7325	1.4418	1	0.6948	0.4837	0.3373	0.2356	0.1649	0.1156	73
74	4.4593	3.06	2.1038	1.7456	1.4491	1	0.6914	0.4789	0.3323	0.231	0.1609	0.1122	74
75	4.5503	3.1066	2.125	1.7588	1.4564	1	0.6879	0.4741	0.3274	0.2265	0.1569	0.1089	75
76	4.6432	3.1539	2.1465	1.7721	1.4637	1	0.6845	0.4694	0.3225	0.222	0.1531	0.1058	76
77	4.738	3.2019	2.1682	1.7855	1.471	1	0.6811	0.4648	0.3178	0.2177	0.1494	0.1027	77
78	4.8347	3.2507	2.1901	1.7990	1.4784	1	0.6777	0.4602	0.3131	0.2134	0.1457	0.0997	78
79	4.9333	3.3002	2.2122	1.8125	1.4859	1	0.6743	0.4556	0.3084	0.2092	0.1422	0.0968	79
80	5.034	3.3504	2.2345	1.8262	1.4933	1	0.671	0.4511	0.3039	0.2051	0.1387	0.094	80

APPENDIX 1: Presidential Guidance – General Case Management (published 14 March 2014)

REMEDY

What is remedy?

1. After a tribunal has decided whether the claimant's claim succeeds it will consider how a successful party should be compensated. This part of the judgment is called "Remedy". Sometimes it is done immediately after the merits judgment, but in long or complex cases it may be adjourned to another day.

2. The tribunal has different powers for each different type of claim. It must calculate loss and order an appropriate remedy for each part of a successful claim. Accurate and often detailed information from both parties is needed to make correct calculations and issue a judgment which is fair to all, but sometimes the tribunal can only estimate the loss, for example for how long a party may be out of work.

Different types of remedy

3. For some claims the only remedy is to order the employer to pay a sum of money – for example wages due, holiday and notice pay.

4. For unfair dismissal the tribunal may:

   • order the employer to "reinstate" the dismissed employee, which is to put them back in their old job, as if they had not been dismissed; or to "re-engage" them, which is to employ them in a suitable different job. In each case the tribunal may order payment of lost earnings etc.

   • If those orders are not sought by the claimant or are not practicable, it may order the employer to pay compensation, calculated in two parts: a "Basic Award", which is calculated in a similar way to a redundancy payment, and a "Compensatory Award", which is intended to compensate the employee for the financial loss suffered.

5. In claims of unlawful discrimination, the tribunal may;

   • make a declaration setting out the parties' rights; and/or

   • order compensation to be paid by the employer and/or fellow workers who have committed discriminatory acts, but if the employer can show that it has taken all reasonable steps to prevent employees from committing such acts (called the "Statutory Defence") the only award which can be made is against the fellow worker, not the employer; and/or

   • make a recommendation, such as for the claimant's colleagues or managers to be given training to ensure that discrimination does not happen again.

Mitigation

6. All persons who have been subjected to wrongdoing are expected to do their best, within reasonable bounds, to limit the effects on them. If the tribunal concludes that a claimant has not done so, it must reduce the compensation so that a fair sum is payable. The tribunal will expect evidence to be provided by claimants about their attempts to obtain suitable alternative work; and by respondents who consider that the claimant has not tried hard enough, about other jobs which the claimant could have applied for. (See "Information needed for the tribunal to calculate remedy" below).

Statement of Remedy

7. The tribunal will usually order the claimant to make a calculation showing how each amount claimed has been worked out (eg. x weeks pay at £y per week). Sometimes this is called a "Schedule of Loss". As tribunals are expected to calculate remedy for each different type of loss - sometimes called "Heads of Loss" or "Heads of Damage"- the statement should show how much is claimed under each head. If the claimant has received state benefits it should also specify the type of benefit, the dates of receipt, the amount received and the claimant's national insurance number (see also "Recoupment" below).

8. Typical heads of loss include;

   • wages due

   • pay in lieu of notice, where no, or inadequate, notice was given

   • outstanding holiday pay

   • a basic award or redundancy payment

   • past loss of earnings

   • future loss of earnings

- loss of future pension entitlements

- in discrimination cases:

  - injury to feelings

  - aggravated or exemplary damages, (which are rare)

  - damages for personal injury- but only when the act of discrimination is the cause of the claimant becoming ill

- any tribunal fee paid

9. The tribunal will usually order the statement to be produced early in the proceedings, as it can help in settlement negotiations and when considering mediation, and when assessing the length of the hearing. It should however be updated near to the hearing date.

Submissions on *Polkey* and Contributory Fault

10. If an employee has been dismissed but the employer has not followed a proper procedure (such as the ACAS Code), tribunals will follow the guidance in *Polkey v AE Dayton Services Limited* and subsequent cases and consider whether, if a fair procedure had been followed, the claimant might still have been fairly dismissed, either at all, or at some later time. This question is often shortened to "*Polkey*". There are also cases where the dismissal may be procedurally unfair but the employee's own conduct has contributed to the position they now find themselves in. This is called "contributory conduct".

11. Where either or both of these are relevant, the tribunal will reduce the compensation awarded by an appropriate percentage in each case. This means that there may be two reductions, which, where there has been really serious misconduct, could be as high as 100%, so that nothing would be payable.

12. Generally the tribunal will decide these issues at the same time as it reaches its decision on the merits of the claim, and sometimes at a separate remedy hearing. It should explain at the start of the hearing which of those options it will follow, but if it does not, then the parties should ask for clarification of when they are expected to give evidence and make submissions (see separate guidance on "Timetabling") on these matters.

Injury to Feelings

13. In discrimination cases and some other detriment claims, tribunals may award a sum of money to compensate for injury to feelings. When they do so they must fix fair, reasonable and just compensation in the particular circumstances of the case, bearing in mind that compensation is designed to compensate the injured party not to punish the guilty one, and that awards should bear some relationship to those made by the courts for personal injury.

14. They follow guidelines first given in *Vento v Chief Constable of West Yorkshire Police*, which have since been updated by *Da'Bell v NSPCC* and *Simmons v Castle*[1], but are still referred to as the "*Vento*" Guidelines. They identify three broad bands of compensation for injury to feelings as distinct from psychiatric or personal injury:

- The lower band is for less serious acts of discrimination. Awards in this band are currently between £660 and £6,600.

- The middle band is for cases which are more serious but do not come into the top band. These awards tend to be from £6,600 to £19,800.

- The top band is for the most serious cases such as where there has been a lengthy campaign of harassment. These awards are between £19,800 and £33,000, but are relatively rare. A case would have to be highly exceptional for any sum higher than this to be awarded.

15. Tribunals will expect claimants to explain in their statement of remedy which *Vento* band they consider their case falls in, and will also expect both parties to make submissions on this during the hearing.

Information needed for the tribunal to calculate remedy

16. This varies in each case dependant on what is being claimed. Each party should look for, provide to the other, and include in the bundle, copies of any of these which could help the tribunal with any necessary calculations in their case:

- Copy contract of employment or statement of terms & conditions with the old employer,

---

[1] **Editor's note:** The Court of Appeal in *De Souza v Vinci Construction (UK) Ltd* [2017] EWCA Civ 879 has now confirmed that the *Simmons v Castle* 10% uplift should be applied to awards for injury to feelings and physical and psychiatric injury.

including the date the claimant started work, and details of any pension scheme

• Copy pay slips for the last 13 weeks in the old employment or any other document showing the claimant's gross and net pay

• Proof of any payments actually made by the employer, such as a redundancy payment or pay in lieu of notice

• Any document recording the day s/he last actually worked

• Any document explaining how many days/hours per week the claimant worked

• Any document explaining how overtime is paid

• Any document recording when the holiday year starts,

• Any document recording when holiday has been taken in that year and what has been paid for those days

• Any documents setting out the terms of the former employer's pension scheme

• Any document showing the claimant's attempts to find other work

• Copy contract of employment and payslips for any new job

• Documents such as bank statements if losses for bank charges are claimed.

• Medical reports or "Fit" notes if unable to work since dismissal

• Any document showing that jobs were/are available in the locality for which the claimant could have applied.

17. The witness statements should tell the tribunal which parts of these documents are important and why. Providing enough information to the tribunal at an early stage could help to promote a settlement and so avoid a hearing.

Is all loss awarded?

18. For claims such as unpaid wages, holiday and notice pay the tribunal will order the difference between what should have been paid and what has actually been paid. Wages and holiday pay are usually calculated gross, but pay in lieu of notice is usually calculated net of tax and national insurance. The judgment should specify whether each payment ordered has been calculated gross or net.

19. In the case of unfair dismissal there are several limits (called statutory caps) on what can be awarded:

• For the basic award there is a maximum sum for a week's pay, which, for dismissals on or after 6 April 2017, is £489 per week. It is usually increased each year.

• For the compensatory award there are two separate limits. The first is an overall maximum, which for dismissals on or after 6 April 2017 is £80,541 and usually increases each year. However, under the Unfair Dismissal (Variation of the Limit of Compensatory Award) Order 2013, where the dismissal took effect on or after 29 July 2013 (subject to rules about the minimum notice having been given) the maximum which can be awarded to any individual is one year's salary.

• There is no limit to the maximum compensatory award where the reason for the dismissal was that the claimant made a Public Interest Disclosure, or complained of certain Health and Safety related matters, and no limit to an award for discrimination, as long as it genuinely compensates for loss actually incurred as a result of the discrimination.

Grossing up

20. The rules on when tax is payable on awards made by tribunals are too complex for inclusion here. When it is clear that the claimant will have to pay tax on the sum awarded, the tribunal will award a higher figure, calculated so that tax can be paid and the claimant will receive the net sum which properly represents the loss. This calculation is called "grossing up".

Interest

21. There are two separate situations where interest is relevant.

22. Firstly, when a tribunal calculates compensation for discrimination, it is obliged to consider awarding interest. If it decides to do so, it calculates interest from the date of the act of discrimination up to the date of the calculation, except for interest on lost wages, where the calculation is done from the middle of that period (as that is simpler than calculating interest separately on each missing wage but leads to a roughly similar result). The tribunal will then include that interest in the award made. For claims presented on or after 29 July 2013 the rate of interest is 8%. For claims presented before that date, it is 0.5%.

23. In addition, interest of 8% is payable on awards for all claims if they are not paid when due. In respect of all claims presented on or after 29 July 2013 interest is calculated from the day after the day upon which the written judgment was sent to the parties, unless payment is actually made within the first 14 days, in which case no interest is payable. For claims presented before 29 July, interest is payable 42 days after the day upon which the written judgment was sent to the parties.

24. Employment Tribunals play no part in enforcing payment of the awards they make. That is done by the civil courts, who issue separate guidance on how to enforce payments.

Recoupment

25. For some claims, such as unfair dismissal, if the claimant has received certain state benefits the tribunal is obliged to ensure that the employer responsible for causing the loss of earnings reimburses the State for the benefits paid. In those cases the tribunal will order only part of the award to be paid to the claimant straight away, with the rest set aside until the respondent is told by the State how much the benefits were. The respondent then pays that money to the State and anything left over to the claimant. This is called "recoupment". The judge should set out in the judgment whether or not recoupment applies, and if it does, how much of the award is set aside for recoupment purposes. If either party is in any doubt about recoupment, they should ask the Judge to explain how it affects them.

APPENDIX 2: Sample schedule of loss

Claimant's schedule of loss – Green v XYZ Ltd

Background

Mrs Green, who was born on 14/02/1981, started work with XYZ Ltd on 24/10/2010. Her gross weekly salary was £1,600 and her net weekly salary, after the deduction of tax and employee national insurance, was £1,200. She was a member of the employer's defined benefit pension scheme, the details of which are added below. On 17/04/2014, she was dismissed summarily for gross misconduct and was given £1,000 as payment in lieu of notice. Her contractual notice period was 8 weeks. Mrs Green found part time work from 23/07/2014 until the date of the Tribunal hearing, earning a net amount of £15,523 up until the date of the hearing. This arrangement was expected to continue for the next few months at least. Mrs Green was not eligible to join the pension scheme in her new job until she had worked for them for 2 years.

The date of the remedies hearing was set to be 03/01/2015.

Mrs Green's claims

- On 28/06/2014 Mrs Green brought claims of unfair and wrongful dismissal and sex discrimination at the ET.

- She maintained it would take a year to find another equivalent permanent job and therefore was claiming future loss of earnings until 17/04/2015.

- She was entitled to a sum representing loss of statutory rights.

- Any award should be increased by 25% for the failure of the employer to comply with the Code of Practice.

- She was entitled to a sum of £850 representing untaken accrued holiday which the respondent had not paid on termination.

- She claimed a sum of £18,000 for injury to feelings and interest on this figure, from 01/01/2012 until 01/01/2014.

- Mrs Green argued that as it would take 2 years for her to become eligible to join the pension scheme in her new job she wants to be compensated for loss of pension for that time.

Pension information

- Mrs Green's normal retirement date is 14/02/2046 (i.e. at age 65).

- Her pensionable pay at the date of dismissal was £1,200.

- Her employer contributed 12% of its wage bill to the private pension scheme.

- The scheme administrator valued Mrs Green's deferred pension at EDT as £3,000.

Respondent's Counter Schedule of Loss – Green v XYZ Ltd

Counter arguments

• The claimant's schedule of loss does not include her expected earnings, which are estimated to be £3,000 from the date of the hearing to the date when the employer's liability ends. This needs to be recorded.

• The respondent disputes the 25% uplift for failing to follow the Code of Practice for unfair dismissal, submitting that the figure should be closer to 10%.

• The respondent also submits that the claimant was also partly responsible for her own dismissal to the extent of 10% (for both the basic and compensatory awards).

• There is a 10% chance that the claimant would not have remained in the pension scheme until normal retirement so this needs to be reflected in the pension calculation.

• A deduction of 2% should also be made for accelerated payment of future sums of compensation.

• The sum of £18,000 for injury to feelings is disputed – there was no discriminatory conduct on the part of the respondent.

• The compensation cap should be applied to the final figure since the dismissal of the claimant was not discriminatory.

IN THE EMPLOYMENT TRIBUNALS
CASE NO: 3452/87

BETWEEN

Green
AND
XYZ

CLAIMANT'S SCHEDULE OF LOSS

1. Details

Date of birth	14/02/1981
Date started employment	24/10/2010
Effective Date of Termination	17/04/2014
Period of continuous service (years)	3
Age at Effective Date of Termination	33
Remedy hearing date	03/01/2015
Cut-off date for future loss of earnings	17/04/2015
Contractual notice period (weeks)	8
Statutory notice period (weeks)	3
Net weekly pay at EDT	£1,200
Gross weekly pay at EDT	£1,600

2. Basic award

Number of qualifying weeks (3) x Gross weekly pay (£464.00[1])	£1,392.00
Total basic award	**£1,392.00**

3. Damages for wrongful dismissal

Loss of earnings: Damages period (8) x Net weekly pay (£1,200)	£9,600.00
Plus failure by employer to follow statutory procedures @ 25%[2]	£2,400.00[3]
Total damages	**£12,000.00**

---

[1] £464 was the limit on a week's pay at an EDT of 17/04/2014

[2] The ACAS uplift can also apply to damages for wrongful dismissal – see *Adjustments and order of adjustments* and Schedule A2 of TULR(C)A

[3] £9,600 x 0.25

4. Compensatory award (immediate loss)

Loss of net earnings: Number of weeks (29.3[4]) x Net weekly pay (£1,200)	£35,160.00
Plus loss of statutory rights	£350.00
Plus accrued holiday pay	£850.00
Less payment in lieu	-£1,000.00
Less earnings: (23/07/2014 to 03/01/2015)	-£15,523.00

Pension loss[5]

Gross weekly pensionable pay (£1,200) x % of pensionable pay paid (12) x Multiplying factor (0.85[6]) x Number of weeks (37.3)	£4,565.52
Loss of enhancement of accrued pension rights: Deferred pension (3,000) x Multiplying factor (4.42[7])	£13,260.00
Total compensation (immediate loss)	**£37,662.52**

5. Compensatory award (future loss)

Loss of future earnings: Number of weeks (14.9[8]) x Net weekly pay (£1,200)	£17,880.00
Future loss of pension	£8,164.08
Number of weeks (66.7[9]) x Gross weekly pensionable pay (£1,200) x % contributed by employer (12) x Multiplying factor (0.85)	
Total compensation (future loss)	**£26,044.08**

6. Adjustments to total compensatory award

Failure by employer to follow statutory procedures @ 25%	£15,926.65[10]
Compensatory award before adjustments	**£63,706.60**

---

[4] 29.3 weeks has been calculated by subtracting the damages period of 8 weeks from the total number of weeks between EDT and the hearing date (37.3)

[5] Pension loss has been calculated according to the Employment Tribunal Guidelines: Compensation for Loss of Pension Rights

[6] This multiplier has been taken from Table 7.2 Appendix 7 of the Employment Tribunal Guidelines: Compensation for Loss of Pension Rights (Age last birthday is 33, Normal Retirement Age is 65)

[7] This multiplier has been taken from Table 4.3 Appendix 3 of the Employment Tribunal Guidelines: Compensation for Loss of Pension Rights (Private Sector Scheme, Age last birthday is 33, Normal Retirement Age is 65)

[8] Number of weeks between 03/01/2015 and 17/04/2015

[9] 104 weeks (i.e. 2 years) – 37.3 weeks immediate loss

[10] (£37,662.52 + £26,044.08) x 0.25. Remember that accrued holiday pay which has not been paid can be classed as unlawful deductions and thus uplifted according to Schedule A2 of TULR(C)A

Total adjustments to the compensatory award	**£15,926.65**
Compensatory award after adjustments	**£79,633.25**

7. Discrimination

Injury to feelings	£18,000.00
Plus interest @ 8%[11] for 730 days	£2,880.00[12]
Discrimination award	**£20,880.00**

8. Summary totals

Basic award	£1,392.00
Wrongful dismissal	£12,000.00
Compensation award	£79,633.25
Discrimination	£20,880.00
TOTAL	**£113,905.25**
TOTAL AFTER GROSSING UP AT 40%	**£155,355.42[13]**

---

[11] The interest rate is 8% from 29/07/2013

[12] £18,000 x 0.08 x 730 ÷ 365

[13] (£1,392 + £12,000 + £79,633.25 - £850) - £30,000 = £92,175.25 - £30,000.00 = £62,175.25. Remember that the £850 holiday pay should not be grossed up since it should be paid gross by the employer. Nor should the injury to feelings figure be included here because it is thought this will not be taxable.

Grossed up at 40% = £62,175.25 ÷ 0.6 = £103,625.42

Add back £20,880.00 + £30,000.00 + £850, and the final award comes to £155,355.42

The statutory cap does not apply since the claimant is claiming that the dismissal was for discriminatory reasons (see respondent's counter schedule).

IN THE EMPLOYMENT TRIBUNALS
CASE NO: 3452/87

BETWEEN

Green
AND
XYZ

RESPONDENT'S COUNTER SCHEDULE OF LOSS

1. Details

Date of birth	14/02/1981
Date started employment	24/10/2010
Effective Date of Termination	17/04/2014
Period of continuous service (years)	3
Age at Effective Date of Termination	33
Remedy hearing date	03/01/2015
Cut-off date for future loss of earnings	17/04/2015
Contractual notice period (weeks)	8
Statutory notice period (weeks)	3
Net weekly pay at EDT	£1,200
Gross weekly pay at EDT	£1,600

2. Basic award

Number of qualifying weeks (3) x Gross weekly pay (£464.00)	£1,392.00
Less contributory fault @ 10%	-£139.20
Total basic award	**£1,252.80**

3. Damages for wrongful dismissal

Loss of earnings: Damages period (8) x Net weekly pay (£1,200)	£9,600.00
Plus failure by employer to follow statutory procedures @ 10%	£960.00
Total damages	**£10,560.00**

4. Compensatory award (immediate loss)

Loss of net earnings: Number of weeks (29.3) x Net weekly pay (£1,200)	£35,160.00
Plus loss of statutory rights	£350.00
Plus accrued holiday pay	£850.00
Less payment in lieu	-£1,000.00
Less earnings: (23/07/2014 to 03/01/2015)	-£15,523.00

Pension loss

Gross weekly pensionable pay (£1,200) x % of pensionable pay paid (12) x Multiplying factor (0.85) x Number of weeks (37.3)	£4,565.52
Loss of enhancement of accrued pension rights Deferred pension (£3,000) x Multiplier (4.42) x % for chance of withdrawal (10)	£11,934.00[14]
Total compensation (immediate loss)	**£36,336.52**

5. Compensatory award (future loss)

Loss of future earnings: Number of weeks (14.9) x Net weekly pay (£1,200)	£17,880.00
Less expected future earnings (04/01/2015 to 17/04/2015)	-£3,000.00
Future loss of pension Number of weeks (66.7) x Gross weekly pensionable pay (£1,200) x % contributed by employer (12) x Multiplying factor (0.85)	£8,164.08
Total compensation (future loss)	**£23,044.08**

---

[14] £3,000 x 4.42 x 0.9

6. Adjustments to total compensatory award

Less accelerated payment	-£460.88[15]
Plus failure by employer to follow statutory procedures (ACAS uplift) @ 10%	£5,891.97[16]
Less contributory fault (compensation award) @ 10%	-£6,396.17[17]
Compensatory award before adjustments	**£59,380.60**
Total adjustments to the compensatory award	**-£965.08[18]**
Compensatory award after adjustments	**£58,415.52**

7. Summary totals

Basic award	£1,252.80
Wrongful dismissal	£10,560.00
Compensatory award	£58,415.52
TOTAL	**£70,228.32**
GROSSING UP AT 40%	**£96,480.53[19]**
AFTER STATUTORY CAP OF £76,574[20]	**£89,236.80[21]**

---

[15] Accelerated payment only applies to future loss. The future loss figure is £23,044.08 and 2% of this figure is £23,044.08 x 0.02 = £460.88

[16] Immediate loss + future loss – accelerated receipt = £36,336.52 + £23,044.08 - £460.88 = £58,919.72. The ACAS adjustment should now be applied to this figure = £58,919.72 x 0.1 = £5,891.97

[17] This has been calculated by first adding together the immediate loss, future loss and ACAS uplift, and deducting the sums for accelerated receipt to get £36,336.52 + £23,044.08 + £5,891.97 - £460.88 = £64,811.69

Next, the contributory fault deduction needs to be applied to this new figure but LESS the £850 holiday pay sum because contributory fault does not apply to holiday pay. This now becomes: (£64,811.69 - £850) x 0.1 = £6,396.17

[18] - £460.88 + £5,891.97 - £6,396.17

[19] (£1,252.80 + £10,560.00 + £58,415.52 - £850) - £30,000 = £69,378.32 - £30,000 = £39,378.32. Remember that the £850 holiday pay should not be grossed up since it should be paid gross by the employer.

Grossed up at 40% = £39,378.32 ÷ 0.6 = £65,630.53

Add back £30,000 + £850 = £96,480.53

[20] This was the statutory cap applicable at an EDT of 17/04/2014 (see Table 1). Compare this with the claimant's gross annual salary of £83,200 (i.e. £1,600 x 52) and the smaller figure applies.

[21] First, we need to find out what the compensatory award is after the grossing up has been done. £18,187.20 was tax free (because £30,000 - £1,252.80 - £10,560.00 = £18,187.20). The balance of £39,378.32 (i.e. £58,415.52 – 18,187.20 - £850) was grossed up to get £65,630.53 (i.e. £39,378.32 ÷ 0.6).

Thus the total compensatory award = £18,187.20 + £65,630.53 (excluding the holiday pay) = £83,817.73 which exceeds the statutory cap. Therefore, the total award is: £1,252.80 + £10,560 + £76,574 + £850 = £89,236.80. Remember that the £850 holiday pay does not count towards the compensation cap.

APPENDIX 3: Calculating holiday entitlement

The calculation of holiday entitlement can be a complicated matter. The calculation ultimately depends upon the construction of the contract of employment, and where relevant the construction of the Working Time Regulations. The Working Time Regulations must themselves be interpreted consistently with the Working Time Directive where it is the four weeks of paid leave that derive from the Directive that are under consideration (see *Bear Scotland & Ors v Fulton & Ors* [2015] ICR 221). Subject to that strong note of caution, the following principles will often assist in calculating holiday entitlement.

Working 5 or more days a week

Most workers who work a 5-day week have a statutory entitlement to 28 days paid annual leave per year which amounts to 5.6 weeks.

Note that the statutory minimum is limited to 28 days - even if a worker works 6 days per week, they will still only be statutorily entitled to 28 days holiday per year (not 6 x 5.6 which is 33.6 days).

Working part-time

Part-time workers are also entitled to a statutory minimum of 5.6 weeks of paid holiday each year, although this may amount to fewer actual days of paid holiday than a full-time worker would get. For example, someone working 4 days per week will be entitled to a minimum of 4 x 5.6 weeks which comes to 22.4 days per year.

Working a fixed number of days per week

Number of days entitlement per year = number of days worked per week (up to a maximum of 5 for the statutory minimum) x number of weeks holiday entitlement (5.6 is the statutory minimum although the contract of employment may provide for more)

> *Example 1*: for a worker who works 3 days per week, and who is contractually entitled to 7 weeks holiday per year, they would be entitled to 3 x 7 days = 21 days

> *Example 2*: a worker who works 4 days a week and is contractually entitled to 35 days a year pro rata would be entitled to 4 ÷ 5 x 35 = 28 days

> *Example 3*: a worker who works 4 days per week but has no contractual right to holiday would be entitled to 4 x 5.6 = 22.4 days

Working a fixed number of hours per week

Sometimes it is easier to calculate holiday entitlement in terms of hours rather than days, especially if the worker does not work whole days. It also means it is easier to calculate how much holiday is due to a worker who leaves part way through the leave year.

> *Example 4*: a worker works 20 hours per week, and is entitled to the statutory 5.6 weeks per year.

> Holiday entitlement is 20 x 5.6 hours per year = 112 hours

Working a different number of hours per week and variable number of days per week

This will apply to many casual workers and again it is usually easier to calculate holiday entitlement in hours, with direct reference to the number of hours actually worked. Note that the WTD provides for entitlement to four weeks paid leave.

Statutory holiday entitlement only

For each hour worked, the worker accrues 0.1207 of an hour or roughly 7 minutes of holiday. The 0.1207 is the proportion of the working year that a worker is entitled to have as holiday by statute, and is worked out as:

> 5.6 ÷ (52 - 5.6) = 5.6 ÷ 46.4 = 0.1207 [The 5.6 weeks are excluded from the calculation as the worker would not be at work during those 5.6 weeks in order to accrue annual leave.]

> *Example 5*: a worker works 20 hours in a week.

> Holiday entitlement = 20 x 0.1207 = 2.41 hours, which is approximately 2 hours and 25 minutes.

Holiday entitlement in excess of statutory minimum where holiday is expressed in weeks (W)

For each hour worked, the worker is entitled to W ÷ (52 - W) of an hour.

> ***Example 6***: a worker works 25 hours per week, and holiday entitlement is 6 weeks per year.
>
> Holiday entitlement per hour of work = 6 ÷ (52 - 6) = 0.1304 of an hour or about 8 minutes.

Holiday entitlement in excess of statutory minimum where holiday is expressed in days (D)

For each hour worked, the worker is entitled to D/5 ÷ (52 - D/5) of an hour (this divides days by 5 rather than 7, since the statutory formula is worked out on the basis of 5 working days).

> ***Example 7***: a worker works 25 hours and holiday entitlement is 34 days per year.
>
> Holiday entitlement per hour of work = 34/5 ÷ (52 - 34/5) = 0.1504 of an hour = approximately 9 minutes

Annualised hours

The following calculations would be suitable for any worker who works a set number of hours per year. The easiest way to calculate holiday entitlement is to treat the worker as a casual worker and calculate the number of hours of holiday accrued per hour of work actually done.

For statutory holiday entitlement

Holiday in hours = hours actually worked x 0.1207

For holiday entitlement in excess of statutory minimum

Holiday in hours = hours worked x W ÷ (52 - W) where W is the number of weeks holiday the worker is entitled to according to their employment contract.

> ***Example 8***: a worker works 1000 hours per year and is entitled to 8 weeks holiday per year.
>
> Holiday entitlement = 1000 x 8 ÷ (52 - 8) = 181.82 hours per year.

Compressed hours

Some workers work compressed hours; for example, they may work 40 hours compressed into 4 days instead of 5.

The easiest way in which this is calculated is by working out the number of hours' holiday that is being accrued. This avoids having to calculate the length of a day for the purposes of taking a day off.

Holiday entitlement (hours) = hours worked in a week x number of weeks of contractual holiday (or 5.6 if only statutory holiday).

Shift workers

The easiest way in which holiday entitlement can be calculated in this case is to work out the number of shifts the worker is entitled to take off. To do this calculate the proportion of the entire shift pattern (including days off) that the worker has actually worked to work out the average number of shifts worked per week, and then multiply this number of shifts by the number of weeks of annual holiday entitlement.

> ***Example 9***: a worker works four 12 hour shifts in a week and then has 2 days off. He is only entitled to statutory holiday.
>
> First find out the average number of shifts worked per week. The complete shift pattern is 6 days, of which the worker works 4. So in a 7 day week they work on average: 4 ÷ (4 + 2) x 7 = 4.67 shifts.
>
> Then, annual holiday entitlement = 4.67 x 5.6 = 26.15 shifts

Entitlement if a worker starts or leaves part way through the leave year
Starters

You need to work out the proportion of the year left from the day the worker started to the end of the leave year, then multiply by the entitlement as calculated above.

> ***Example 10***: leave year is from 1 January to 31 December. A worker starts on 18 September. Full years' entitlement (as calculated using the above formulae) = 28 days.
>
> First, the number of days between 18 September and 31 December, including both days = 105.
>
> Holiday entitlement for the remaining period = 28 x 105 ÷ 365 (or 366 in a leap year) = 8 days

Leavers

You need to work out the proportion of the leave year actually worked, then multiply by the entitlement as calculated above. Finally subtract any holiday actually taken.

> **Example 11**: leave year is from 1 June to 31 May. A casual worker worked a total of 600 hours and left on 24 October and had already taken 20 hours holiday. Statutory holiday entitlement applies.
>
> In this case, because holiday is being accrued for each hour worked, we don't need to work out the proportion of the leave year worked.
>
> Holiday entitlement = 600 x 0.1207 hours = 72.42 hours
>
> Holiday pay due = 72.42 - 20 = 52.42 hours

> **Example 12**: leave year is from 1 June to 31 May. A worker, who worked 3 days a week, left on 24 October and had already taken 4 days holiday in that leave year. Statutory holiday entitlement applies.
>
> Annual holiday entitlement = 3 x 5.6 = 16.8 days
>
> Then, number of days between 1 June and 24 October inclusive = 146 days
>
> Holiday entitlement = 16.8 x 146 ÷ 365 (366 in a leap year) = 6.72
>
> Holiday pay due = 6.72 - 4 = 2.72 days

Term time only workers

There is no specific calculation for working out the holiday entitlement for term time workers and the easiest and fairest calculations might be those used for annualised hours or casual/irregular hours.

Calculating accrued holiday pay on termination of employment

If an employee has left employment part way through a leave year, and at the effective date of termination he has taken less holiday than he is entitled to up to that date, the employer should make a payment in lieu to the employee, either according to a relevant agreement (see below) or, if no such agreement exists, then the accrued holiday is calculated according to Reg 14 WTR 1998 which then needs to be multiplied by a day's pay or an hour's pay:

> (A x B) - C
>
> where:
>
> A is the period of leave to which the worker is entitled;
>
> B is the proportion of the worker's leave year which expired before the termination date; and
>
> C is the period of leave taken by the worker between the start of the leave year and the termination date.

What is a day's pay?

The calculation of a days' pay can be a complicated matter. The calculation ultimately depends upon the construction of the contract of employment, and where relevant the construction of the Working Time Regulations and ss221 to 224 ERA 1996. The Working Time Regulations must themselves be interpreted consistently with the Working Time Directive where it is the four weeks of paid leave that derive from the Directive that are under consideration, such that provisions in the ERA 1996 for calculating a days' pay cannot be relied upon at face value (see *Bear Scotland & Ors v Fulton & Ors* [2015] ICR 221). Subject to that strong note of caution, the following principles will often assist in calculating holiday entitlement.

A day's pay for the purposes of working out holiday pay is calculated according to a 'working' year rather than a full 365 day calendar year. This approach was adopted by the EAT in *Leisure Leagues UK Ltd v Macconnachie* UKEAT/940/01. It held that a year's pay should be divided by 233 because this was the number of actual days worked by the claimant in the year.

What is an hour's pay?

For workers for whom it is easier to calculate holiday entitlement in terms of hours rather than days, it will be necessary to calculate the appropriate hourly rate of pay. Where there is a straightforward hourly rate of pay with no variations or additional sums, this will be simple to establish. Otherwise, this may be calculated by identifying the total remuneration over the last 12 weeks and dividing this by the total number of hours worked over the last 12 weeks, in accordance with the calculation of a day's pay, but using hours worked instead of days.

Relevant agreement

Podlasiak v Edinburgh Woollen Mill Ltd is an ET decision where the tribunal held that a clause in the claimant's contract of employment, providing that they would receive £1 in respect of any accrued holiday pay on termination of employment, was unlawful and unenforceable. It was incompatible with the Working Time Directive, even though otherwise consistent with the wording in the WTR.